BUFFALO, N. Y., COURIER

Sunday, Nov. 12, 1877

DAILY TRIBUNE: SATURDA

One of Her Best Works.

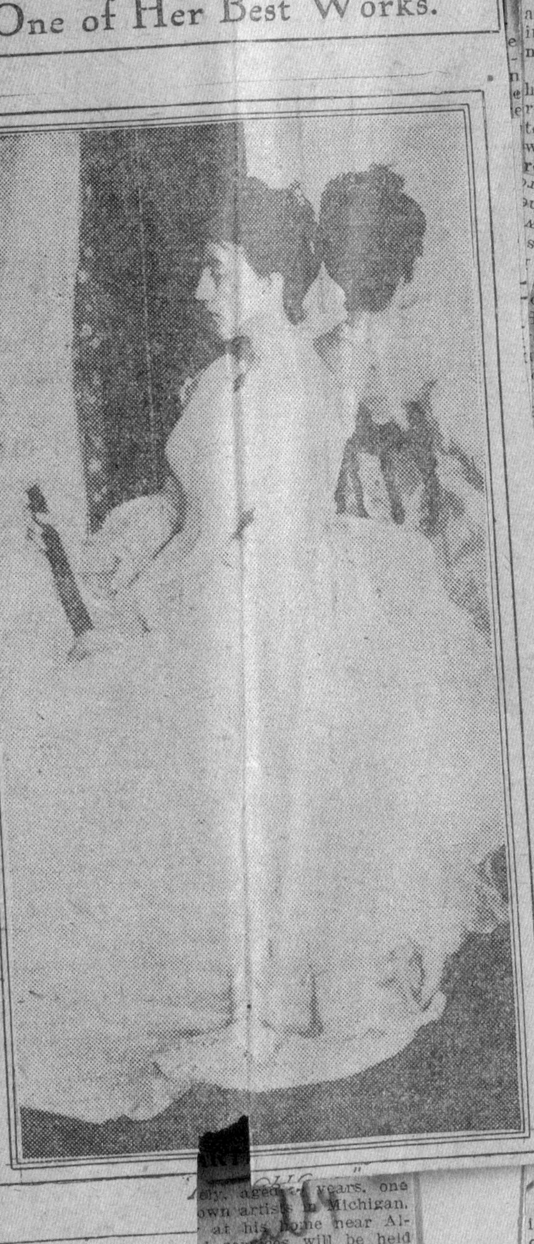

ROCHESTER, N. Y., Chronicle (25)

Tuesday, Oct. 10, 1911.

DEATH OF WELL-KNOWN ARTIST

Wilson Marlatt Succumbs to Sudden Illness at His Home.

Wilson Marlatt, an artist, 73 years of age, died suddenly early yesterday morning at his home, No. 17 Plymouth avenue north.

Mr. Marlatt had been in failing health for some time. Sunday night he reclined in an easy chair and appeared to be in a normal condition when his wife left him shortly after midnight to retire. About 5 o'clock she found that he had been dead an hour or more.

Mr. Marlatt was born in Steuben county, this state, in 1837, and was for a number of years a photographer in Harrisburg, Pa. He displayed such talent with his brush that he gave up photography to devote his time to painting. He came to Rochester about fourteen years ago and became one of the leading landscape artists of this city. His son, Irving Marlatt, of New York, is also well known in Rochester as an artist.

BROOKLYN, N. Y., EAGLE (25)

Sunday, Oct. 22, 1911.

Charlotte E. Thetford.

Charlotte E., widow of William Thetford, formerly a well-known artist of Brooklyn, died at her home, 892 Myrtle avenue, Friday. She was born in England, July 22, 1822, and had lived in Brooklyn eighty-seven years, coming with her parents when about two years old. She was a member of the Episcopal church, and leaves five sons, eleven grandchildren and eight great-grandchildren. Funeral services will be held at some time Monday afternoon at 2 o'clock.

N. Y. TIMES (2876)

Friday, Oct. 6, 1911.

J. Aumonier, Artist, Dead.

LONDON, Oct. 5.—J. Aumonier, the artist, died here to-day. He was a member of the Royal Institute of Painters in Water Colors.

J. Aumonier became a member of the Royal Institute of Painters in Water Colors in 1879, a society which claimed such famous men as Ruskin, Whistler, Burne-Jones, and Rossetti. He was also a painter in oil. Richard Muther in "The History of Modern Painting," says that he is the heir of Walker and Mason, and praises his lanscapes. Aumonier, he says, reveals a sense of poetry in his paintings of valleys, and he speaks of the "odor of earth from his meadows." One of Aumonier's best-known paintings is called "The Silver Lining to the Cloud," and is the property of the City of Manchester, England.

MRS. LAURA S. POMEROY, ARTIST, DIES AT 78

Mrs. Laura Skeel Pomeroy, sculptor and artist, aged seventy-eight, died on Wednesday at her home, in Grand avenue, the Bronx. She was the widow of Mr. Walter H. Pomeroy, a Greek scholar and literary critic. Her early life was spent in Poughkeepsie, N. Y., where, when still young, she executed a bust of Matthew Vassar, which stands to-day in the college that bears his name. She was the first to introduce art pyrography in this country and left many examples of her skill.

For more than twenty years Mrs. Pomeroy had one of the few "salons" in New York, at which were gathered on Wednesday evening young and old in intellectual intercourse, and at which live topics of the day were discussed, interspersed with music and readings by many of the men and women who were accustomed to gather. She knew many of the leading women of her day personally, including Lord Tennyson and Charlotte [...]

Miss Adelaide Skeel, of New York, a nephew, Roswell Skeel, Jr., of Hudson, survive her. The funeral will be held this afternoon at New York avenue, the Bronx, and the body taken to Rutland, Vt., where it will be buried.

Jersey City, N. J., Journal (892)

Thursday, Aug. 17, 1911

—Mr. Sleesman, with his two little daughters, Adelaide and Ellen, spent a delightful day in Steeplechase Park on Coney Island last week. Mrs. Sleesman will be for a few days this week at Keansburg, N. J.

—Frank Keim, who died in Jersey City on Sunday, Aug. 6, was a lifelong friend of Maj. Edward P. Reichhelm of West Thirty-fourth Street. He, with his wife and three sons formerly resided in West Thirty-fifth Street. From here he removed to Jersey City, shortly after which he lost his son Edgar from typhoid fever. He was a young artist of unusual merit. It is said that Mrs. Keim never recovered from the shock of her son's death and that she died of a broken heart. Mr. Keim was a veteran of the Civil War. Mr. Reichhelm was at the bedside of his comrade when he passed away. Mr. Keim was a firm believer in cremation. He had his wife and son cremated and it was at his request that he was himself cremated on Tuesday, Aug. 8.

CINCINNATI, O.

Saturday, Nov. 18, 1911

[...] on the Chicago skyscraper was stopped because the doors had finished by nonunion men in this city added that had the work been done by union men it would have been [...] union men in any city.

ARTIST DIED SUDDENLY

SPECIAL DISPATCH TO THE ENQUIRER.

Bellefontaine, Ohio, November [...] Simeon Sweet, well known portrait painter, died suddenly to-day at the breakfast table. He was 82 years old and formerly resided in Cincinnati. He had studied in Cincinnati and New Orleans.

[...] years, one [...] known artist [...] Michigan. [...] at his home near Albion [...] services will be held [...] his son, Walter S. Conely, 48 [...]ton avenue, Highland Park, Saturday afternoon at 2 o'clock. The services will be conducted by Rev. F. S. Roland of the Cass Avenue M. E. church and interment will be in Woodmere cemetery.

Mr. Conely was wounded in the Civil War and had suffered greatly since, but with great fortitude he continued to paint. Many of his pictures have been well received and a number hang in the Museum of Art. Mr. Conely was born in New York and came to Detroit as a boy. He studied art here and soon showed talent. He was married in 1860 at Ann Arbor to Miss Anna McCallum. He is survived by the widow, the son and one daughter, Mrs. L. F. Margah.

DEATHS OF ARTISTS

BER
SELF

...uts Throat
...l With
...ors.

APRIL

...l Infirmities
...t Time.
...amily.

...71, a life resi-
...t and for some
...unty treasurer's
...t the Columbus
...result of an at-
...Saturday morn-
...und in his neck
...s.

...f the Republican
...Republican Club,
...s lodge of Elks,
...popular citizen.
...dates back to the
...tion of the opera
...Apr.. by the Elks.
...e, he slipped and
...receiving injuries

...Ledger.

...tails of their finan
...management are ex
...holding companie
...d no tax whateve
...ay under the ne

...T A SUICIDE
...Nov. 27. — John Ja
...a scenic artist
...the Columbus State

Eden Musee's Designer Dead.

Eden Musee's Designer Dead.

Constant Thys, 56 years old, an ar
...mployed by the Eden Musée, died
...heart disease yesterday afternoon in
...studio at the Musée while he was at w
...gures portrayin
...came to Ame
...y-eight years
...d ever since at
...esigned practic
...ups displayed t
...asbrouck Heis
...er of the Hasbr
...ucation. He is
...d four children

ORK, FRIDAY, DECEMBER 2,

Artist, Dying of Starvation, Paints Picture of Herself

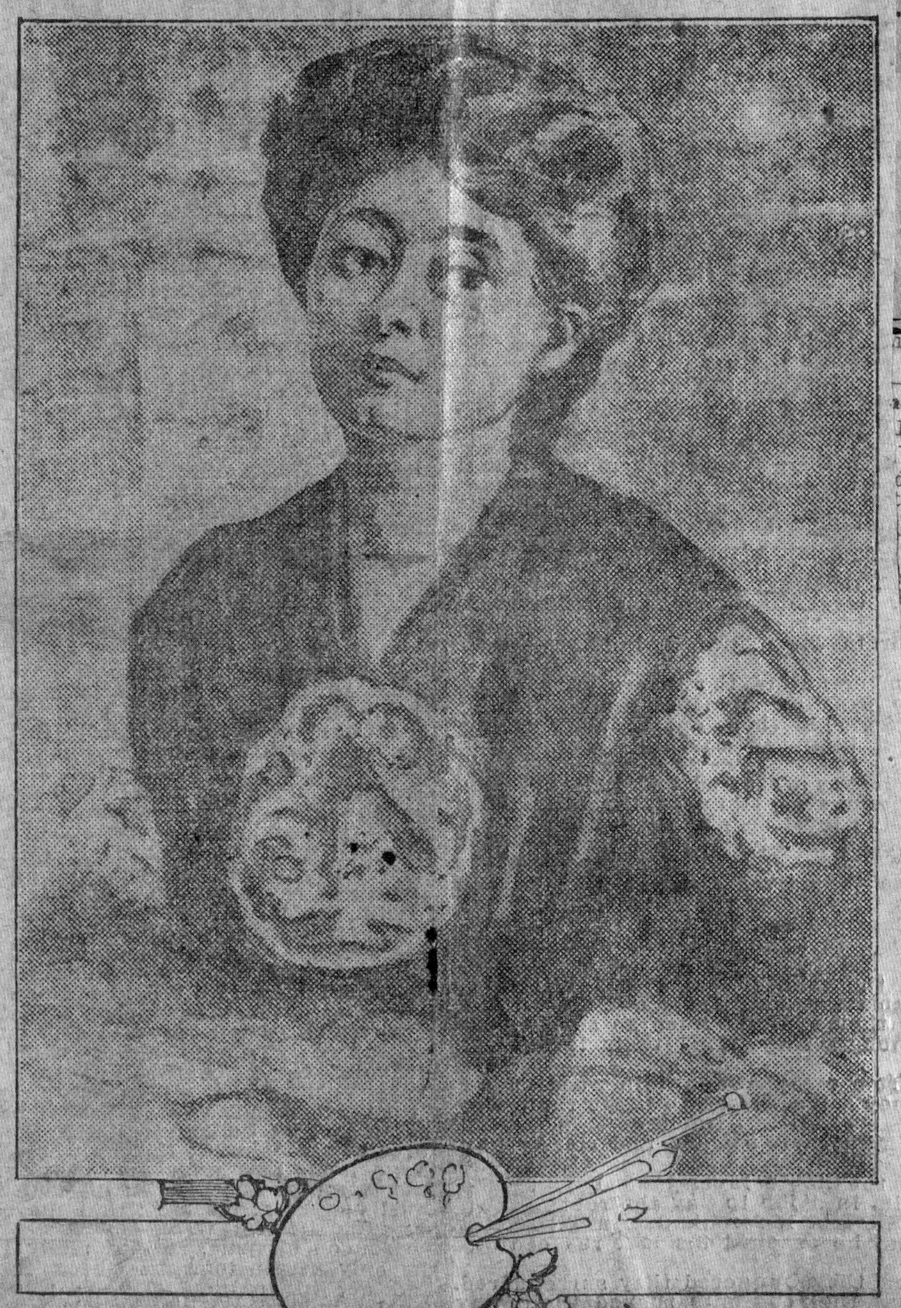

MISS ELLA FINLEY.
Photographed from the picture she painted just before she
died.

...Durand Wood
...Woodman, and
...d of the late A
...the founders of
...of Design, and
...years, is dea
...West Ninety-
...man, who her
...born in New Y

...S (23379)

...ER 27, 191

...was the on
...made their fo
...ned a resident
...life. He left a

...H. Osgood.

...rriett Osgood
...Art School
...treet in 1878
...ease yesterday
...She was a da
...Winthrop Osg
...olumbus, Ohi
...in 1842. The
...the pioneer
...ted States, ar
...troduce dec
...of a factory.
...ther, Winthr
...ers, Mrs. A
...ist, and Mrs
...will be bur

DEATHS OF ARTISTS

From the Archives of The Metropolitan Museum of Art

COLLECTED BY A. B. DE ST. M. D'HERVILLY

JIM MOSKE

Foreword by Robert Storr

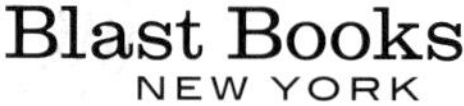

Blast Books
NEW YORK

Published by Blast Books, Inc.
P.O. Box 51, Cooper Station
New York, NY 10276-0051
www.blastbooks.com

Edited and designed by Laura Lindgren
Proofreader: Don Kennison
Indexer: Cathy Dorsey
Set in Eames Century Modern and Rational Text
Separations by Professional Graphics, Inc., Rockford, Illinois
Printed and bound by Printer Trento, Italy
Printed on Gardamatt 150 gsm

Image credits unless otherwise stated in captions: pp. 29, 96 right Internet Archive, pp. 35 and 49 Project Gutenberg, p. 58 Wikimedia Commons, pp. 71, 73 right, 92, HaithiTrust Digital Library, p. 94 JSTOR, p. 96 left Wikimedia Commons, p. 105 right Library of Congress, p. 118 Photo-Ellebe, Duchamp family tomb in Cimetière monumental de Rouen, Marcel Duchamp Exhibition Records, Philadelphia Museum of Art, Library and Archives

Library of Congress Control Number: 2023947892

ISBN: 978-0-922233-53-3

First Edition 2024

10 9 8 7 6 5 4 3 2 1

"I should die if I no longer painted, and I prefer to paint and die of it.
Besides, my will is nothing in the matter.
Nothing exists beyond art; let the world burst!"

Claude Lantier, artist
L'Œuvre, Emile Zola

← NEWSPAPER CLIPPINGS →

CONTENTS

D ARTIST
NG AFTER
TO WRECK

Bedside in Liberty
Car Fell ...

... Hospital at 8 o'...
... accident at S o...
... when his sedan auto...
... tumbled into the Little
... and he was caught in
... reckage, suffering internal
...

... Fowler was driving the car,
... became unmanageable and
... over an embankment on the
... turn north of Parksville. The
... automobile rolled across the
... stream and the heavy back fell
... Fowler, crushing him under-
... the baggage, inflicting inter-
... injuries.

The Fowlers were returning
from Buffalo where Mr. Fowler
had held, or had attended an exhibition of his own works. Several of the paintings were in the
car, but escaped damage. Mrs.
Fowler escaped with scratches
and is at the hospital awaiting the
crisis.

Brown County
Artist Dead

(By United Press)

Nashville, Indiana, September
23.—The body of Frederick Nelson
Vance, prominent Brown county
artist, will be taken today to
Crawfordsville, Ind., where funeral services will be conducted.
Vance, a well known member of
the local artist's colony, died from
an attack of acute indigestion late
yesterday.

... Artist Dies

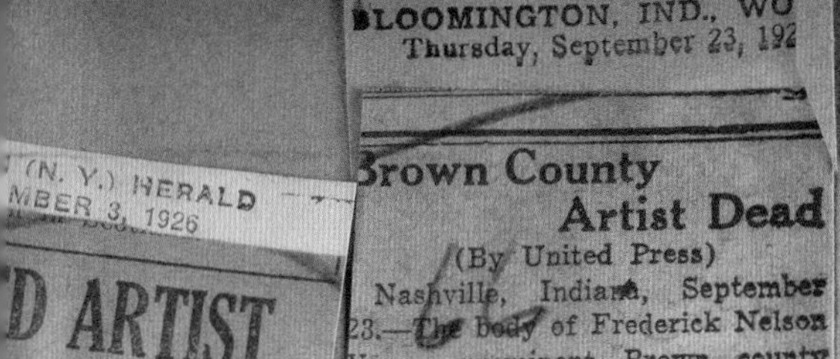

Death Saddens Many

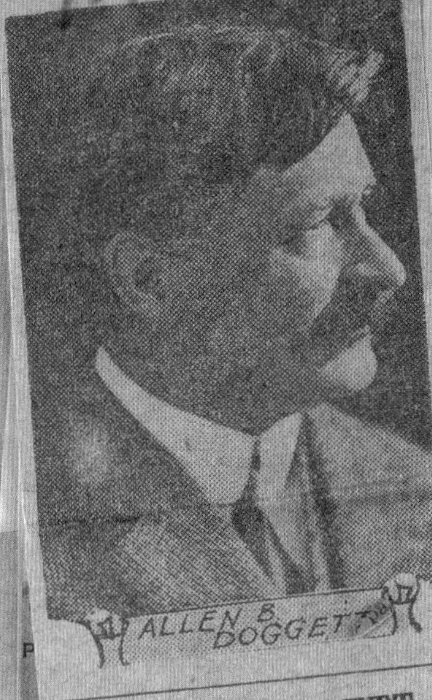

ALLEN B. DOGGETT,
ARTIST, EDUCATOR,
WIDELY MOURNED

Funeral of Great Nature Lover
and Erasmus Teacher Will
Be Held Tonight.

Funeral services for Allen B. Doggett, well known in educational and
art circles throughout the city, will
be held tonight at the Flatbush Con-
gregational Church, Dorchester rd.
and E. 19th st., where he was a
member and active worker. Mr.
Doggett died suddenly on Saturday
at his home, 360 E. 19th st.

Mr. Doggett was born at Grove-
land, Mass. He was the son of
Thomas Doggett, D. D., and Frances
M. Barrows. He received his early
...

Claude Monet,
Noted Nature
Painter, Dies

...ther of Impressionism and
Dean of Modern School of
Artists Succumbs in 86th
Year at Home in France

...menceau at Bedside

...er Premier Overcome
...End of Life - Long
...end; Helped in War

Herald Tribune Paris Bureau
... 1926, New York Tribune Inc.

... Dec. 5.—Claude Monet, world
... painter and intimate friend
... Clemenceau, died at 10
... morning at his home in
... colony at Giverny, in the
... Department. M. Clemenceau was
... at the bedside. The former Premier
was overcome by death of his lifelong friend, who had been an inspiration in war time.

The artist, who had recently celebrated his eighty-fifth birthday, had
been seriously ill for several weeks and
failed slowly during the last week.
The funeral will be held on Wednesday, according to advices reaching
Paris to-night.

Pioneer of His School

The last of the famous "Impression-
ists" of French pictorial art in the
nineteenth century might in a direct
sense be called also the first of them,
since it was he who gave them the
name. In 1874 he exhibited a painting
entitled "Impression — Rising ...,"
which attracted much attention and
was hailed as the harbinger of a new
school of art, which thereafter became
known as Impressionist. This ...,
Claude Monet, was born in ...
November 14, 1840. When he ...
developed a technic ...
brought him fame.
... to picture the ...

OE MAR,
...ONIST, DIES

... as Brake-
...awing ... ...ted
... Publisher

...ITH THE RECORD

... Mar, noted newspaper ...
... yesterday morning at ...
...field, Delaware County, ...
... of six months.
... was born in Philadelphia
... 1865, and was the ...
... Mar, an architect ...
... parents moved to ...
... 7 years old ...
... first job he lived in ...
... a groc clerk successon a ...
... drug store and a ...
brakeman ... as a railroad
... But ...
... was to ... talent which
... noted ... ranks of ...
... sion in sound expres-
... manifest first became ...
... a drawing 6 he won ...
... had its ... career ...
... man be ... a brake-
... side of ... represen on the
... holding sketche ...
... ear and ...

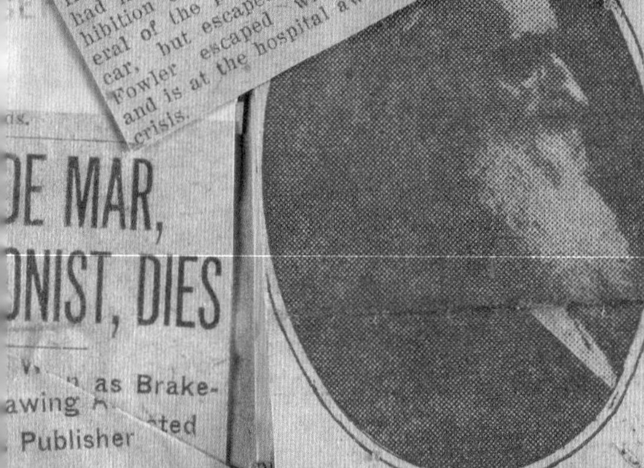

Prof. John B. Whittaker was
for forty years instructor at
Adelphi College. He retired in
1916 on a pension.

JOHN B. WHITTAKER,
FAMOUS ARTIST, DIES,
IN NINETY-FIRST YEAR

Was Instructor for Forty
Years at Adelphi College and
Painted Portraits of Many
Notables.

Prof. John Bernard Whittaker,
... reporter: "I am feeling pretty
... On his 87th birthday he said
... he would round out a century
... and often expressed a hope
... of his strength as he grew ...

CLIPPINGS IN THE WIND   Robert Storr

It is conventional wisdom that all artists seek immortality. And, furthermore, that they are different from other mere mortals in actually having a chance at achieving it through their works. Even so, this volume attests to what a crowded field they must contend with while alive and what a long shot they're betting on thereafter. For it seems safe to say that the majority of the artists who've made or are making a Faustian wager on their own lasting renown do so in willful denial of the odds against them as well as of the banality of their exalted dreams. On that score, I vividly recall an exchange with the late French Conceptual artist Christian Boltanski while we both looked up at the facade of the old Italian Pavilion in the Giardini of the Venice Biennale. During that installment of the casting call for eternal prestige, it was covered with dozens of names of erstwhile participants lettered in eye-crossing ranks. Christian wistfully asked what his chances were of being remembered after his name joined theirs when few that we could read at that moment registered with us.

Artists who succeed in becoming household names in better, more cultivated households, or who are notorious among the general public, for a variety of reasons usually owing less to their art than to their wealth or transgressive actions or personae, are a painfully small minority of the total number of aspirants. Which only adds pathos to their determination. In keeping with Bohemian ethos back in days when actual outcomes were more in keeping with mythologies of poverty, disease, and the myriad and macabre forms of death traditionally attached to their vocation—tales graphically retold by quite a number of these newspaper cuttings—many professed indifference to if not contempt for the rewards available in this life here below. And, while being far from entirely cynical about such elevated principles, since I share their sentiments when it comes to the aesthetically self-defeating choice between selling little and "selling out," I am reminded of the dictum of the Abstract Expressionist generation painter of the nominally black and otherwise ostensibly monochrome abstractions and art humorist extraordinaire, Ad Reinhardt, to wit: "A myth is as good as a pile." That's a version of the no-nonsense truism delivered by a newspaperman who recognizes the divergence between fact and fiction when it comes to how he should write up the triumph of the mild-mannered and inexperienced young lawyer played by James Stewart over the vicious gunslinger played by Lee Marvin in *The Man Who Shot Liberty Valance*—a triumph ensured by self-effacing, sharpshooting cowboy John Wayne. "Print the legend," the journalist wisely determines despite learning the truth.

Or, along an intersecting line of skeptical bet hedging, I think of the desperate plea of the protagonist of Eugene Ionesco's absurdist drama *Le Roi Se Meurt* (The King Dies), who begs for a temporary reprieve that he calls "une immortalité provisoire." One possible definition of such "provisional immortality" might be the press that many but by no means most artists of even modest distinction receive at the time of their death: an obituary that focuses on their career. Naturally, the discomforting irony is that the subject will never read it, and hence will never know the consensus verdict on his or her endeavors. In that connection, it is no secret that like many public figures, artists anticipate such obituaries with keen alertness to any indication of its probable length and slant. Never forgetting the legendary art dealer Leo Castelli's remark that fundamentally what matters when it comes to reviews is less whether they are positive or negative than how many column inches they fill. For that as much as anything may be taken as an indicator of whether the conversation about the artist and their work will continue. Otherwise, artists wonder, has the writer made a concerted effort to take stock of my accomplishments? Has the artist or those close to him or her been interviewed by a notable critic in the dailies of record or some writer or editor in the trade glossies? And have their friends and enemies been approached by the same short-deadlined, frequently trigger-happy arbiters of reputations—the hard-bitten wiseguys and wisegals of the reporting pool who, on assignment, double as art historians?

Parenthetically, art critics seldom get, or for that matter, merit, full-dress obituaries despite their claims to having spoken for their more lauded artistic heroes or for the zeitgeist. A word of caution

ANCISCO (CAL.) CALL-POST
ebruary 6, 1925

Artist Suicide
Assured Funeral
By S. F. Dentist

Touched by the dramatic death
[let]ter left by Maurice Mock, youth-
painter who on Wednesday killed
[h]imself by inhaling gas in his attic
[stu]dio at 957 Fillmore street, where
[he] had surrounded himself with his
old paintings of beautiful women
[t]he nude, Dr Painless Parker, lo[cal]
dentist, today advised an under[tak]-
[in]g firm that he would pay the
[exp]enses of a decent funeral for the
[dead] artist.

[T]he painter, in his farewell mes-
[sage] addressed to the world at large,
[will]ed his body to sience and his
[teet]h to Dr. Parker. The dentist
[said] today that he had never known
[the] artist and could not understand
[why] Mock had willed his teeth to

[break]fast room in Randolph Hall, at
[Harv]ard University, and also of the
[Worc]ester Country Club. He pub-
[lish]ed "Holland Sketches" in 1907 and
[Spa]nish Sketches" in 1911.
[Fo]r many years he lived at Pelham
[o]r amid a colony of fellow artists,
[fin]al arrangements have not been
[com]pleted.

MRS. CLIO H. BRACKEN, SCULPTRESS, DEAD

Mrs. Clio Hinton Bracken, American sculptress, widow of William Bar-
rie Bracken, lawyer, of this city, died
the other day of pneumonia in her
home, 31 Washington square west.

Mrs. Bracken was 55 years old, was
a daughter of Howard Hinton, editor
of the old Home Journal, and a direct
descendant of the royal Stuarts, her
grandmother having been Lady Grace
Stuart. Her mother, Luck Brownson
Hinton, was one of the early suffra-
gists. Mrs. Bracken studied first at
the Art Students' League here and
then in Paris with Rodin, MacMon-
nies and St. Gaudens. She won honors at the Salon while still a girl,
when only 20 captured a $10,000
for her statue of General Fre[mont].

She made her name chiefly in
decorative work, the vogu[e of stat]-
ettes being largely credited to

Landscape Painter, Dies

Arthur Virgil Howe, a noted
landscape painter, died last evening
at the residence on Lake Avenue,
after a long illness. Mr. Howe was
born in Troy 65 years ago.

He was the roommate in his student days of Frederic Remington.
They attended the Episcopalian Institute at Burlington, Vt., together,
and it was there that both resolved
to enter upon careers in art. Later
Mr. Howe and Frederic Remington
occupied a studio together in New
York, with Frederick Macey, Rob[ert]
Penny, and other celebrities in
artists' who's who.

Mr. Howe was a grandson of
Ebenezer Hatch Virgil, founder of
the National Express.

He married Elizabeth Morse, who
survives, as do the children,
Alfred Morse, Elizabeth Morse,
and Ina Howe Morse, and the sons
William, Ezra, George, Henry and
Richard Howe.

The funeral will be held Sunday
afternoon from the residence. Rev.
Marvin J. Thomas, the rector
of the Oakwood Avenue Presbyterian
Church, will officiate.

WASHINGTON (D. C.)
March 11, 1925

FUNERAL OF METC[ALF,]
NOTED ARTIST, TO[MORROW]

Was Well Known in Wash[ington]
for Connection With Cor[coran]
Art Gallery.

Funeral services for W[illiam]
Metcalf, noted artist, who d[ied Tues]-
day from a sudden heart at[tack, will]
be held in New York City [tomorrow]
afternoon. Pallbearers wi[ll include]
G. Powell Minnigerode, di[rector of]
the Corcoran Art Gallery, [at which]
institution a special exhibi[t of Met]-
calf's paintings was rece[ntly held.]
This retrospective display, [arranged]
through the personal effor[t of the]
artist, included the best ex[amples of]
his work.

Mr. Metcalf, who was ranked by
most critics as the leading American
landscape painter and as an outstanding figure in the art world of today,
was born in Massachusetts in 1858.
He was thoroughly grounded in art
[funda]mentals and during his life did

CLIPPING FROM
NEW YORK TIMES

carry on the banking busin[ess, also pos]-
sessed a natural inclination toward art.
He indulged this inclination by making
valuable collections of art, by becoming
an art critic who attained fame in
Europe, and by encouraging the art
ambitions of his son.

Edward was sent to an art school in
Dusseldorf. While the son was attending school, the elder Van Reuth gave
up banking, came here and purchased
an estate of 300 acres on the Harford
Road.

For a short time after finishing at
Dusseldorf, young Van Reuth came here
to visit his family, but preferring the
Old World manners and the artistic at-
mosphere of Europe he soon returned.
For ten years he studied and painted in
the art colonies of Antwerp, Dresden,
Brussels, Paris and Berlin.

APR 4 1925

of Detroit, are relatives of Pro[f.]
[ ]alta.

SUPERVISOR DROPS DEAD

Eduard Gruetzner, Painter, Dies
MUNICH, April 4.—Prof. Eduar[d]
Gruetzner, celebrated for his painting[s]

CLIPPING FROM
NEW YORK AMERICAN

APR 16 1925

John S. Sargent,
Famous American
Portrait Painter

LONDON, April 15 (By Associa[ted Press]
).—John Singer Sargent, the
[famous] artist, died suddenly at his
[home in] Chelsea this morning. Mr.
[Sargent] suffered
[a heart attack] at 3
[o'clock and] died
[soon af]ter.

and treasurer of trustees;
music, Mrs. G. D. Stover, Mrs.
Weston, George Mantell, H. B[il]-
lard; estimating and finance,
Goodrich, G. R. Russell, J. H[ar]-
rill, W. H. Sargent, H. O.
George Mantell, A. W. Littl[e];
examination of local preachers
tor, H. O. Cole and C. A. Goo[drich].

Order Hill's Ginger Ale in [large]
and small size bottles. It is [good.]
Try it.

At the Baptist church Thu[rsday]
evening, Feb. 19, Mrs. Comma[nder]
D. Johnson of the New En[gland]
headquarters at Boston, will [talk]
on some of the activities of the [Sal]-
vation Army. An interesting [meet]-
ing is promised and everyone [is in]-
vited to hear this unusually [fine]
speaker.

[structors were Bourgereau, [ ]
Bromtot and Doucet, acknowle[dged]
masters of their art.

After completing his course in [the]
academy he opened a studio at Rue
De Pont, Paris. After being
three years he located at Rue [Cha]-
teau Brient, where he rem[ained]
three years. After eighteen m[onths]
spent in travel and study, and
years in Boston, he removed [to]
Framingham in September 190[ ]
he purchased the old Wheel[er es]-
tate on Worcester road and [made]
it one of the picturesque an[d at]-
tractive homes of Massach[usetts.]
The original fireplace is a s[pecial]
feature of his studio.

In 1904 while in Holland [Mr.]
Butler made many very inte[resting]
studies of Dutch interiors an[d land]-
scapes. His work has been [exhibit]-
ed at the Paris Salon for a [number]
of years, an honor that wil[l be bet]-
ter appreciated when it is [under]-
stood that of about eig[ht thousand]
subjects offered, only th[ose that]
are selected for the ex[hibition.]
Landscape painting was his [special]-
ty.

Mr. Butler was a member [of a]
lodge of Masons, by affiliati[on of]
Hamilton lodge, N. Y., Cone[rod Roy]-
al Arch chapter, Orient of [ ]
E. S., St. John's Episcopa[l church.]

[char]ter member and form[er]
[ ] of the Framingham [ ]
and he was formerly a r[ ]
[of] the New York State [National]
Guard.

He married Hattie E. W[ ]
Jan. 15, 1895, and she pass[ed away]
several years ago. He is sur[vived by]
two brothers, Eugene of Ca[lifornia,]
E. C. Butler of Hamilton, [and]
three sisters, Mrs. George [ ]
of Liberal, Kansas, Mrs. G. [ ]
lard and Mrs. [ ] A. Oren[ ]
caut, Ohio, and a nephew [ ]
LaVerne Butler, who has [made his]
home here for the past tw[o years.]

The funeral services w[ill take]
place Sunday afternoon [at]
o'clock with services at S[t.]
Episcopal church, Framing[ham.]

DEMOCRA[T]

[ ]ee sisters
[B]eauregard,
St. Louis,
L. Harney
B. Harney

[ ]eld at 9 [o'clock]
[ ]from the
[ ] will be in
the family lot in Calvary Cemetery.

is in order: don't go into the profession if your unacknowledged or undisciplined *im*modesty is likely to betray you by erupting into vainglorious comparisons with Charles Baudelaire—the father of modern art criticism, who wrote *Les Fleurs du mal*—or Oscar Wilde, the man who set the tone for postmodern critique in English but also penned *The Importance of Being Earnest* and *The Ballad of Reading Gaol*. Even if your style is fluent, your judgments are memorably on target, and your put-downs are the equal of a stand-up comic's best zingers, you must produce a substantial body of work in your own right—poems, plays, stories, art—before making the leap in status sufficient to being considered the Baudelaire or Wilde of one's day. In most fields "genius" is vanishingly rare—if not a wholly suspect category—but its presence is scarcer than hens' teeth in cultural criticism, where sharp beaks and claws are standard offensive and defensive equipment. As that great settler of scores Clint Eastwood (in the guise of Dirty Harry) put it, "A man's got to know his limitations." And a woman does, too, though all too few "opinionators" of either gender who make their living by dispensing summary aesthetic justice, do.

This anthology of clippings commemorates the demise of the artists in question decades and, in several instances, a century or more after their deaths occurred. The interest we may have in the obituaries of names that were "big" that long ago and sometimes still remain so, is primarily in recognizing and pondering their stature's staying power, or in speculating on differences between their reputations then and now. So it is with an uncontested old master such as Auguste Rodin, who garnered several pages of pasted death notices in the Metropolitan's scrapbooks. Or Claude Monet, who garnered fewer but was undeniably a major artist. However, there are also once-laureled figures like Jules Breton, whose glory has been eclipsed by time. Although Breton's dramatically silhouetted sunset panorama of peasant women at their labors, *The Weeders* (1868), remains in the permanent collection of The Metropolitan Museum of Art, it is doubtful that contemporary gallery goers will breathlessly seek it out or be much moved by it when they come upon it in the Museum's galleries. Nevertheless, there is some chance that imaginative readers with a feeling for the human cost of fleeting adulation will experience a pang, correlating Breton's fate with that of more recent "art stars" raised up by sudden acclaim and left dangling in limbo. As for those who succumbed to misery or violent deaths, their stories anecdotally might usefully complement the microhistories currently being written by professors in the field inspired by the Annales school of historiography, or echoed in the kind of anecdotal literature pioneered by the Post-Impressionist critic and anarchist bomb thrower Félix Fénéon in his "Novels in Three Lines," published anonymously in the French newspaper *Le Matin* in 1906, which were based on incidental press items—or *faits divers*—used as filler in the Paris tabloids of the Belle Époque, and have been recently gathered and translated by Lucy Sante for publication by The New York Review of Books.

Meanwhile, the sometimes colorful, tantalizingly concise funerary portraits-in-prose in this book are the first draft of art history. And in most cases they may simultaneously have been the next to last word on the career of the long since departed talent to whom each was dedicated. Or, these assembled clippings may constitute a collective *vanitas* or collage *memento mori* for the art worlds of the past, differing from our own more in detail than in substance. Consequently, in the aggregate these short texts represent a warning from beyond the tomb not to take our current reality too seriously or its bitter ironies for genuine tragedy. In any event, if, in flipping the pages and scanning the entries of this book, you experience a chill, it is the forever cold of oblivion with these yellowed scraps being the last thin layer of protection against its penetrating jabs.

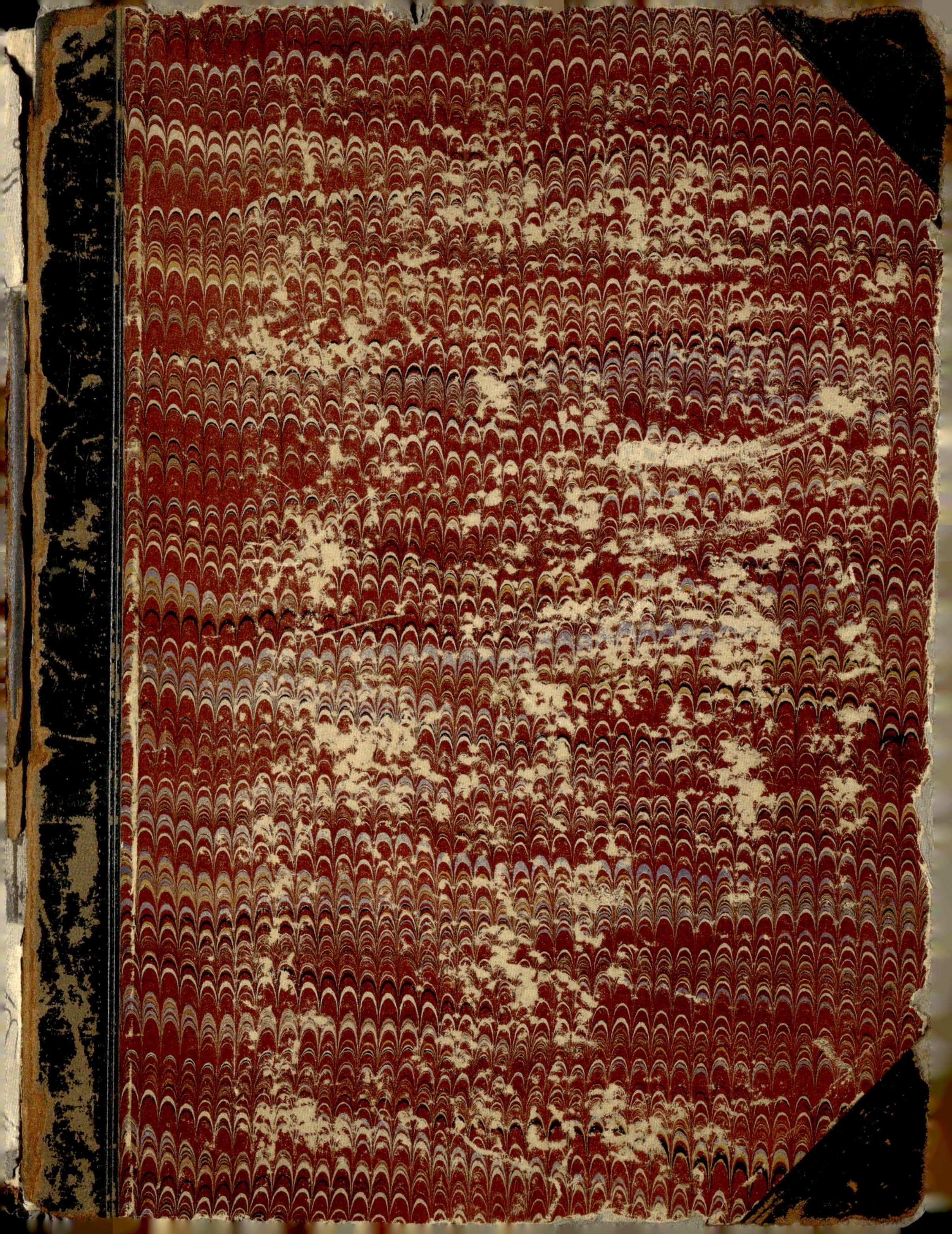

INTRODUCTION

One afternoon in 2018, I was searching through old files and papers
in The Metropolitan Museum of Art Archives for material to feature in an exhibition that would celebrate the Museum's upcoming
150th anniversary. I worked for much of my career in The Met's
archives, a formidable repository of fascinating artifacts and documents of the Museum's founding and early years. As I surveyed the
contents of one cabinet in the collection for suitable items, my eye
was caught by a pair of large clamshell boxes, the kind typically
used to protect rare books. Their dimensions were odd for storage of
archival records, and when I lifted one of them from the shelf, I was
surprised by its heavy weight. I set it down on a table, opened the
lid, and found inside a thick scrapbook with a frayed cover, its spine
hand-titled in black ink "Newspaper Clippings Relating to Artists."

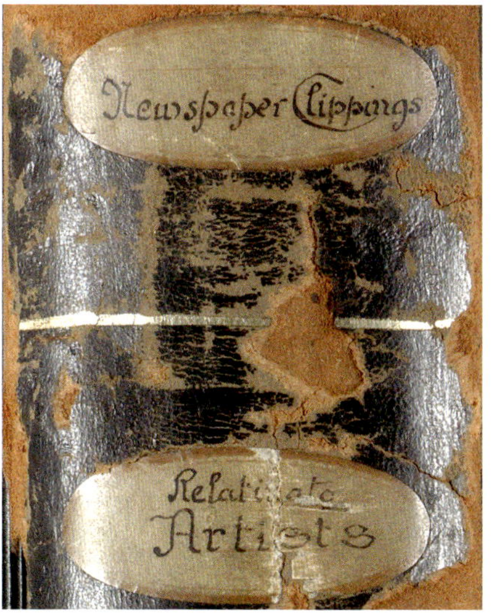

As I turned to the first page, tiny flakes of brittle, brown paper
crumbled from its edge, warning me that my impulse to look would
surely hasten this fragile volume's demise. The irony of this risk
was instantly apparent when I discovered the scrapbook was packed
with thousands of newspaper clippings that reported the deaths of
painters, sculptors, and photographers of the early twentieth century.

HARRY FENN PREFERS TO RISK DEATH FROM KNIFE.

Artist Underwent Operation, Although Warned It Would Be Dangerous—Rallied Well.

Harry Fenn, artist and illustrator, yesterday at his home in Montclair, N. J., underwent an operation for the removal of a tumor. The operation was performed by Dr. J. Hubley Schall, of Brooklyn.

Mr. Fenn, who is sixty-eight years old, has suffered for some time from the tumor. He was warned that the operation would be attended by grave danger because of his advanced age, but he nevertheless determined to submit to the surgeon's knife. He selected Dr. Schall. Mr. Fenn rallied well from the operation and his chances of recovery are good.

Mr. Fenn was born in Richmond, Surrey, England. He came to this country [in 18]57, and immediately won a name [for h]imself in art circles. He was one [of the] founders of the American Water [Color S]ociety, and since the organiza[tion] the institution has been an an[y] [contr]ibutor.

[He] is best known as an illus[trator. Exa]mples of his work in this [country are] contained in "Picturesque [America,]" "Picturesque Europe," and ["Picturesque] Palestine."

OBITUARY.

JULES ADOLPHE BRETON.

Paris, July 5.—Jules Adolphe Breton, the noted genre painter, is dead. He was born in 1827.

Jules Adolphe Breton was born in Courrières, France, May 1, 1827. He studied painting under Drolling and Devigne and devoted himself chiefly to rural life and scenes among the peasants of France, where he passed most of his life. He only occasionally visited Paris, to see the salon exhibitions and go to studios. Among his principal paintings are "The Recall of the Gleaners," "Evening," "The Weed Gatherers," "Blessing the Grain," "The End of the Journey," "The Benediction," "Washerwomen of the Coasts of Brittany," "The End of the

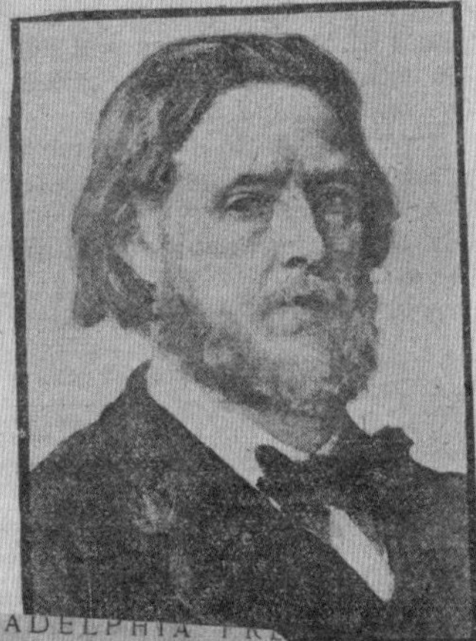

THE PHILADELPHIA PRESS

JULES BRETON, POET-ARTIST. DIES IN PARIS, AGED 79

[...] BRETON.
[... yest]erday.

[...]ay" and "A Brittany [...]

[...] literature as well as [...] "Les Champs et la [M]er[ve], Jeanne," a poem, which [took a pri]ze from the French [...Life] of an Artist," which [...] "The Painters of the [Fa]r[myar]d," and "A Peasant [...]

[...com]mander of the Legion [... a m]ember of the Académie [... he] received many medals [... "Life of] an Artist" is regarded [... He is] frankly an artistic tem[peramen]t, [emo]tions and feelings. His [... i]n genre painting [...are] owned in this [country...pub]lic galleries [... have a]lways been [in great] [demand...] sold for high [pri]ces."

[...]Soir—Les [Décor]ation de l'Eglise [... La Chas]se de Dindons," "Un [...] "Les Lavandières," [... Les] Vaches," "La Gla[neuse... Les] Communiantes," [...] "L'Etoile du Berger" [... Les] Fleurs."

Greatest Painting Hangs

Regarded as [...]

THE death Thursday of Jules Breton, the famous French painter, calls attention to the fact that one of his masterpieces is owned in Minneapolis. "The Evening Call," "L'Appel du Soir," now in the Walker art gallery, is considered by art critics as the cream of Breton's work. Mme. Demont-Breton, his daughter, and her husband and his friends rank "The Evening Call" as the best thing Breton ever did. T. B. Walker was in Paris in 1889, when this picture was first exhibited at the Universal exhibition. It was hung several weeks later in the room which had been reserved for the works of the French painter.

Critic Is Spellbound.

[... rea]sons were that she understood his [... is] the finest collection in America. [... and] she liked to have "Her Man Is on [the] Sea" in the same collection with [her] father's "The Evening Call." [... "The An]gelus Bells," a larger sized and [mor]e beautiful and immeasurably finer [tha]n Millet's "Angelus," is in the [Chi]cago Art Institute, tho it was [brou]ght to this country for Mr. Walk[er.] But he was unable to make the [pur]chase owing to an impending panic [in t]he financial world.

[Pr]ofessor French, director of the in[stitu]te, and Mr. McCormick, president

The second box contained a continuing volume. The obituaries were pasted into the two books in chronological order by publication date, starting in 1906 and ending in 1929. Most were about American and European artists. I recognized some familiar names, but many of the articles reported the deaths of artists I'd never heard of.

It wasn't long before I'd looked through enough of the crowded pages to see there was no clear connection between all these obituaries and the history of the Metropolitan Museum. In general, The Met's extensive archives house curatorial correspondence, trustee memoranda, and other press clippings that shine a spotlight on the Museum's past milestone events and achievements, like the acquisition of masterpiece paintings and sculptures, special exhibition openings, and ribbon cuttings for new galleries. These ponderous volumes bulging with historical data about random artists, most of them too obscure to merit a place in the Museum, seemed misfits in the stacks.

Even if such clippings might be useful to curators or historians with a specialized interest in the art scene of a century ago, I thought, they certainly appeared irrelevant for a Met history exhibit. I was about to close and reshelve the tomes when my attention fixed on a startling headline.

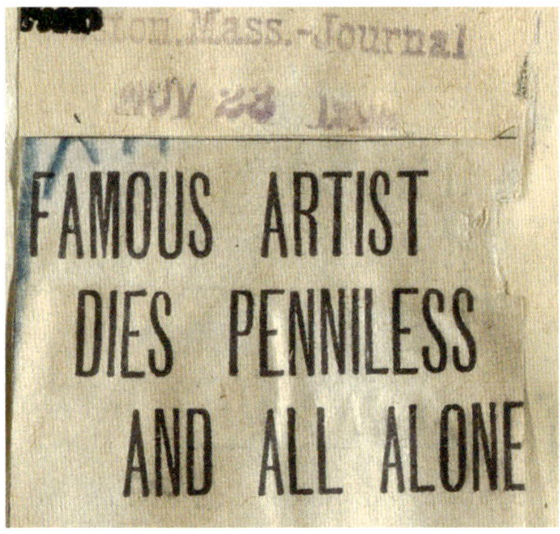

FAMOUS ARTIST DIES PENNILESS AND ALL ALONE
Practically penniless and seemingly without friends, Mrs.
Imogene Robinson Morrell, one of the most noted women
painters of this country . . . died early today in her humble
room in a cheap boarding house.

MISS CAROL H. BECK

Talented Woman Artist Who Did Many Fine Portraits.

Miss Carol H. Beck, one of the best known and most talented of Philadelphia women artists and a portrait painter of distinction, died yesterday, after a brief illness in Hahnemann Hospital, where she had been under treatment. She was a sister of ex-United States Assistant Attorney General James M. Beck, now living in New York, and he came at once to the city on learning of her death. The funeral will be held Saturday morning from the residence of a brother-in-law, Dr. W. K. Ingersoll, No. 4008 Chestnut street.

Miss Beck studied in the schools of the Pennsylvania Academy of the Fine Arts and also in Paris, Dresden and Madrid, having won the Mary Smith prize at the Academy in 1899. She made a specialty of portrait painting and fine examples of her work now hang in the halls of the University of Pennsylvania, Masonic Temple, Odd Fellows' Temple, Musical Fund Society, Penn Charter School, Wesleyan, Swarthmore and Women's Medical Colleges, and the State Capitol at Harrisburg and Trenton. She arranged and edited the catalog of the Wilstruch collection in Memorial Hall, Fairmount Park, and did other important work. She was a member of the Plastic Club and a manager of the Fellowship of the Academy of the Fine Arts.

M. HEBERT, PAINTER, DIES IN FRANCE

[SPECIAL DESPATCH TO THE HERALD VIA COMMERCIAL CABLE COMPANY'S SYSTEM.]

HERALD BUREAU,
No. 49 AVENUE DE L'OPERA,
PARIS, Thursday.

M. Ernest Hébert, a famous French painter, died yesterday at La Trouche, near Grenoble, aged ninety-one.

M. Hébert was one of the most prolific painters of nude figures and portraits in France. He was born at Grenoble in 1817, and after having studied law at the University of Paris entered the studio of David d'Angers. He exhibited his first work, "Tasso in Prison," at the Louvre in 1839. This painting was purchased by the government for the Grenoble Museum. Gaining the Prix de Rome the same year, he went to Italy to study, remaining there eight years.

After his return he produced his first masterpiece, "La Malaria," which was placed in the Luxemburg Museum, and has been reproduced in lithograph scores of times. Several other notable works, among them "Les Filles d'Alvito," for the Exposition of 1855; "La Jeune Fille aux Puits," purchased by the Empress Eugénie, and numerous portraits.

M. Hébert was a commander of the Legion of Honor, a member of the Academy of Fine Arts and professor of painting at the Ecole des Beaux Arts.

ROSWELL G. SHURTLEFF.

Death of a Well Known Springfield Artist.

Roswell G. Shurtleff, a landscape artist, who was as well known about Springfield as Roswell Morse Shurtleff of New York is known in Hartford, died at the State Hospital at Northampton, Mass., at 11 o'clock Sunday morning. Since the death of his wife two years ago, Mr. Shurtleff has been steadily failing, suffering a paralytic shock about six months ago and growing much worse during the last week.

Mr. Shurtleff was born in Bath, N. H., in 1826, but with his parents moved to Rochester, N. Y., at an early age. Later the family moved to Springfield and in this latter city he received his academic education and became chief clerk and private secretary to General Dyer, who was in charge of the United States armory there. This post he occupied for twenty-one years, during which time he took painting lessons and exercised to a considerable extent his natural ability in this line, most of his training being what he got in practice. In 1857 he was married to Sarah Mills of Springfield, and he leaves one child, Miss Clara Mills Shurtleff of that city. After leaving his work at the armory Mr. Shurtleff devoted all his time to painting, opening a studio at his home, painting landscapes of the Connecticut Valley and the Berkshires. He delighted in painting the brilliant colors of the autumn foliage. He was a brother of the late Judge William S. Shurtleff, and the brothers were much devoted to each other.

JOHN ORTGIES, FOR HALF CENTURY ACTIVE IN ART TRADE, IS DE[AD]

Pioneer in His Business in New York City Dies at His Country Home in Ardsley.

CAREER OF HALF A CENTURY

Was on Intimate Terms with Many Noted Artists, Collectors and Connoisseurs of America.

John Ortgies, identified in the business relating to fine arts for nearly half a century, died last Thursday night, at his country home, in Ardsley, after an illness of a few months. He was in his seventy-third year, having been born in February, 1836, in this city.

Mr. Ortgies was thoroughly trained in everything connected with the disposal of works of art, and enjoyed the friendship and confidence of the best known collectors in this country. He was the pioneer of his calling in this city, and among his papers are records of auction sales of paintings and bric-a-brac sold for the last forty-eight years.

Mr. Ortgies in his earlier years was associated with his brother-in-law, Robert Somerville. The firm had charge of the disposal of many important collections, including that of John Taylor Johnson, which in 1876 was sold in Chickering Hall.

Mr. Ortgies and Thomas E. Kirby were partners from 1878 to 1883, when Mr. Kirby withdrew to join the American Art Association, with which he is still connected. Mr. Ortgies remained at No. 845 Broadway until 1888, when he and Mr. Somerville moved to the upper city and established the Fifth Avenue Art Galleries. During this period he was in close personal relations with Samuel P. Avery, Sr. Others with whom he was on intimate terms were the late Henry G. Marquard, once president of the Metropolitan Museum of Art, and R. M. Olyphant. He also knew well many of the American artists of

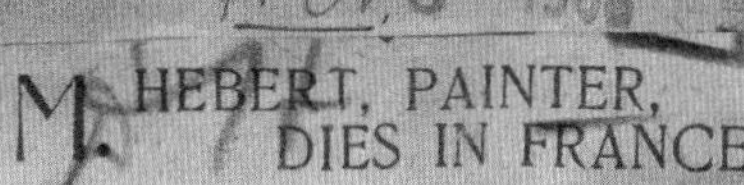

generations ago, such as Frederick E. Church, Sanford R. Gifford, Kensit and the Harts.

Mr. Ortgies remained with the Fifth Avenue Art Galleries until 1899, when he withdrew and became associated with the American Art Association, where he resumed relations with his friend, Mr. Kirby. He was until within a few days of his death the superintendent of the galleries, where he was practically an architect, designer of electrical lighting effects, an expert judge of many classes of art objects and also a successful executive.

He was the manager of many of the largest art sales which took place in the metropolis, and for several decades there was scarcely a dispersal of important paintings and bric-a-brac in the country with which he was not in some way identified.

Mr. Ortgies was attacked last summer by stomach trouble and gradually lost in weight and in vitality. His death was not unexpected. He leaves a widow, two daughters and a son. Mr. Ortgies was of a gentle, kindly nature and in an unostentatious way gave largely to charity.

St. Mary's Church at 9 o'clock.

FAMOUS ARTIST DIES PENNILESS AND ALL ALONE

Mrs. Imogene Robinson Morrell Dead in Lodging House.

HER BEST WORK IS THE DIX PORTRAIT

Attleboro Woman Had Painted the Pictures of Many Famous Men.

Washington, Nov. 22. — Practically penniless and seemingly without friends, Mrs. Imogene Robinson Morrell, one of the most noted women painters of this country, a daughter of Attleboro, Mass., and at one time a Boston school teacher, died early today in her humble room in a cheap boarding house. She [died in] Malden, Mass. [No relatives] heard of her death and no arrangements for her funeral will be made until he is heard from.

In all my years of employment at a museum with a premier American paintings collection, I had never heard of this artist. The poignant summary of her passing aroused my curiosity, and I made a mental note to learn more about her. Then, rather than put the books away, I gently leafed my way further into the past they recorded and was soon spellbound.

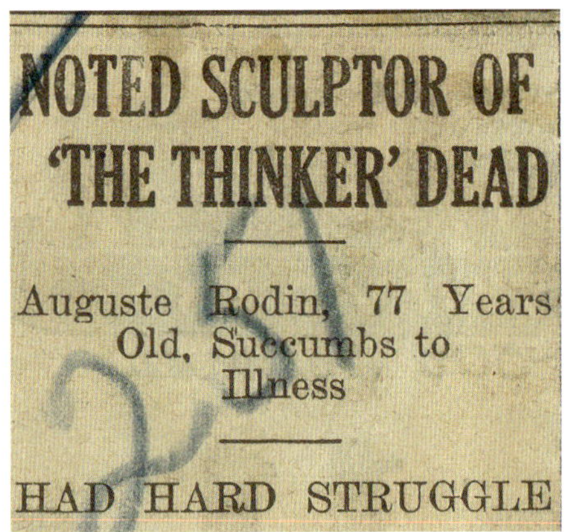

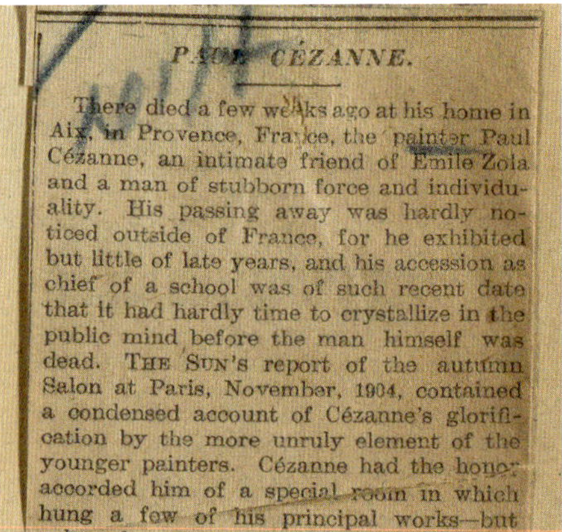

As I continued to look, I saw a few stately remembrances of art world luminaries whose works remain familiar beacons in museum galleries today. Several pages were crammed with stories about the revered sculptor Auguste Rodin, who died in 1917 at his country home outside Paris. Elsewhere I saw clippings about Paul Cézanne and Claude Monet. But many others told stories of the decease of artists who were celebrated in their own time but have since fallen from fashion and are hardly remembered today. The majority recounted the passing away of people now completely forgotten, some of them victims of bizarre accidents, murders, or disease. I felt dismayed that plenty of the decedents were suicides.

After my first awestruck encounter with these macabre volumes, I was compelled to investigate and find out who had compiled them. Examining the scrapbooks closely, I found clues in their margins that pointed to an overlooked Met paintings curator. What could have been his motivation? To understand the context and intellectual backdrop of his endeavor, I delved into public archives and online genealogy sources that held shadowy traces of the curator's early life. Next, in the Museum's outstanding library, I broadened

my scope of research and read of the ways that art historians and
authors from as long ago as the Renaissance described artists'
deaths. Going still further, I searched the art collections of The Met
and of other museums for rare objects of all eras that portrayed how
notable painters and sculptors met their ends.

Meanwhile, I methodically read through the two obituary scrapbooks themselves, transfixed by the brutal poetry of news headlines
that sensationalized tragic and violent deaths. Typical of the crass
tabloid journalism of the Progressive Era, these titles were crafted
to wring maximum drama from misfortune and to excite and grip
readers' voyeuristic attention through raw emotion.

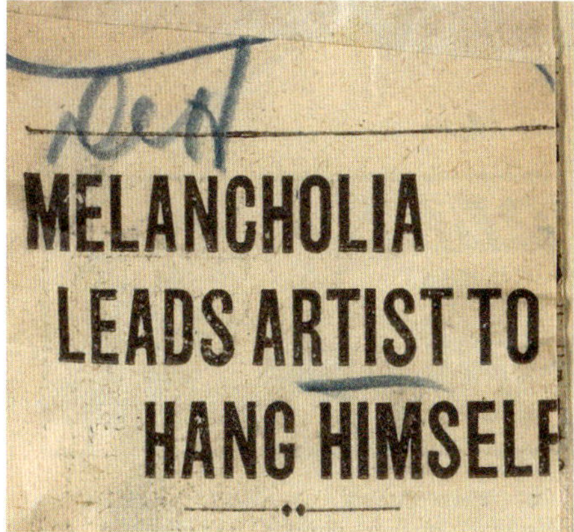

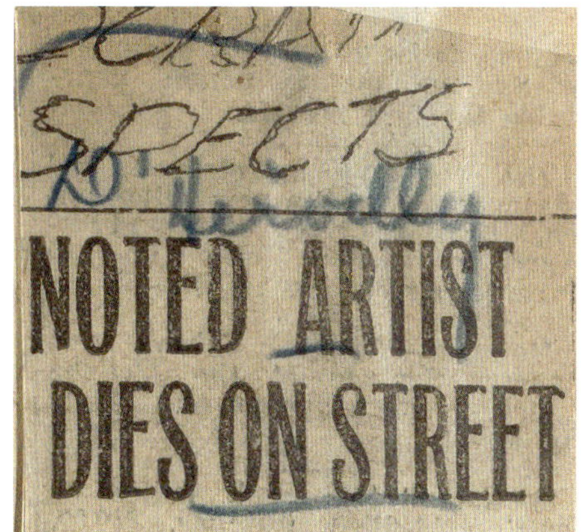

I photographed the most startling headlines—creating a new
digital death archive of my own—and compulsively scoured the
internet for more information about their unfortunate subjects.
This online exhumation felt eerie and invasive, as though I were an
archaeologist opening an ancient tomb. I sometimes questioned my
impulse to expose these forgotten stories to the light of the present day, and during especially bleak, early phases of the COVID
pandemic, I broke away from the effort entirely.

The imposing physical mass of the two volumes and the steady,
infinitesimal disintegration my hands caused as I turned their
pages amplified my mixed feelings of curiosity and apprehension.
From many years of professional experience with old documents
like these made from degraded wood-pulp paper, faded black ink,
and desiccated glue, I knew that the scrapbooks were vulnerable.

...STE RODIN DEAD; ...D FRENCH SCULPTOR

... Nov. 17.—Auguste Rodin, ... great sculptor, died to-day.

... Rodin was born in Paris ... and began the study of ... under Barye, the famous ... f lions. For many years ... overty, and general recog- ... genius came only when ... And then,

...GUSTE RODIN, ...FAMOUS FRENCH SCULPTOR, DIES

Been Suffering From Congestion of the Lungs for Some Time.

WAS 77 YEARS OF AGE

...ENCH SCU ...OUGHT LON...

AUGUSTE RODIN, NOTED FRENCH SCULPTOR, DEAD

Paris, Nov. 17.—Auguste Rodin, France's great sculptor, died early to-day.

He had been ill for only a short time of congestion of the lungs.

Auguste Rodin was born in 1840 in Paris, but it was not until he had struggled forty years that he achieved recognition from the art world.

He was known for his disregard of all preconceived standards in art. His figures were bold and some almost crude in their force. He was married only a few months ago.

RODIN, FAMOUS SCULPTOR, DEAD

Frenchman Distinguished for His Realism Dies at His Villa Near Paris at 77.

FOUGHT CRITICS 50 YEARS

His "La France" Presented by France to America—"The Thinker" in Metropolitan Museum.

... yet he struggled on and submitted his work at every public examination that was held, always without success. Fortunately he came at last under the notice of Barye, the painter and sculptor of animals, who carried his artistic education to the point from which Rodin could pursue it alone. At the age of 23, before embarking on a determined struggle to fame and fortune, the future sculptor married. This move served as an incentive, and spurred him on in his task, for in less than twelve months he had produced his first

Salon. He smashed academic convention, scandalizing the popular artists and the public, as is always the case with new ideas of sufficient force to overturn the old.

... but for years ... misun... and recognized by ... judgment of the time as ... master in sculpture, the most original creative force in the art since the Renaissance. His vitality and vigor...

...STON GLOBE—SATUR...

AUGUSTE RODIN, SCULP...

Called "Michaelangelo of ... —His Works Un...

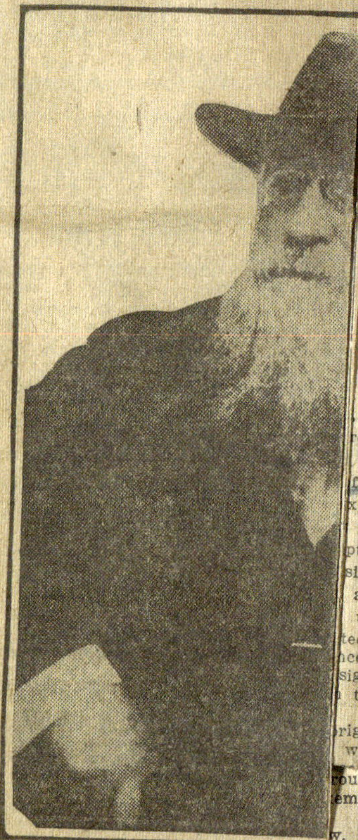

AUGUSTE RODIN, PHOTOG...
(From "Rodin, The War and His Art." Co...

PARIS, Nov 17—Auguste Rodin, the famous sculptor, is dead, of congestion of the lungs.

... past two months, and so far they have not been able to catch him.

F. LE BRUN KIRKPATRICK

Frank Le Brun Kirkpatrick, an artist whose home was at 3213 Dauphin Street, died yesterday in the Osteopathic Hospital after a week's illness of heart disease. His wife, who before her marriage was Miss Josephine Gruber, died last July. Three daughters survive, Misses Josephine, Octavia and Charlotte Kirkpatrick.

His chief pictures were interiors, monasteries and monks.

Mr. Kirkpatrick was born in this city August 19, 1853, the son of Rev. John Kirkpatrick, a Methodist minister. He was educated in this city and completed his art studies in Munich. One of his pictures is in the permanent collection of the Academy of the Fine Arts. He was a member of the Ma...

FRANK L. KIRKPATRICK, MURAL ARTIST, DIES

Succumbs to Heart Disease in Hospital After Week's Illness

Frank Le Brun Kirkpatrick, a professor at the Academy of the Fine Arts and a widely known artist, died yesterday morning in the Philadelphia Osteopathic Hospital after a week's illness. Death was due to heart disease.

Born in Philadelphia sixty-four years ago, Mr. Kirkpatrick received his early education in the public schools. He studied for three years in Munich, Germany, and on his return to America took up the art of mural decorating.

Last July his wife died and it is thought her death hastened his end. He is survived by three daughters, Josephine, Charlotte and Octavia. His father was the Rev. John Kirkpatrick, a widely known Methodist Episcopal minister.

The funeral will take place Wednesday afternoon and the interment will be made in South Laurel Hill Cemetery.

Buy Coal at Mine

NEW YORK HERALD   2377

Sunday, November 18, 1917.

Mr. Auguste Rodin Dead Near Paris

End Comes to Man Whose Works Have Charmed the World.

HAD BEEN ILL ONLY SHORT TIME

Story of How He Succeeded in Face of Years of Criticism and Ridicule.

results, watched him at work. To his astonishment, . . .

, of the death on October 24, of Paul Tilton, an artist of note and a resident of this city, for 18 years. Tilton's last residence in Trenton was at 55 Colonial Avenue.

It is likely that at some future time his body will be removed to Rome, for final interment along the side of his father, John Rollins Tilton, also an artist, who died there several years ago. His mother was buried in Chicago.

Paul Tilton accepted a position last September as assistant purser for the White Star Line Steamship Company and was sent to England. On his arrival there he was promoted to chief purser of the steamer Sedgwick, and was on his way from the company's office in Liverpool to the vessel when he was stricken. He had reached the dock and was ascending the gangplank when he collapsed. He was taken to a hospital, where he died the next day. Word of his death was sent to the New York office and through this means his friends in Trenton learned of his death.

Clipping from

Bloomington, Ill. Bulletin
Sunday, November 18, 1917.

Clipping from

St. Louis, Mo. Globe-Democrat
Sunday, November 18, 1917.

Rodin, Noted Sculptor, Is Dead at 75

"Modern Michelangelo" Struggled Fifty Years Against Poverty, Criticism and Abuse.

Born of Poor Parents.

Born in Paris in 1840, of wretchedly poor parents, he was first heard of in 1864, when, after a short time spent in studying under Barye, he sent his mask, "The Man with the Broken Nose," to the salon. Although this interesting head contained the germ of all that was great in his later work, it was refused, and his poverty obliged him to spend the next six years in the drudgery of an artist's assistant, doing all the tedious, mechanical, profitless labor of an artisan. Later, he collaborated with a Belgian sculptor in carving figures for the Brussels Bourse,

---

Artist ... from Pneumonia

William H. Loomis, one of the most widely known illustrators in the country, died suddenly late Thursday night at the Heinemann Hospital from pneumonia. He had been ill only two days. He worked as an artist on many prominent papers in the United States. One of his best known character creations was the "Widow Wise," which appeared in "The New York Herald." A play, "The W...

other ... newspaper in New ... "Widow Wise" pictures are well remembered. For the last three or four years he had been a member of the staff of the Ethridge Association of Artists.

TO CHARGE LOWER PRICES

INDIANA

WORLD FAMOUS SCULPTOR

(By United Press)

Paris, Nov. 17—Auguste Rodin, France's great sculptor, ... early today, at the age ... He had been ill only ... from congestion of the ...

Rodin was born in ... gium. But it was not until ... the 40 years that he he ... chance ... like recognition ... the ci ... ment to ... cemetery at Evere, the ... stature at the end of A ... in Brussels and the hand ...

...ings in the museum of ...russels.

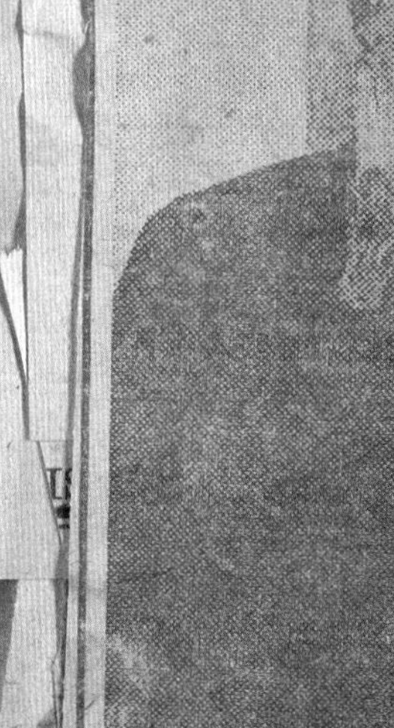

French sculptor ... away in Paris aft...

RODIN BE...

day, February 19, 1916.

Tuesday. November 27, 1917.

Corporal David Bryan Watkins, of the
Fifth Company, coast artillery, stationed
at Fort Totten, died on Sunday in the
post hospital. He enlisted in Kansas, his
native State, where he had been a farmer.

Mr. William E. Clark, for the last fifteen years connected with the Butterick
Publishing Company in Manhattan as a
fashion artist, died on Sunday in his home,
No. 875 Twelfth street, Brooklyn, at the
age of fifty years. He leaves his wife,
one son and two daughters.

*...who talks pacifism now thinks
disloyalty.*

Conn. Disp...
NOVEMB...

CONGDO...
...ASSED A...

...and Etcher Di...
...things of His in...
...Public Library...

...R" MASTERPI...

When He and His
...sioned to Paint
...Rothchilds

...on, the well known
...painter, died in
...and complications

...as a resident of
...rly days and will
...the older resi-

---

d, Minn., Tribune
NOVEMBER 30, 1...

THOS. CONGDON

Former Resident of
...ies in Boston.

...on, who was a resi-
...in the 80's, died re-
...f diabetes and com-
...ongdon was 59 years
...by profession. He
...886 and went to New
...studied three years
Europe, accompani-
spent sixteen years...

Y, NOVEMBER 29, 19...

...ainerd Artist, Die...

...mmissioned by Roths-
...o Paint Landscapes
in Holland.

Nov. 29.—Thomas R. Cong-
...s old, a well-known artist,
...ainter, is dead in Boston,
...word received here. Mr.
...a resident of Brainerd in
...s and will be remembered
...dents here and in Duluth
...throughout the Northwest
...of his productions grace

...left Brainerd for New
...he studied three years and
...Paris where he established
...where later he and his
...o is an artist, were given
...by the Rothchilds to
...in Holland, their native
...whole year.

Thursday, November 22, 1917

NICOLE STAITS, ARTIST, DIES AFTER OPERATION

Nicole Staits, well-known artist of
St. Louis, living at 4115 Shenandoah
avenue, died yesterday afternoon at the
Missouri Baptist Sanitarium following
an operation. He was 64 years old.
Staits was a native of Hungary and
came to St. Louis in 1885. He studied
art in the schools of Europe and began
his career here as an illustrator for
the daily newspapers when that art
was first introduced into journalism.
Later, when photogravure made its appearance, Staits turned to mural painting, and many specimens of his work
now adorn several churches of St. Louis
and other cities. Some of his paintings
depicting the life of Christ were chosen
for the new Kenrick Seminary.

MRS. JOSEPHUS DANIELS
...EST IN ST. LOUIS

St. Louis Min... Jou...
FRIDAY, NOVEMBER 30, 1917.

...his attack has noticeably lessened.

THOMAS R. CONGDON IS DEAD IN BOSTON

Brainerd, Minn., Nov. 30.—Thomas
R. Congdon, 59 years old, artist, teacher
and painter, is dead in Boston, according to word received here.

Mr. Congdon was a resident of
Brainerd and Duluth in the early days.
In 1886 he left Brainerd for New
York, where he studied three years
and then went to Paris, where he established a studio, and later he and his
wife, who also is an artist, were given
a commission by the Rothchilds to
paint scenes in Holland, their native

NOTED FRENCH SCULPTOR DEAD

Auguste Rodin Expires Near Paris After Short Illness.

Paris, Nov. 17.—Auguste Rodin, the
famous sculptor, is dead.
M. Rodin died in his villa at Meudon,
on the outskirts of Paris, after an illness of a few days.
Had he lived M. Rodin would have

Fargo, N. D., Forum
TUESDAY, NOVEMBER 20, 1917.

ARTIST WELL KNOWN HERE, DIES IN EAST

Mrs. G. H. Shaver, Mapleton, received word today of the death of her
brother, Thomas Congdon, of Boston,
Mass., which occurred Nov. 15. The
word came by letter.
Mr. Congdon was very well and
most favorably known in Fargo and
its vicinity, where he frequently visited, and was an artist of considerable
note. In the study of painting he
traveled quite extensively in Europe,
and for some time had a studio in
Paris. He was also a brother of the
late Mrs. C. N. Swart, Fargo, who
died only a few weeks ago.

Duluth, Minn., Herald
WEDNESDAY, NOV. 28, 1917

Bargain store, for $265 claimed to be
due on a sale of a bill of goods. The
trial is being heard before a jury in
Judge J. D. Ensign's court.

NOTED PAINTER, ONCE OF BRAINERD, DIES

Brainerd, Minn., Nov. 28.—(Special to
The Herald.)—Thomas R. Congdon, 59,
artist, etcher and painter, who died
in Boston of diabetes recently, was a
resident of Brainerd in the early days
and is remembered by the old residents.
In 1886 he left for New York, where
he studied three years and then went
to Paris, where he established a studio.

---

day, November 18, 1917.

AUGUSTE RODIN, SCULPTOR, IS D...

By the Associated Press.
Paris, Nov. 17.—Auguste Rodin, the
famous sculptor, is dead. M. Rodin
died in his villa at Meudon, in the outskirts of Paris, after an illness of a few
days.

Auguste Rodin struggled 50 years
against poverty and abuse and ridicule
for his unconventional ideas before he
achieved undisputed celebrity as one of
the most famous sculptors of the world.
Continuing his work until past his 75th
year, he had, however, notwithstanding
... Later he collaborated
with a Belgian sculptor in carving
figures for the Brussels Bourse, and
...ress that Kerensky... villa at Meudon, in
the outskirts of Paris, after an illness of
a few days.

Met with Abuse and Ridicule.

Auguste Rodin struggled nearly fifty
years against poverty, abuse and ridicule
for his unconventional ideas before he
achieved undisputed celebrity as one of
the most famous sculptors of the world.
Continuing his work until past his 75th
year, he had, however, notwithstanding
these early handicaps, still time to en-
rich the world with innumerable examples of his...

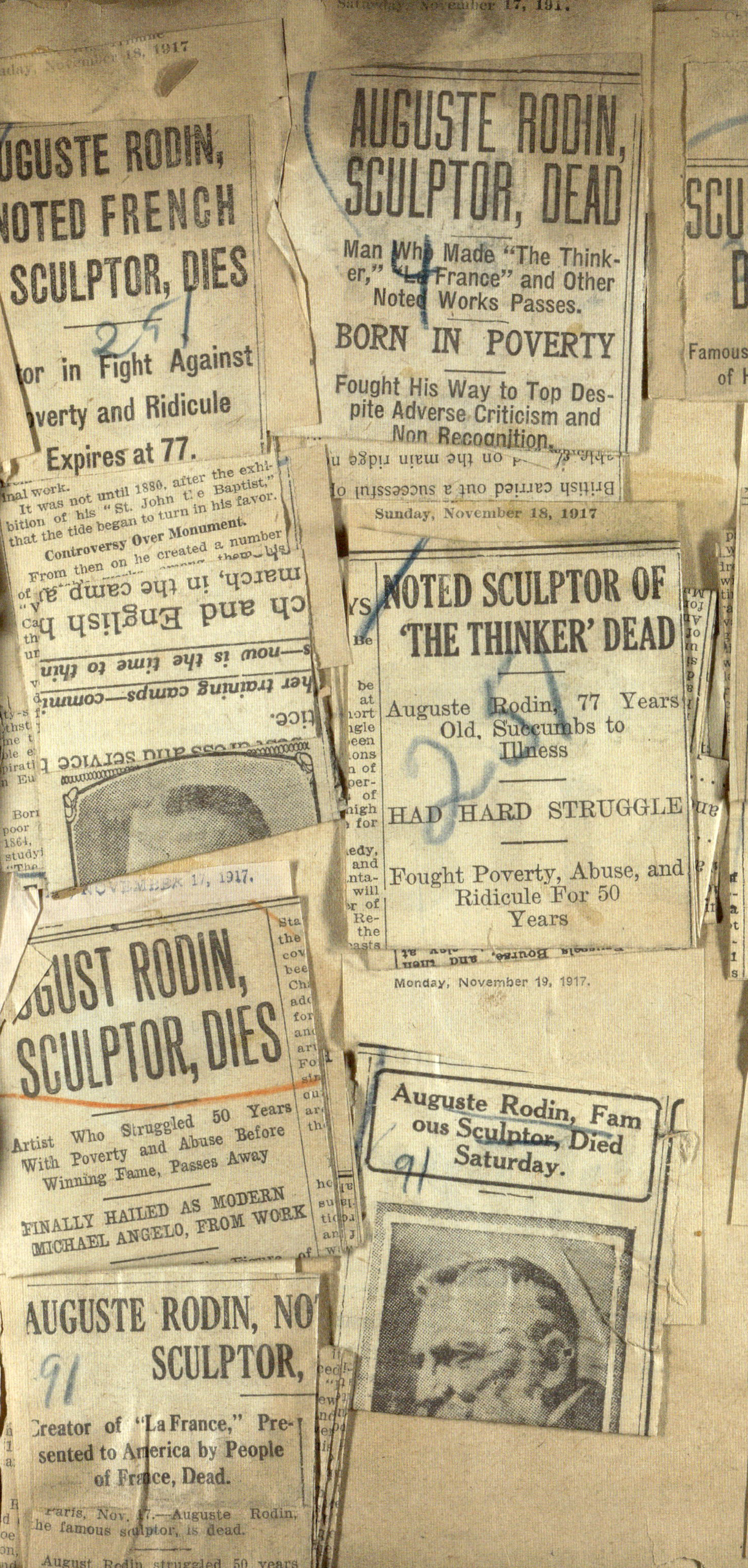

Saturday, November 17, 191.
Chicago, Ill. Examiner
Sunday, November 18, 191.

Sunday, November 18, 1917

AUGUSTE RODIN, NOTED FRENCH SCULPTOR, DIES
251
tor in Fight Against overty and Ridicule Expires at 77.

inal work.
It was not until 1880, after the exhibition of his "St. John the Baptist," that the tide began to turn in his favor.
Controversy Over Monument.
From then on he created a number of

ch and English h
march, in the camp, a
—now is the time to thin
her training camps—comm
ice.

Born
poor
1864,
study
"The

NOVEMBER 17, 1917.

GUST RODIN, SCULPTOR, DIES
Artist Who Struggled 50 Years With Poverty and Abuse Before Winning Fame, Passes Away
FINALLY HAILED AS MODERN MICHAEL ANGELO, FROM WORK

AUGUSTE RODIN, NO SCULPTOR,
91
Creator of "La France," Presented to America by People of France, Dead.
Paris, Nov. 17.—Auguste Rodin, the famous sculptor, is dead.
August Rodin struggled 50 years against poverty and abuse and ridi-

AUGUSTE RODIN, SCULPTOR, DEAD
Man Who Made "The Thinker," "La France" and Other Noted Works Passes.
BORN IN POVERTY
Fought His Way to Top Despite Adverse Criticism and Non Recognition.

NOTED SCULPTOR OF 'THE THINKER' DEAD
251
Auguste Rodin, 77 Years Old, Succumbs to Illness
HAD HARD STRUGGLE
Fought Poverty, Abuse, and Ridicule For 50 Years

Monday, November 19, 1917.

Auguste Rodin, Famous Sculptor, Died Saturday.
91

CHICAGO EXAMINER
SCULPTOR RODIN DIES IN PARIS
Famous Artist Endured 50 Years of Harsh Criticism Before Being Recognized

Friday, September 28, 1917.

OBITUARY
EDGARD DEGAS.
Edgard Degas, the noted French er, died yesterday in Paris, at th of eighty-three years. He was bo Paris July 19, 1834, his full name Hilaire Germain Edgard Degas, an Flaubert, he never married. In his days he associated with Manet, Whistler, Fantin-Latour, Duranty critic, and the crowd that first we the Café Guerbois in the Batig quarter, later to the Nouvelles Ath and, finally to the Café de la R
Sold for $87,00

PARIS, Sept. 27.—Hilaire Ge Edgard Degas, the painter, died he day. He was a noted painter o various phases of Parisian life, pa larly the ballet and horse races. "Les Danseuses a la Barre" re $87,000 at the Roman sale, held se years ago, though Degas had orig sold it for $87.
Degas was born in 1832 and st law, but later took up art. Several ago his eyesight failed him, an lived almost as a hermit. His ca years ago for his newspaper magazine work, particularly in Cosmopolitan and other Hearst lications, died Tuesday from a plication of diseases at his hom Ridgewood, N. J.
Mr. Hering was born on Staten and forty-five years ago and l much of his life in this city. H studied art under Julian in Paris Marr in Munich. He is survive three sons.

promoted. For years he was Fr Consular agent and agent of Cunard line at Bermuda.

EMIL HERING.
Funeral services of Emil Her artist and illustrator, who died his home in Ridgewood, N. J., Tu day, will be held to-day privately Hering became widely known for newspaper and magazine work, p ticularly in The Cosmopolitan other Hearst publications. He born on Staten Island forty years ago and lived much of h in Manhattan. He studied art un Julian in Paris and Marr in Mun He is survived by three sons.

Overhandling would likely make them decompose entirely within a relatively brief time.

And yet this delicate, piteous material called out to me to immerse myself in it, and museum colleagues, archivists, and artists with whom I shared the discovery encouraged me to go deeper. Over time, I realized these grim fragments of the past were much more than just compelling records of artists' deaths; they stimulated ideas and questions about artists' lives. By presenting the scrapbooks and the story of their creation to a wider audience, I hope to inspire a sense of wonder at the unique challenges that artists face, the exceptional risks they take, and the cruel turns of fate that often thwart their efforts.

1. Lives and Deaths

For centuries, art aficionado gossip has persisted that too much sex killed Raphael, the creative genius of the High Renaissance. His admiring biographer Giorgio Vasari can be credited with the rumor.

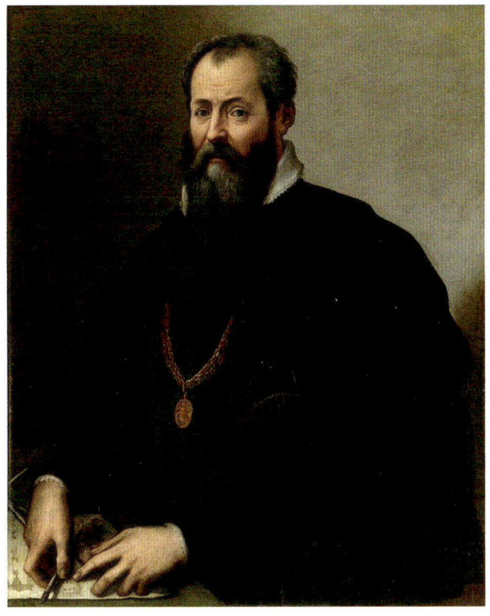

Attributed to Jacopo Zucchi, *Giorgio Vasari*, ca. 1571–1574. Uffizi Gallery

Vasari claimed that the notoriously promiscuous painter routinely "pursued his amorous pleasures beyond all moderation" and that after one occasion in 1520 "even more immoderate than usual," Raphael was stricken with fever. His doctor prescribed bloodletting, then a common remedial practice for all manner of ailments. In Raphael's case the cure proved worse than the illness. Recent research suggests the artist suffered from an underlying pulmonary disease that was likely aggravated by the administered precipitous blood loss, resulting in his death. Vasari himself suspected as much and speculated that, contrary to doctor's orders, the unfortunate artist had been "in need rather of restoratives."

Hagiographic images of Raphael on his deathbed have circulated widely ever since. They spread an apocryphal story that the master was surrounded in his last hours by notable peers and rivals. In a stirring nineteenth-century rendition of the scene, Johannes Riepenhausen depicted Michelangelo standing at the foot of his competitor's deathbed, his hands clasped together and his head tilted in contemplation.

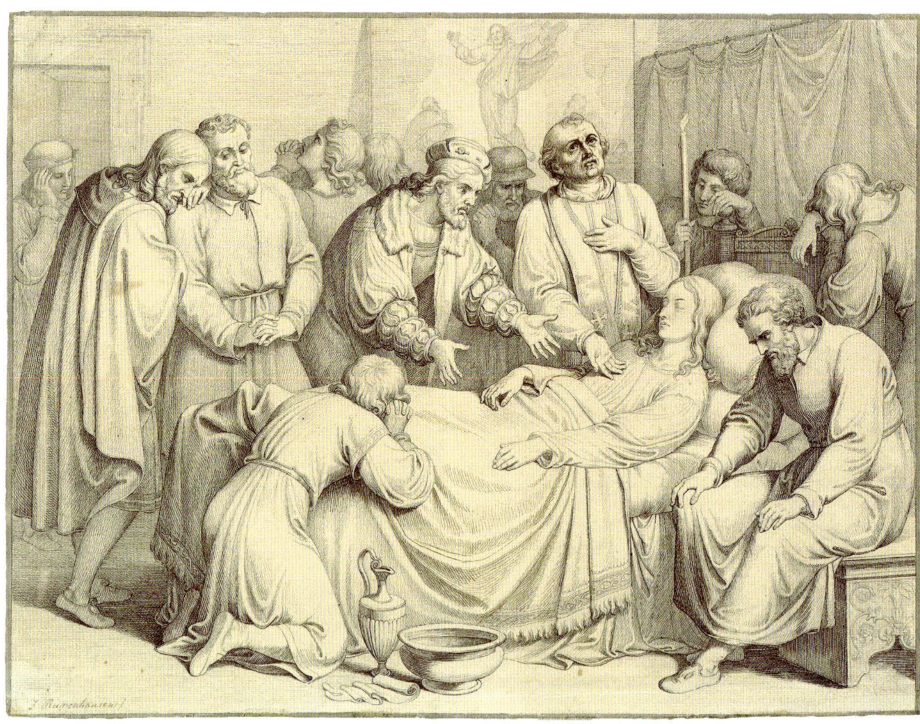

Johannes Riepenhausen, *The Death of Raphael*, 1832 or before. The Metropolitan Museum of Art, Mr. and Mrs. Francis D. Logan and Van Day Truex Funds, 2012 (2012.366)

The notion that artists lived recklessly and were apt to die young as they strove for fame in a professional world crowded with ambitious, inflated egos was a recurring theme of Vasari's great book *The Lives of the Most Eminent Painters, Sculptors, and Architects* (a title often shortened in English to *Lives of the Artists*). This sixteenth-century bestseller established a mode of art history scholarship that thrives to this day, in which exhaustive catalogues raisonnés and

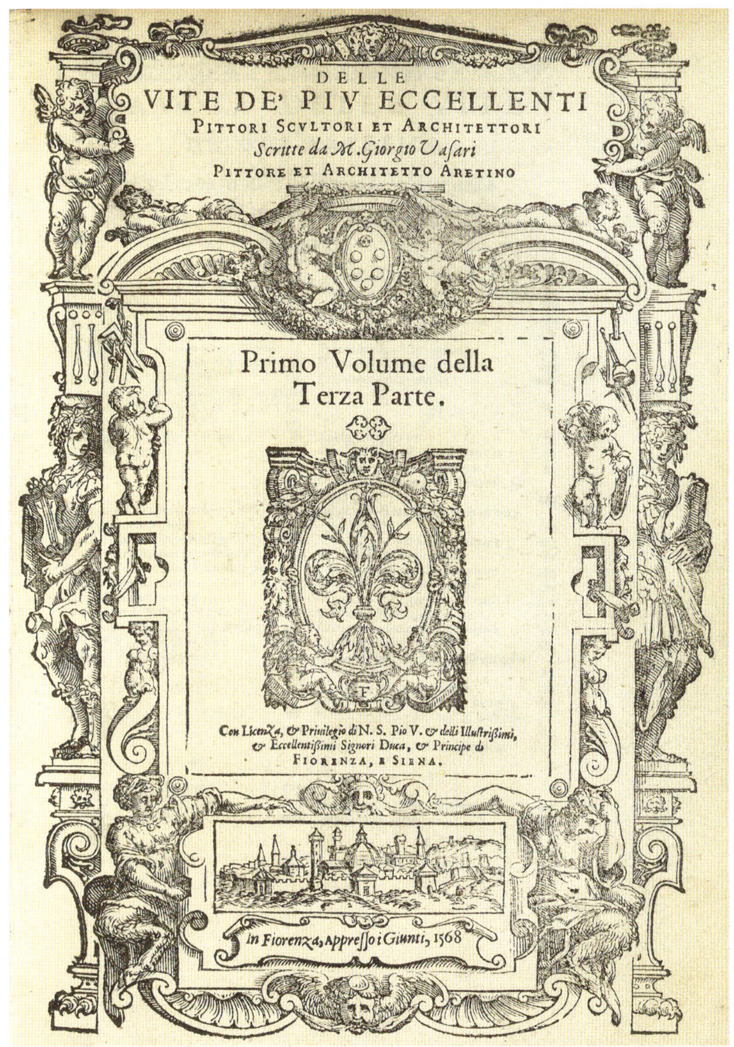

Giorgio Vasari, *The Lives of the Most Eminent Painters, Sculptors, and Architects*, vol. 1, part 3, 1568 edition

copious biographical data support the portrayal of artist-subjects against richly detailed cultural backdrops.

Vasari's sprawling text chronicles the bustling activity of hundreds of artists and inventories the many spectacular objects they made. But a more somber theme of mortality haunts the *Lives*. In his introduction to the first edition of 1550, Vasari voiced fear that the finest creators of his time would be forgotten and that "nothing can

be foretold for them but a certain and well-nigh immediate death."
He aspired in his magnum opus "to preserve them as long as may be
possible in the memory of the living," for they "do not deserve to have
their names and their works wholly left . . . the prey of death and of
oblivion." Tellingly, he sequenced nearly all the profiles that comprise
the book not by the artists' birth dates but, rather, by their dates of
death. When he published an expanded second edition in 1568, Vasari
proclaimed with satisfaction that because of his successful book, "it
can never be said that the artists had truly died, nor that their works
had remained buried." He knew that his subjects, and their achievements—and his own—would be known for centuries to come.

As I dug into the morbid contents of The Met obituary scrapbooks,
I thought of Vasari and his mission to survey comprehensively and
preserve for posterity the accomplishments of all artists of his place
and era. As an archivist, I understood that the scrapbooks contained
news that could be useful to historians and that might also inspire
fresh creative work now and in the future. From a twenty-first-
century perspective, the fascinating qualities of this collection were
abundantly clear, but I was driven to understand its original purpose
at its inception and throughout the years of its creation.

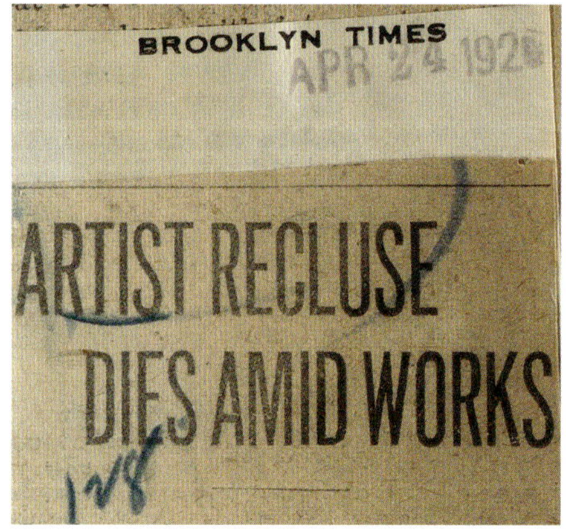

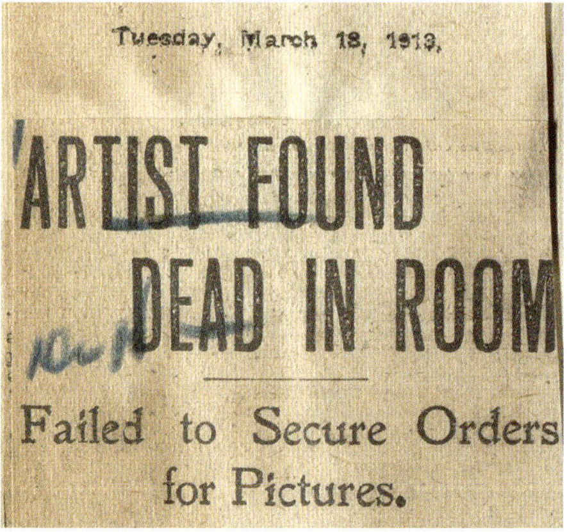

The twentieth-century obituary collector seemed a kindred spirit
to Vasari, his Renaissance forebear, just as obsessed with heaping
up biographical data that might delineate the contours of an art
historical epoch. By odd coincidence, the scrapbook clippings appear

in chronological order by death date, rather than an alphabetical or other organizational principle, mirroring Vasari's arrangement in his *Lives*. Like Vasari's biographies, the scrapbooks present beguiling, colorful vignettes of the rough and tumble bohemian milieu, rife with passion, intrigue, and occasional violence. The cumulative effect of reading through hundreds of dead artist profiles felt very much akin to wading through Vasari's daunting masterpiece: it was enlightening and exhausting. I wondered if the maker of The Met scrapbooks had deliberately aimed to create a modern-day analogue to Vasari's *Lives*—and I began to think of this work as *Deaths of Artists*.

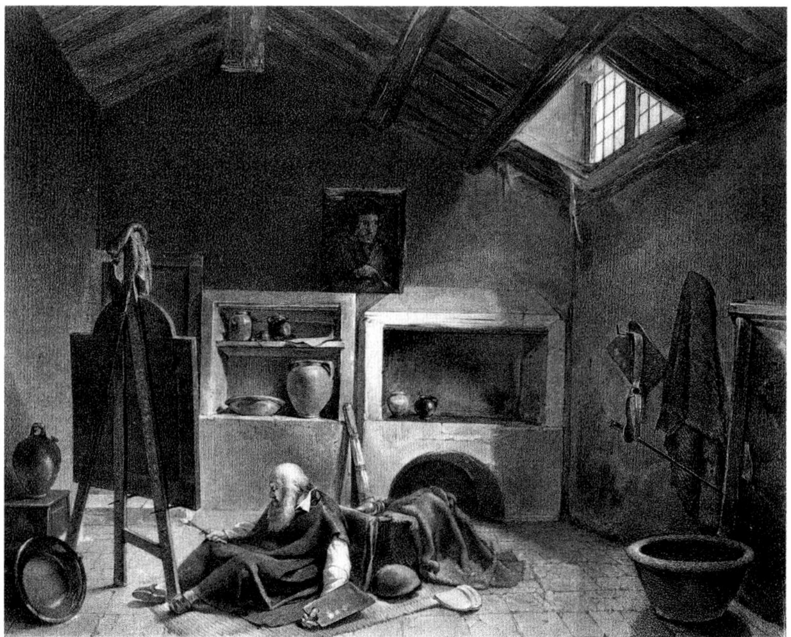

Paul Jourdy after François-Marius Granet, *Mort de Jacone*, 1825–1829. The British Museum (1860,0728.282)

Vasari described many artists' deaths in a moralizing tone. He associated unfortunate or even miserable circumstances that some faced at the end of their lives with creative weakness, and he used history to settle old scores with enemies and antagonists. He derided a fellow Florentine, Jacone, as lazy and more interested in partying than cultivating his artistic ability. Vasari dismissed this minor talent and his friends as "swine and brute-beasts . . . filthy and brutish in mind as their outward appearance." One consequence of a disorderly life, Vasari suggested, was a squalid death. "Finally . . . reduced by infirmity . . . poor, neglected, and paralyzed in the legs . . . Jacone died in misery in a little hovel . . . on a mean street." Centuries later, in the Romantic era, the death scene was imagined by the French artist François-Marius Granet, whose depiction was the basis for a popular print by Paul Jourdy.

Vasari characterized others as impoverished, eccentric, or suffering from delusions that hindered the full flourishing of their genius. In Vasari's estimation, Paolo Uccello, a talented fifteenth-century painter, frittered away his gift by doggedly "seeking to solve the problems of perspective" and squandered his last years as a homebound recluse, chasing an elusive vanishing point to the grave. The lesson was that "Artists who devote more attention to perspective than to figures develop a dry and angular style because of their anxiety to examine things too minutely; and moreover, they usually end up solitary, eccentric, melancholy, and poor, as indeed did Paolo Uccello himself."

Vasari even detailed a self-destructive eccentricity of his great hero Michelangelo, who "wore buskins of dogskin on the legs, next to the skin, constantly for whole months together, so that afterwards, when he sought to take them off, on drawing them off, the skin often came away with them." By relating anecdotes like these, he affirmed and popularized stereotypes of creative personalities that have endured for centuries. Reading Vasari in tandem with The Met scrapbooks confirmed that the tabloid-style reporting by writers of the early twentieth century is consistent with a long tradition of such storytelling about artists.

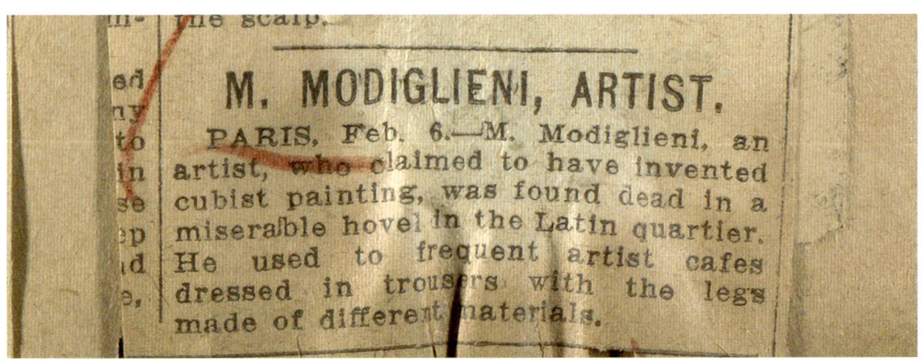

M. MODIGLIENI, ARTIST.

PARIS, Feb. 6.—M. Modiglieni, an artist, who claimed to have invented cubist painting, was found dead in a miserable hovel in the Latin quartier. He used to frequent artist cafes dressed in trousers with the legs made of different materials.

M. MODIGLIENI, ARTIST

M. Modiglieni, an artist, who claimed to have invented cubist painting, was found dead in a miserable hovel in the Latin quartier. He used to frequent artist cafes dressed in trousers with the legs made of different materials.

In a mere two sentences a 1920 news story reported to American readers the death of a little-known avant-garde artist, "M. Modiglieni." Today this Italian artist's name, Amedeo Modigliani, is anything but obscure; one of his paintings fetched $170 million in 2015. Modigliani, the quintessential bohemian, had been a notorious character on the Paris art scene. Like Jacone, he was a hard partier whose appetite for alcohol and drugs wrecked his already fragile health and cut short a promising career. When Modigliani perished of tubercular meningitis at thirty-five, he was destitute and his pictures were unknown beyond a small circle of cognoscenti. The tragedy was magnified the day after his passing when his partner and most frequent model, Jeanne Hébuterne, also a painter, twenty-one and pregnant with their second child, leapt to her death from the window of her parents' apartment.

Friends aspired to create a lasting memento to Modigliani by casting a death mask from his corpse. They nearly botched the job, tearing skin from the face and winding up with a poor likeness. From the wreckage, sculptor Jacques Lipchitz patched together a version serviceable to cast multiples later acquired by private collectors and museums, including one now in The Met. Modigliani's funeral was thronged by Montparnasse locals including Pablo Picasso, Fernand Léger, and Constantin Brancusi. The spectacle drew the attention of a jour-nalist who filed the poorly fact-checked story that is glued to the bottom margin

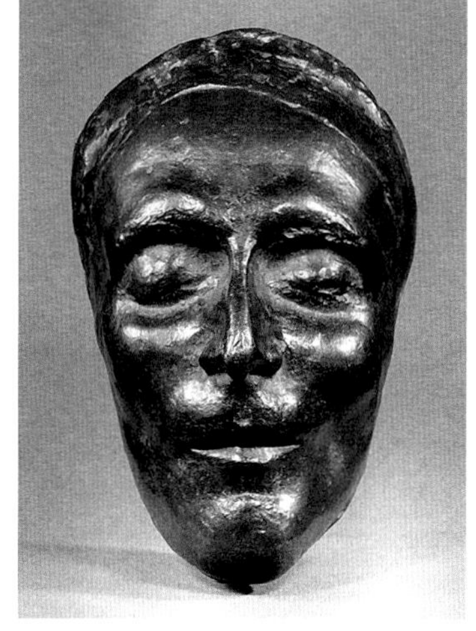

Jacques Lipchitz and Moïse Kisling, *Death Mask of Modigliani*, ca. 1920. The Metropolitan Museum of Art, Gift of Phyllis Lutyens, 1972 (1972.219) © 2023 Artists Rights Society (ARS), New York

of a scrapbook page. In addition to misstating the artist's first-name initial and misspelling his surname, the obituary wrongly associated him with Cubism and mislocated his place of death as a hovel rather than a hospital. Finally, it raised an eyebrow at Modigliani's fashion sense, echoing Vasari's description of Jacone as "brutish" in "outward appearance."

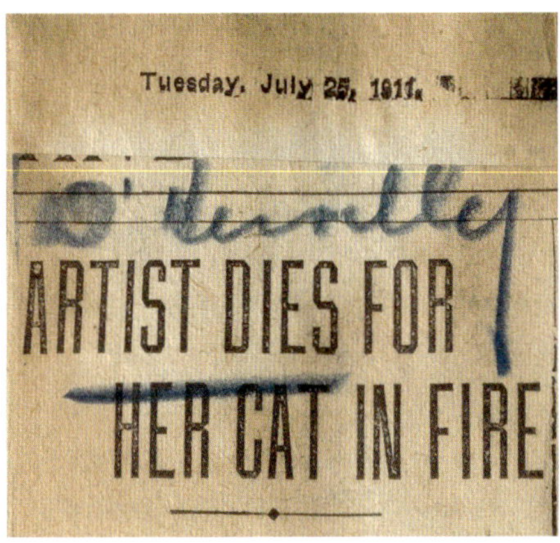

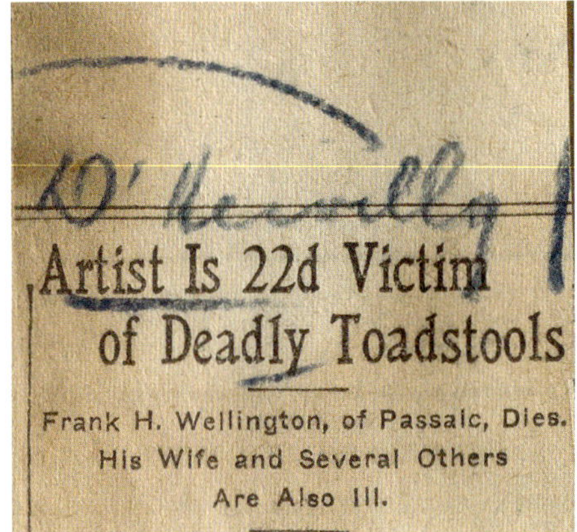

One day I noticed a significant detail that I had overlooked during many prior viewings of the scrapbooks. Almost every clipping was marked with a bold stroke of blue pencil that underlined the word *artist* where it first appeared in each text. Additionally, scrawled across many obituaries was *D'Hervilly*, or sometimes *D'H.* I wondered—could this be the surname of someone at The Met?

I searched in old file card indexes in The Met archives and I quickly found a match for the unfamiliar name that led me to a dusty bundle of museum payrolls bound with thin, mauve twine. It looked like it had not been opened for a very long time. On a neatly penned ledger sheet from 1894 I discovered that an Arthur D'Hervilly was hired that year as a gallery attendant, the era's parlance for a guard. I chased this hint and sifted through meeting minutes and correspondence of The Met's first chief executive, where surprising details came to light. Over the next decade, D'Hervilly ascended the ranks and was ultimately appointed assistant curator of paintings around the time that the first artist obituaries were pasted into a scrapbook volume. I resolved to uncover all that I could about him.

2. The Path of Strict Rectitude

Arthur D'Hervilly was born on August 20, 1850, the last of eight
children of Felix and Laura D'Hervilly. His parents were New
Yorkers of French descent, possibly related to white colonizer refu-
gees who fled Haiti during the revolutionary uprising of the 1790s.
Felix was a stockbroker with an office on Exchange Place in Manhattan's financial district. His large family, supported by three ser-
vants, lived farther north near what is now SoHo. Laura gave birth
to Arthur in bucolic Morris County, NJ, perhaps while on summer
holiday not far from the metropolis. When Arthur was about ten
years old, a crisis upset the domestic order and part of the family
moved to Philadelphia. The Panic of 1857, an economic crisis that
sent railroad stocks and bonds plummeting, may have had significant ramifications on the family's fortune and forced a change.

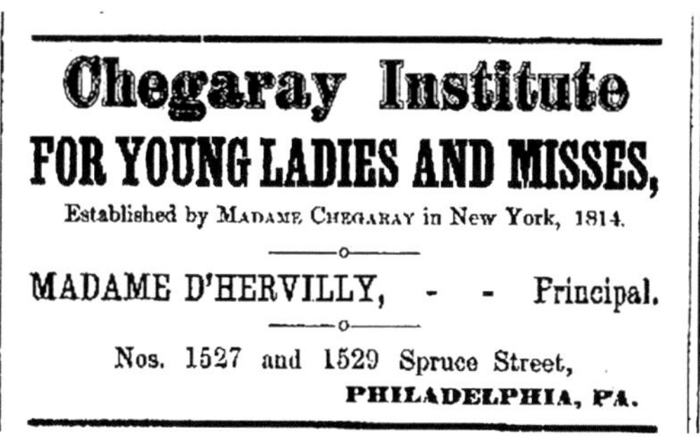

Advertisement for Chegaray Institute published
in Thomas A. M. Ward, *Punch and Judy*, 1874

By 1862, some of the D'Hervilly clan were resettled in Center
City Philadelphia, where Arthur's mother, Laura, opened a boarding
and day school for young ladies. She called it the Chegaray Institute,
after her aunt Eloise Chegaray, who earlier ran a similar establishment in New York. Advertisements for students boasted "French is
the language of the family and is constantly spoken at the Institute."
Arthur attended public school until age seventeen. He learned to
write a beautiful script and was sharp at math, and after graduating

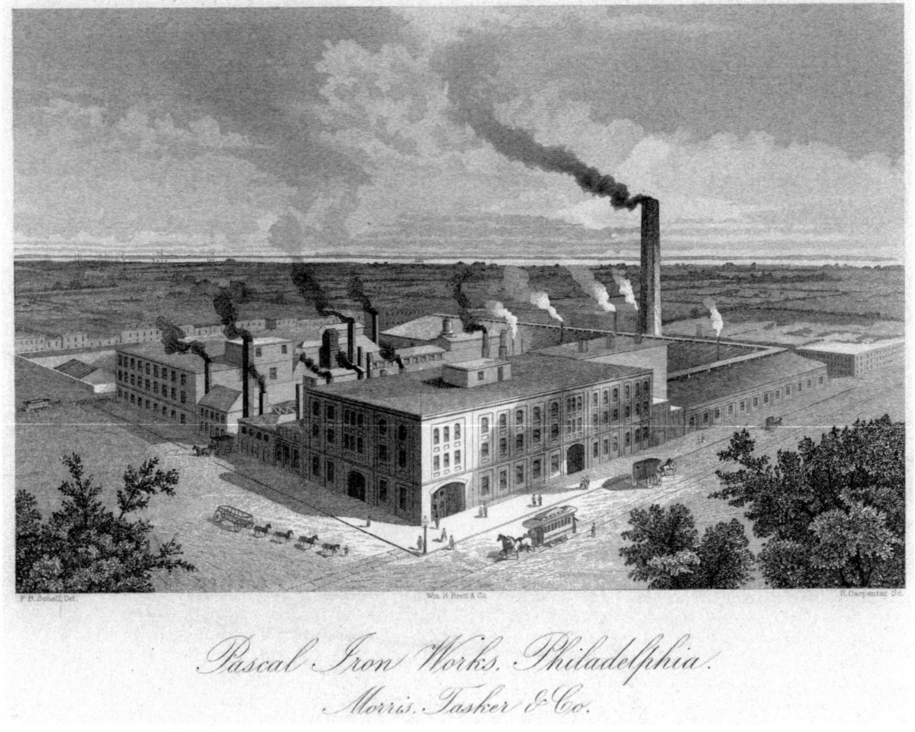

Pascal Iron Works, Morris, Tasker & Co., Philadelphia, PA, 1867. Hagley Museum and Library, Wilmington, DE, 1986.268

he found work as a bookkeeper. Both penmanship and accounting were skills he drew upon much later at The Met.

In 1876 he was listed in a Philadelphia city directory as a resident of 1527 Spruce Street, the Chegaray Institute address, which was home base to members of the family for years to come. He clerked in the head office of Morris, Tasker & Co., which made industrial pipe, plumbing parts, machinery, tools, and ornamental lighting at the Pascal Iron Works on the city's south side. In the booming postwar American economy, an administrative position with a large manufacturing firm was lucrative enough to support a family and was a good bet for a secure future. An 1880 census taker listed Arthur still living at the Chegaray Institute, married to a woman named Ida.

Around this time the sibling closest to Arthur in age, James, was discharged from the U.S. Marine Corps suffering from a debilitating mental illness. He was shipped back to Philadelphia from the other side of the world in Samoa, where he'd been stricken aboard the USS *Lackawanna* with symptoms including an acute fear of electricity. He soon died at age thirty-four. Another brother, Charles, was killed when he fell and fractured his skull in a Philadelphia street brawl. A sister, Emma, had also passed away by this time, as had their father, Felix.

In the Victorian era, death felt closer at hand than it does today. Rather than in hospitals, many died at home, surrounded by family. Arthur D'Hervilly may have watched with his own eyes as loved ones suffered their final illnesses. As I learned about D'Hervilly's early life, I wondered if his later obsession with obituaries stemmed in part from witnessing many deaths in his family.

ARTIST, DYING OF STARVATION,
PAINTS PICTURE OF HERSELF

Philadelphia is the location in the dateline of some harrowing stories in The Met scrapbooks. Ella Finley, a painter and sculptor, died there in 1910 after spending a month before a mirror creating a self-portrait she believed would win her the fame accorded her hero James McNeill Whistler. She was fifty years old, and in her youth she had placed a few sculptures in group shows at the Pennsylvania Academy of Fine Arts. But critical acclaim and commissions eluded her, and for many years she lived on the largesse of a wealthy brother. After he died, Finley drifted into penury. According to an obituary writer, the overproud artist rejected a friend's suggestion that she hire out as a commercial illustrator. "I would rather starve to death than do the trash you are doing," she shot back.

A physician who happened to visit Finley's Chestnut Street studio found her emaciated and subsisting on moldy bread while daubing at her own painted image. He whisked her to a hospital, but it was too late, and she soon died. The *N.Y. Evening Journal* published a remarkable photograph of her final creation, while another tabloid reported Finley's death under the headline WOMAN ARTIST FOUND STARVED and suggested her ambition had been "to paint a likeness of herself which would keep fresh in the minds of her friends how she looked before the pangs of starvation demanded their toll."

JOHN J. BARBER KILLS HIMSELF

Well-Known Artist Cuts Throat in State Hospital With Pair of Scissors.

INJURED IN APRIL

Physical and Mental Infirmities Date From That Time. Leaves no Family.

John J. Barber, aged 71, a life resident of Columbus, artist and for some time a clerk in the county treasurer's office, died last night at the Columbus State Hospital as the result of an attempt at suicide made Saturday morning. He inflicted a wound in his neck with a pair of scissors.

Barber, a member of the Republican Glee Club, Buckeye Republican Club, G. A. R. and Columbus lodge of Elks, a prominent and popular citizen. mental infirmity dates back to the presentation of the opera given last April by the Elks. performance, he slipped and n stairs, receiving injuries

taxes. Many details of their financial standing and management are ex however, and holding companie formerly paid no tax whateve compelled to pay under the ne

CENIC ARTIST A SUICIDE

LUMBUS, O., Nov. 27. — John Ja er, at one time a scenic artist died tonight at the Columbus State ital for the Insane, of which he had an inmate a little over a week, from ds self inflicted with a razor. His ity was due to a fall last April.

Artist, Dying of Starvation, Paints Picture of Herself

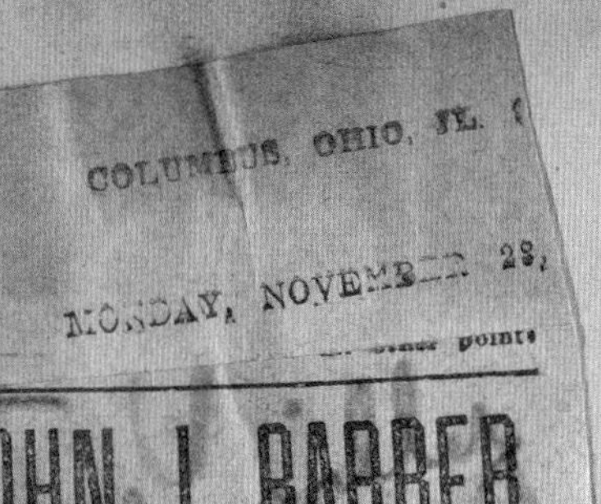

MISS ELLA FINLEY.

Photographed from the picture she painted just before she died.

Eden Musée's Designer Dead.

Constant Thys, 56 years old, an artist employed by the Eden Musée, died of heart disease yesterday afternoon in the studio at the Musée while he was at work figures portraying America y-eight years ago ed ever since at the esigned practically ups displayed there Hasbrouck Heights er of the Hasbrouck ucation. He is sur d four children.

ndoned her original

an—

Durand Woodman, Woodman, and the d of the late Asher the founders of the of Design, and its years, is dead at West Ninety-first man, who herself born in New York

was the only one made their fortunes ned a resident of the life. He left a large

H. Osgood.

rriett Osgood, who Art School at 120 treet in 1878, died ase yesterday in her She was a daughter Winthrop Osgood, a olumbus, Ohio, and in 1842. The school the pioneer decorated States, and was introduce decorative of a factory. Miss her, Winthrop A. ers, Mrs. Annette ist, and Mrs. Mary will be buried in

Ulrich Hoegger died in Philadelphia from burns suffered in a shocking studio fire—a disaster eerily presaged by his most popular work of art. In 1897 he finished a painting he titled *Verstummt* (Silenced), which depicted the charred wreckage of a burned-out music conservatory including a singed cello and a framed picture of Beethoven. Strangely, the original *Verstummt* was itself partially destroyed in a 1904 fire in the artist's atelier. Inspired by the near-disaster, in 1905 Hoegger had an engraving and prints made that showed the now actually burned canvas. The prints sold well and

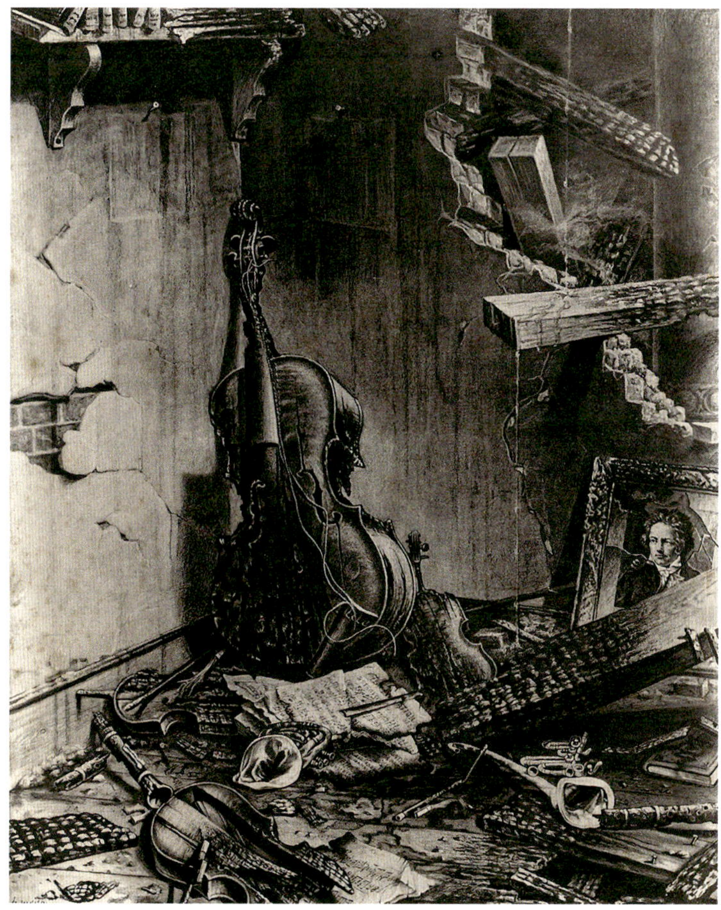

Max Zeitler, *Verstummt* (Silenced), 1905, engraving from the original painting by Ulrich A. Hoegger

ARTIST LAMBERT DIES OF A BROKEN HEART

Grief Over Loss of Sight Hastened End of Painter and Art Critic.

HAD BRILLIANT CAREER

were wrecked. [...]

John Lambert [...]
and a broken [...]
The brilliant [...]
beautiful coun[...]
Jenkintown, de[...]
best medical s[...]
ing physicians [...]
were responsi[...]
those who kn[...]
loss of his sig[...]
In September [...]
underwent trea[...]
Pennsylvania [...]
he was kept w[...]
ered room wi[...]
of his eyes, bu[...]
to treatment h[...]
removed to his [...]
It was in Sp[...]
Lambert was s[...]
that his sight [...]
was the glare [...]
roads that ca[...]
in the mounta[...]
condition was [...]
to go to Paris [...]
specialist. [...]
"Drop all wo[...]
you will be b[...]
the specialist. [...]
ENDED [...]
At the heigh[...]
and just as h[...]
ance of nearl[...]
had had a har[...]
on Seventh s[...]
back to this [...]
Drs. De Sch[...]
They did all that science and [...]

ARTIST BURIED WITH SIMPLE CEREMONY

John Lambert Laid Away in North Laurel Hill Cemetery After Impressive Services

HOLGER HENRIK DRACHMANN.

Copenhagen, Jan. 14.—Holger Henrik Herholdt Drachmann, the Danish poet and author, died yesterday at Hornbaek from a long standing affection of the nerves. When he was young he made two visits to the United States.

Holger H. H. Drachmann was born in Copenhagen on October 9, 1846. He was educated at the university of that city and at its Academy of Fine Arts, beginning his career as a painter of the sea, and achieving success in that field of art, both in Denmark and in England. To Georges Brandes's influence is largely due his serious entrance upon the field of letters. He had already, as early [...] short sketches in [...] to Brandes, who [...]ged him. In the following titles: "Young Blood," [...] the Frontier." [...]place about this [...]o years, and re[...]tion of devoting [...]nations and the [...]him to write a [...]ned his future [...] author.

[...]eader by th[...]
of Young Den[...]
to abdicate, a[...]
e of Danish li[...]
the national a[...]
He became th[...]
on, and as suc[...]
work. He wa[...]
eligious theme[...]
ge of bourgeo[...]
ise of libert[...]
was above [...]
deep impul[...]
a realist. [...]
[...] Feuer," [...]
astical in[...]
uced r[...]
mong [...]
n and [...]
Time, [...]
desk[...]

ARTIST HOEGGER, BURNED IN STUDIO, DIES MEETING FATE WHICH HE LONG DREADED

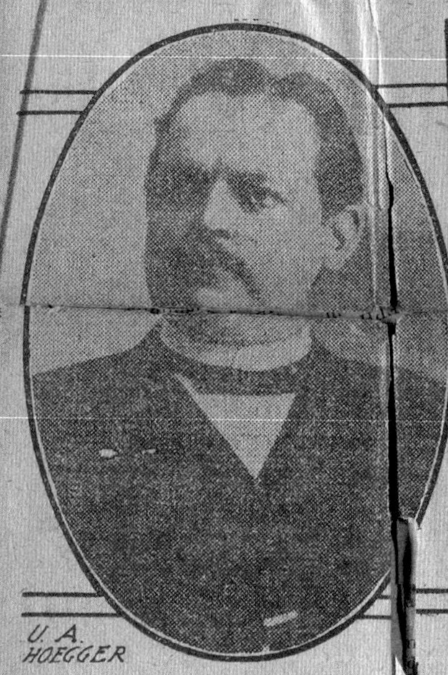

"SILENCED," THE DEAD ARTIST'S MASTERPIECE.

Continued from Page 1.

in the room, valued at $110,000, were charred fragments.

His Famous Picture of Fire.

The fear of fire that obsessed Hoegger inspired the picture that gained him more fame than any of his numerous pastels and portraits. He called the picture "Silenced." It portrayed in vivid and graphic tints a partially wrecked music studio with broken and burned violins. This picture was pronounced a masterpiece and received the most favorable attention from critics. Many offers were made for the painting, but for a reason that he never made plain, Hoegger refused to part with it.

[...] will be held at [...] o'clock Wednesday afternoon from his Camden home.

child slept. This picture, which was a fine conception, the Mother standing pensively over her sleeping child, was to be sold to the St. Columbia's Catholic School for $5000. It awaited only a few finishing touches.

Notable Paintings Destroyed.

Another noted painting destroyed was entitled "Caught at Last," and depicted an aged woman setting a trap for a mouse, the little rodent being shown caught fast in the door of a cupboard. "The Lioness and Her Cubs," an animal study from life, was painted by Mr. Hoegger at the local Zoological Gardens.

The "No Name" picture, also destroyed, was a favorite of the artist, to which an interesting story attaches. It portrayed an humble cottage overshadowed by stately mansions. In quest of an appro-

BURNED ARTIST SUCCUMBS TO FATE HE LONG DREADED

[...] Hoegger Dies as Result of Fire Which Destroyed Li[...]ork—Obsession May Have Caused Blaze.

When Ulrich A. Hoegger, the artist who was burned with his priceless paintings, Thursday night, in a fire at his studio, 2337 North Thirty-first Street, died yesterday in the Woman's Homeopathic Hospital, a tragedy was completed whose sinister shadow has for years been hanging over its victim and darkening his life.

The fear of death in flames, and with his own destruction and that of his works of a lifetime, was so strong that it played an important part in his actions and [...] toward the concep-

[...]TOR
[...]EATH

were reproduced in magazines like *The Etude,* which also shared the image's odd backstory.

Unbelievably, a second conflagration in 1908 destroyed the last remnant of *Verstummt,* along with a valuable stock of other art. Hoegger was pulled alive from the flames but soon died of his wounds. Studio fires are a recurring motif in the scrapbooks, and it often happened that such disasters consumed troves of art and cut short the lives of their creators. These true-life tales recall the demise of the French novelist Honoré de Balzac's fictional painter Frenhofer, who sets his oeuvre ablaze and dies at the climax of the 1831 novella *The Unknown Masterpiece.*

Creative writers like Balzac and chroniclers of current events alike resorted to age-old stereotypes of struggling artists when describing their tragic fates. But tabloid writers of a century ago refracted their narratives through the dark, gritty lens of yellow journalism. The nickname of this reporting style derived from a cartoon character called "The Yellow Kid," a newsprint fixture at the turn of the twentieth century. Joseph Pulitzer's *New York World* and its rival *New York Journal* published by William Randolph Hearst pioneered the genre, which attracted a huge audience by exploiting the minutiae and banality of raw human tragedy, violent crime, and political scandal. Sensational images and riveting headlines drew readers into stories rife with salacious details and sometimes dubious quotations.

The tabloids characterized artists as prone to abject poverty and presupposed that even those of great renown were liable to die

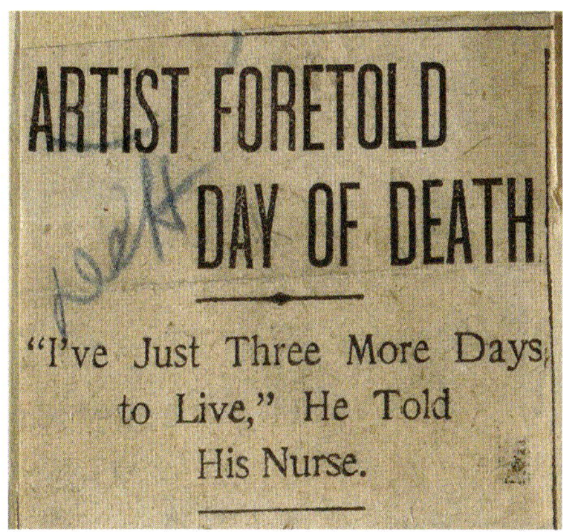

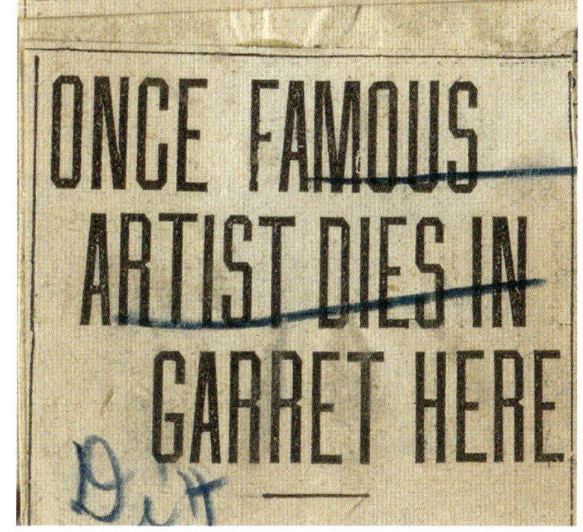

of hunger or in squalor while fanatically pursuing their vocation. Failure to sell work or secure patronage drove many to depression and suicide, and the most insensitive news writers divulged exactly how such troubled souls ended their own lives, dishing out startling details as lowbrow literary entertainment.

Sometimes these sad stories prompted reflection on the whims of fate, narrating chance mishaps that could have taken the life of anyone, artist or not. Car crashes and train wrecks, drownings, and poisonings were accidental means of death that tabloid writers played up even when a story lacked the struggling artist angle. After the outbreak of the First World War, tabloids reported too on artist-soldiers maimed and killed on the battlefields of Europe.

A remarkable number of the artists' obituaries in the scrapbooks involve criminal acts. The most shocking of these detail brutal murders stemming from love quarrels or unorthodox living arrangements associated with the bohemian demimonde.

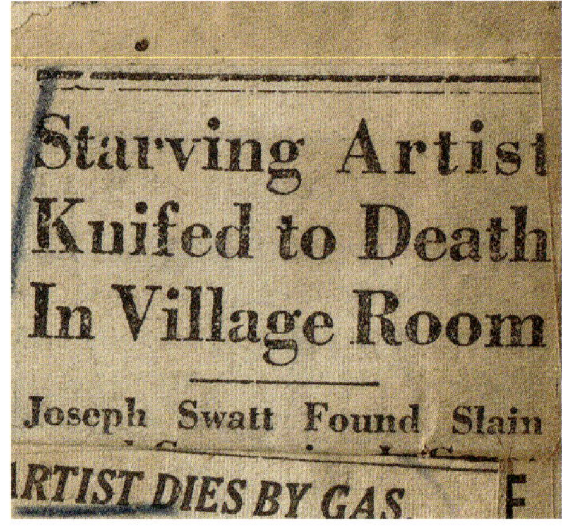

STARVING ARTIST KNIFED
TO DEATH IN VILLAGE ROOM

The *New-York Tribune* identified the victim of this blunt headline as twenty-eight-year-old Joseph Swatt, "a painter of impressionistic portraits . . . stabbed to death with a bread knife in his room. . . . He had been stabbed in a dozen places." Police speculated Swatt's boardinghouse roommate was the culprit.

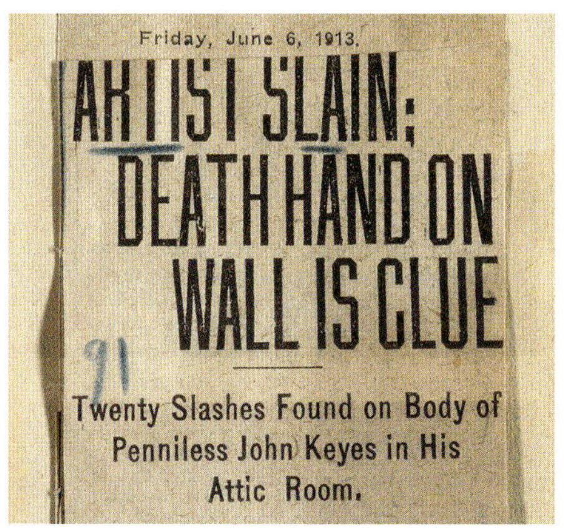

ARTIST SLAIN; DEATH HAND ON WALL IS CLUE
Twenty Slashes Found on Body of Penniless John Keyes in
His Attic Room.

John Keyes, also knifed in his New York City abode, was "one
of the drifting thousands who draw pictures—not salaries. . . . His
books and sketches were the dignity of his gloomy room."
True-crime stories of artist homicides like those of Swatt and
Keyes evoke the fictional murder of painter Basil Hallward in Oscar
Wilde's 1891 novel *The Picture of Dorian Gray*. After enduring years of
psychic torment brought on by the supernatural qualities of his portrait by Hallward, Gray impulsively stabs the artist to death in front of
the painting. If Wilde was a reader of tabloids, he might have ripped
the idea for one of his most enduring works from their headlines.

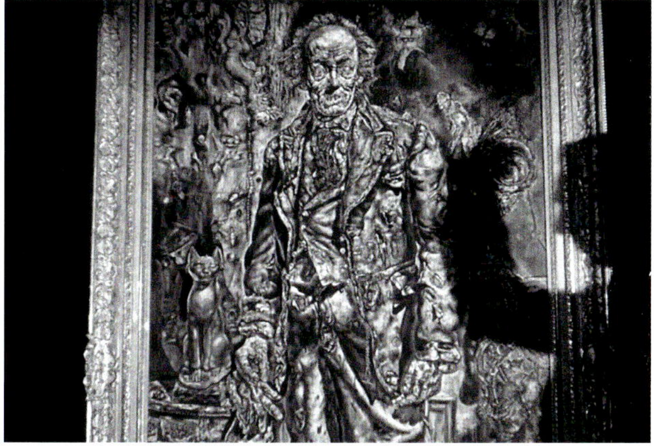

Film still, *The Picture of Dorian Gray*, directed by Albert
Lewin, 1945

Tuesday, Oct 7, 1912.

GIVES HIS BODY FOR DOG MEAT

Artist, a Suicide, Also Leaves Note in Which He Repudiates God and Religion.

ENDS LIFE AMONG HIS PAINTINGS

Arranges Works of His Brush and Writes Letters to Wife and Friends Before Turning On Gas Jets.

ARTIST FIRES BULLET INTO BRAIN WHILE IN HOTEL DINING ROOM

Name of Harry B. Longacre on Suspender Only Clue to Identity of Dying Victim

ARTIST CUTS THROAT, DIES

Wife Tries to Save Him—Injured in Struggle.

John Sweeney, 36 years old, an artist, of 144 Grove street, committed suicide early today by slashing himself across the throat with a table knife.

He was in ill health and despondent. His wife was preparing breakfast when, in the mirror, she saw her husband take up the knife and attempt to cut himself. She ran into the room and wrenched the blade away from him.

PLEADED IN VAIN WITH GIRL ARTIST TO AVERT SUICIDE

ARTIST SELECTS PARK TO COMMIT SUICIDE

Relatives in this city have been advised of the suicide in Portland of Henry Epting, a landscape artist, well known in San Francisco.

A telegram to Nicholas Epting, 1005 Diamond street, a brother of the suicide, conveys the information that Epting's body was found yesterday in a Portland park and that he had shot himself through the head.

ARTIST KILLED

WHILE HURRYING TO CATCH A TRAIN.

Guy Ewing, a Nephew of W. A. Urquhart, Met Death in a Tragic Manner.

STRANGE DEATH OF WELLKNOWN ARTIST

Frank C. Ormsby Dies From Attack of Apoplexy Due to Nightmare.

Frank C. Ormsby, the well known cartoonist and newspaper illustrator,

YOUNG ARTIST KILLED BY FALL FROM WINDOW OF HIS "DEN" AT HOME

Back of Seat in Which He Dozes Breaks and He Tum-

WOMAN ARTIST KILLED IN AUTO ACCIDENT

Machine Skids and Overturns in Yonkers——Three Injured,

WOMAN ARTIST DIES ENVELOPED IN FLAMES

Mrs. Gustav Faber Victim of Gasoline Stove

SAN BERNARDINO, July 22.—Mrs. Gustav Faber, a well known artist, was burned to death this afternoon as a result of trying to fill a gasoline stove while it was lighted. She was instantly enveloped in flames, and, running from the house, was a human torch and beyond relief when aid arrived. She died a few hours later. The home was destroyed. Mrs. Faber was an artist of rare talent, her pictures having been awarded prizes at many art exhibits.

ARTIST DIES IN FIRE THAT BURNS WORK

DEATH REVEALS STRUGGLES OF ARTIST

FORTUNE GONE IN STOCKS, ARTIST KILLS HIMSELF.

Albert Chittenden, a Hunchback,

WOMAN ARTIST, OF OLD FAMILY, DIES IN WANT

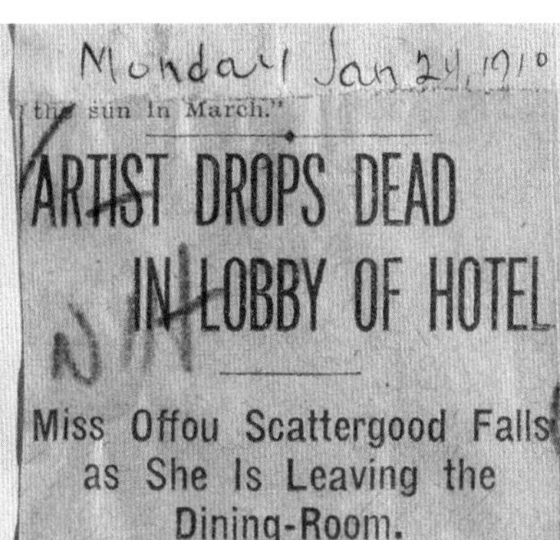

Monday Jan 24, 1910

"the sun in March."

ARTIST DROPS DEAD IN LOBBY OF HOTEL

Miss Offou Scattergood Falls as She Is Leaving the Dining-Room.

ARTIST KILLED BY SIGHT-SEEING AUTO

Harry O. Landers, Struck While Crossing Street, Dies in Hospital.

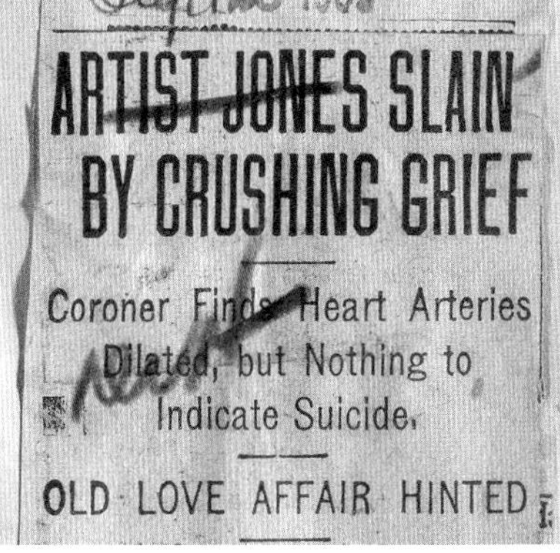

Sep 1908

ARTIST JONES SLAIN BY CRUSHING GRIEF

Coroner Finds Heart Arteries Dilated, but Nothing to Indicate Suicide.

OLD LOVE AFFAIR HINTED

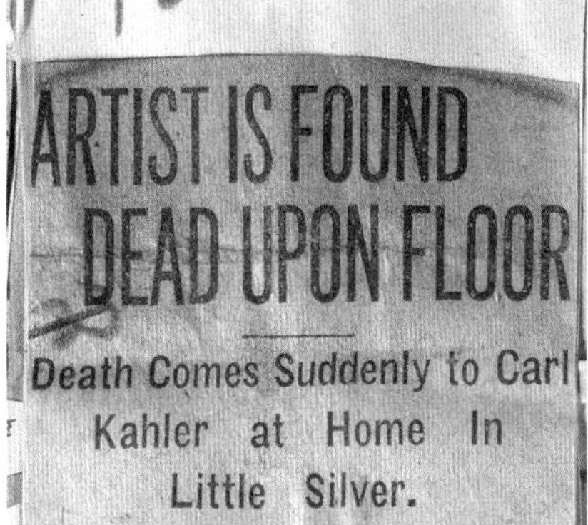

ARTIST IS FOUND DEAD UPON FLOOR

Death Comes Suddenly to Carl Kahler at Home In Little Silver.

BURST ARTERY KILLS ARTIST IN GOLF GAME

Samuel Isham Dies on the Links of the Maidstone Country Club.

Samuel Isham, a well-known artist, bled to death on the golf links of the Maidstone Country Club at East-ampton, L. I., to-day. He suffered

ARTIST, BROKE, ENDS HIS LIFE

Art did not bring money for Carl Lugo, believed to have held a national reputation for his designs, to purchase food and pay his rent. So yesterday he ended his career in a gas filled room at 3611 Twenty-third street.

SPREADS GRIEF IN ART CIRCLES

Painter Died Amid His Treasures.

1x8-23

As a bride would array herself

WOMAN ARTIST, AS SHE ENDS LIFE ILL, BEGS DOCTOR

Mrs. Beck-Browndun Writes Card Calling Physician and Then Shoots Herself.

SAD ARTIST ENDS LIFE

Karl Vogel Inhales Gas at Home.

Second Time He Had Sought Death, According to Police, Who Tell of Previous Shooting.

February 19, 1916

Clipping from

San Francisco, Cal., Call
Thursday, September 13

...R ARTIST'S ASHES TO BE CAST ON THE SEINE

A request that, following an unpretentious funeral, his body be cremated and cast to the four winds on the banks of the Seine, is contained in the will of John William Klumpke, one time San Francisco grocer, brother of Anna E. Klumpke, famous artist of Paris, himself an artist. The will was filed for probate here today, following a filing of the same document in Paris. The ... have lived in the French cap-

---

Chicago, Ill., Tribune
Saturday, September 8, 1917

late res...
Lady of Sorrows church...
to Calvary cemetery.

OBITUARY.

H. C. SAMMONS, THE ARTIST, DEAD

Frederick Harrington Cruikshank Sammons, the artist, one of the most expert restorers of paintings in the United States, died yesterday at the Passavant Hospital in his seventy-ninth year.

He was the painter of some beautiful landscapes. He was born at Bath, England, and was the godson of the illustrator Cruikshank. He was a resident of the north side for the last forty years. Before then he lived in many foreign countries.

Mr. Sammons was best known in Chi-

DONALD MACKENZIE, veteran of the civil war and the first Commodore of the Robbins Reef Yacht Club of Bayonne, N. J., died yesterday at his home, ... West Forty-fourth Street, Bayonne. Mr. Mackenzie was at one time a noted scene ... He retired ten years ago.

FRANK ... DICKEY, former night editor of The New England Associated Press and ... a member of the staff of the Boston ... of The Associated Press, died yester... at Boston. He was born at Milford, ..., in 1852.

Artist Seeking D... Found Killed by Gas

Sumner Robinson, ... interior decorator, was found dead in the kitchenette of his bachelor apartment at No. 64 West Ninth street, with gas flowing from four open jets on a gas range. Mr. Robinson, fully clothed, was stretched on the floor, his head pillowed on a cushion. Apparently he had died of asphyxiation several hours before. He had been in ill health, and had said he wanted to die. A cousin of Mr. Robinson, William Johns, an artist, found the body.

Mr. Robinson was thirty-eight years old, the son of Thomas R. Robinson, a wealthy Pittsburgh insurance man. His cousin said Mr. Robinson had gained a reputation as a lecturer on interior decorating.

Saturday, September 22, 1917

T. K. PEMBROKE, PAINTER, IS FOUND DEAD

Theodore K. Pembroke, a well-known landscape painter, was found dead in his apartment in the studio building at No. 27 West Sixty-seventh street to-day. Death was due to

---

ARTIST IS FOUND DEAD IN STUDIO

Theodore K. Pembrook Was Native of Elizabeth.

Theodore K. Pembrook, formerly of this city, was found dead in his studio in New York on Saturday, apparently ... of heart disease. He was

...s by keeping them in a Saf...

PEMBROOKE, ARTIST, DIES ALONE IN HIS ROOM

Turns From Easel to Rest and Expires on Couch—Body Undiscovered for Two Days.

Theodore Pembrooke, a painter of landscapes, who was known as the "hermit artist," was found dead yesterday in his studio in the apartment house at 27 West Sixty-seventh Street. On an easel was an unfinished painting, upon which he had been working a few minutes before he expired. Pembrooke, who had been troubled with a weak heart for some time, had apparently tired of painting, and, still wearing his painter's smock, he had taken a novel and lay down on a couch to rest and read. The ... the artist were ...

...administration. To saddle the expense on the county if his possible successor did not favor the move would be unfair, he believes.

Theodore Pembrook Dies

Artist's Body Found in His Studio 2 Days After Death

Theodore Pembrook, fifty-five years old, a landscape artist, was found dead yesterday in his studio, at 27 West Sixty-seventh Street. Dr. Boland, of Polyclinic Hospital, said heart disease was the cause of death, and that Mr. Pembrook had been dead about forty-eight hours.

Sunday, September 23, 1917.

...unconscious. At the Holy Family Hospital it was said that his skull had been fractured and that he would die. He is about thirty-five years old, 5 feet ... inches tall and has dark hair. No arrests were made.

ARTIST IS FOUND DEAD.

Theodore Pembrook, Landscape Painter, Succumbs to Heart Disease.

Theodore Pembrook, fifty-five, a landscape painter, was found dead yesterday morning in his studio at No. 27 West Sixty-seventh Street, where he had lived for several years. Dr. Boland of Polyclinic Hospital said death had occurred about two days before, and heart disease was the cause.

In early life Mr. Pembrook was connected with the dry goods firm of Sweetzer, Pembrook & Co., in which his father was a partner. His paintings have been shown in the Hotel Plaza and the Folsom Galleries. His wife and married daughter, both living in Boston, survive him. The time for the funeral, which will be held from the Funeral Church, Broadway and Sixty-seventh street, has not been set.

Theodore Pembrook, a landscape artist, who had lived for several years in the studio at No. 27 West Sixty-seventh street, was found dead in his room yesterday. Dr. Boland, of Polyclinic Hospital, said death occurred two days before from heart disease.

Mr. Pembrook was born in Elizabeth, N. J. He has exhibited his paintings at the Plaza and the Follsom Art Galleries. He is survived by a widow and a married daughter, both of whom live in Boston. He was fifty-five years old.

T. K. PEMBROOK, NOTED LANDSCAPE ARTIST, DIES

NEW YORK, September 22.—Theodore K. Pembrook, 55 years old, well-known landscape artist, was found dead this morning on a couch in his studio. A janitor, alarmed because he had not seen the artist for two days, entered his apartment shortly before noon and found his body.

An ambulance surgeon said that Pembrook had been dead for nearly two days. Death resulted from heart disease, the doctor said. Pembrook is survived by a wife and daughter, who live in Boston. He was the son of the late Theodore K. Pembrook of Sweezer, Pembrook & Co., dry goods merchants. Pembrook was born in Elizabeth, N. J.

Before devoting himself entirely to landscape painting fifteen years ago, Pembrook was a designer of fabric prints. He was completing work to give to the Red Cross.

SHERMAN APPEALS TO ...

...ceived Measly $30 brings $17,000 in London.

Matthew Maris, or, to give him the name under which his birth was registered at The Hague, Matthias Maris, died in London the other day, 78 years old.

With him disappears the last of three Dutch artist brothers, who all became famous. If Matthew was perhaps less known, so that only a very restricted circle of friends was aware...

Saturday, October 6, 1917.

Monday, October 1, 1917.

allowance of

ARTIST KILLED IN AUTO CRASH

Dunbar Wright Victim of Accident.

PINNED UNDER CAR

absences because of sickness.

Oil Magnate Wright's Son Dies in Auto Crash

John Dunbar Wright, son of J. Howard Wright, Standard Oil millionaire, was instantly killed in an automobile smash near Otisville, N. Y., yesterday afternoon. He was fifty-five, an active philanthropist, amateur painter and a member of many clubs. His town house was at No. 41 East Fifty-first street.

Mr. Wright was driving Helen Langford toward her home at Milford, Pa. While going down a steep hill between Middletown and Port Jervis, he swerved to avoid a rut. The car skidded into a telegraph pole. Miss Langford was bruised.

Mad Ex-Countess Dies Pauper Here

ARTIST DIES UND... JERVIS AS A GIRL

Port Jervis, Oct. 6.—J. Dunbar Wright of 1 West Sixty-seventh street, New York, artist and clubman, lay dying beneath his motor car in the Shawangunk Mountains, eight miles from this city on Friday, while his companion, Miss Helen Langford, made hopeless attempts to extricate him. He was dead when another motoring party found them an hour after the accident.

Mr. Wright and Miss Langford started from New York in the morning on their way to Mr. Wright's country he...

ago as a member of one of the earlier Harvard units, but is now home. For the last few years Mrs. Cheever has made her home in Dedham.

DISTINGUISHED ENGLISH ARTIST

Charles Napier Hemy Had Exhibited His Work in Foremost Galleries of London

A cable message from London announces that Charles Napier Hemy, the marine painter, died on Sunday at Falmouth, England. Mr. Hemy was born in Newcastle-on-Tyne, May 24, 1841, the son of the late Henri F. Hemy, a distinguished musician, and Margaret Hemy. After attending the Newcastle schools he was graduated from St. Cuthbert's College, Durham, England, and later studied art at Antwerp Academy and became a pupil of Baron Henri Leys. He exhibited his first picture at the Royal Academy at the age of twenty...

English Marine Painter Dead.

London, Oct. 1.—Charles Napier Hemy, the marine painter, died yesterday at Falmouth. Among his most prominent pictures are "Homeward," "The Trawler," "Silent Adieu" and "Home Wind."

NEW YORK COMMERCIAL   76

Tuesday, October 2, 1917.

automobiles caused the death of 636 persons on streets and highways in New York State.

Charles Napier Hemy, who painted "Silent Adieu," "Home Wind" and other famous marine pictures, is dead at Falmouth.

Announcement was made that 281 interned German sailors will be transferred from Boston to the detention camp at Hot Springs.

upon the demand for permission $1.7 cute the deputy.

CHARLES N. HEMY NOTED PAINT...

LONDON, Monday.—Char... Hemy, the marine painter, ...Falmouth.

Mr. Hemy was born a... Tyne in 1841. Among his... pictures are "Homeward," "Silent Adieu" and "Homery," one a member of the Royal A...

MISCELLANEOUS button

EDWARD STRAEFFLER, an artist with the Empire State Photo-Engraving Co., died at his home, 143 Tompkins Avenue, Brooklyn, on Thursday. He was 69 years old, and was born in Cincinnati, Ohio.

Mrs. PHOEBE GIBES, widow of Captain George C. Gibbs, who established the Montauk Line of steamboats, died at her home in Sag Harbor, L. I., on Wednesday. She was 74 years old.

Mrs. MARY J. HAVENS, 52 years old,

...ght to Philadelphia.

After relations were broken off with Germany, the crews of the two raiders were taken South and interned. Since his arrest early this summer, Capt. Thierichens has been confined in the county prison here.

LT. ROBERT WILLIAMS DIES AT HOME OF HIS PARENTS

Lt. Robert Williams died at the summer home of his parents in Scituate on Sunday afternoon. He was born on March 28, 1889. He attended the Volkmann School and entered Harvard University in 1907, graduating in 1911 with the degree of A. B. He then went into business with his father, Arthur Williams, Jr. of Arthur Williams, Jr., & Co., where he took an active interest.

In May, 1916, he attended the military camp at Fort Ogelthorpe, Ga., and was in the 2d cavalry, under Capt. G. A. Purington, U. S. A. Last May he went to Plattsburg, where he stayed three months, and was commissioned at the end of that time a first lieutenant...

ARTIST CASARINI KILLED IN BATTLE

Italian Painter Well Known Here, Falls at San Gabriele.

Lieutenant Athos Casarini of the Italian army, who was killed in the recent battles for Monte San Gabriele, was well known in Brooklyn as an artist and for several years made his home here. He was a painter of talent. His works were displayed at several local exhibitions...

Tuesday, October 9, 1917.

more than 6,000,000 tons.

ARTIST KNOWN HERE IS KILLED IN BATTLE

Among the Italian officers killed in the recent taking of Monte San Gabriele was Lieut. Athos Casarini, well known as an artist in New York. He was the son of a merchant in Bologna, studied art in Venice under Ettore Tito and came to America about six years ago. The World was the first in this country to recognize his talent.

His introduction to the American public was a double page of drawings in The World's Sunday Magazine Section. Afterward his paintings were exhibited in several galleries and many places in the homes of artists. While in America Casarini had a studio in Poplar Street, Brooklyn. He was among the first to answer his country's call to arms.

Artist Dies After Fighting Arrest

An autopsy to be held to-day will determine the exact circumstances surrounding the death of Louis B. Caney, forty-eight, an artist, whose skull was fractured by a fall as he was trying to escape from a policeman early yesterday morning. Caney fell in front of No. 101 West Forty-sixth street and died soon after in the Polyclinic Hospital.

According to Policeman Gunson Caney was fighting in the street with William P. Connors, a seaman assigned to the Navy Yard. On complaint of Connors the artist was placed under arrest. The group headed for the West Forty-seventh street when Caney turned and

FREDERICK STURGES, PHILANTHROPIST, DIE...

Frederick Sturges, of No. 36 Park avenue and Fairfield, Conn., where the family has been established for more than two hundred years is dead at home in this city. He was eighty-... years old. Since the death of his fat...

AMUSEMENTS.

PENNILESS ARTIST SOUGHT TO DIE BY STARVATION

Henry Carleton Jones Taken to Hospital in a Critical Condition.

HAD TURNED ON THE GAS

Agony of Slower Method of Death Had Been Too Much for Discouraged Youth.

Henry Carleton Jones, the young artist and decorator, was yesterday morning found dying in his room on the top floor of a boarding house at No. 123 East Twenty-eighth street, after an attempt to end his life by illuminating gas and morphine.

The young artist comes of a prominent family and moved in good society in this and other cities. He had travelled extensively and was a member of a number of clubs up to a year ago, when ill-health robbed him of an income from his work.

Unimproved in health and with empty pockets the young man returned last Thursday from the South, where he had gone to recuperate, and engaged a room in the boarding house. It is tenanted by hard-working men and women, and the landlady, Miss Elberson, did not want to admit Jones, because she feared from his appearance he would not be satisfied.

Said He Needed a Shelter.

"No, no," replied Jones, with a bitter smile. "You will find that I am easy to please, and I promise that I shall make no compaints and give you no trouble. I am ill and need a shelter. Please take me in."

Thomas Hill, well known as a painter of Yosemite views, died yesterday at Raymond, near Famous Valley, Cal., which he did so much to bring to the world's attention. Although 79 years old, he kept his studio at Wawona, in the Tuolumne big tree grove, and worked there regularly on his paintings. Hill's first work to attract attention was a view of the Yosemite which hangs in the Crocker Art Gallery at Sacramento. He painted the Yosemite in all the seasons, and he also made striking canvases of the Yellowstone, Muir Glacier, in Alaska, and other Pacific Coast scenes. He made a fortune, but lost it in the collapse of Bonanza Mining stock.

ARTIST SLAIN IN PARIS HOME BY STRANGLERS.

His Wife Gagged, Bound, Left to Die and Helpless, Hears Her Mother Struggling in Vain for Life.

FORMER MODEL LED GANG OF THREE MALE ROBBERS.

"Kill Her Quick!" She Commanded as Pals Lingered at Wife's Bedside.

PARIS, May 31.—Adolphe Steinheil, a distinguished painter, and his mother-in-law were found strangled this morning in the former's residence in the Rue de Vaugirard, which adjoins the studio of Seymour Thomas, an American portrait painter.

The house was ransacked and everything of value was stolen.

Aside from the brutality of the crime, a feature of the affair is the almost inconceivable audacity with which it was perpetrated.

The artist's house is close to a large printing house, where work is going on all night. A night watchman and a timekeeper are employed there, and workmen come and go all the time in an almost constant stream.

The double murder was discovered by Steinheil's man servant, who got up at 6 o'clock in the morning to get breakfast. Hearing groans coming from Mme. Steinheil's sleeping apartment he entered and found her lying bound hand and foot on the bed. A gag of cotton wool, which she had somehow succeeded in ejecting from her mouth, lay on the floor. A thin cord was around her throat.

In the hall he found the painter dead, resting on his knees, the body bent backward. He had been strangled by a whip-cord, like that around his wife's neck; his face was black and his lips were stiff.

In another bedroom was the dead body of Mme. Steinheil's mother, Mme. Japy. She also had been strangled and the body was fastened to the bed.

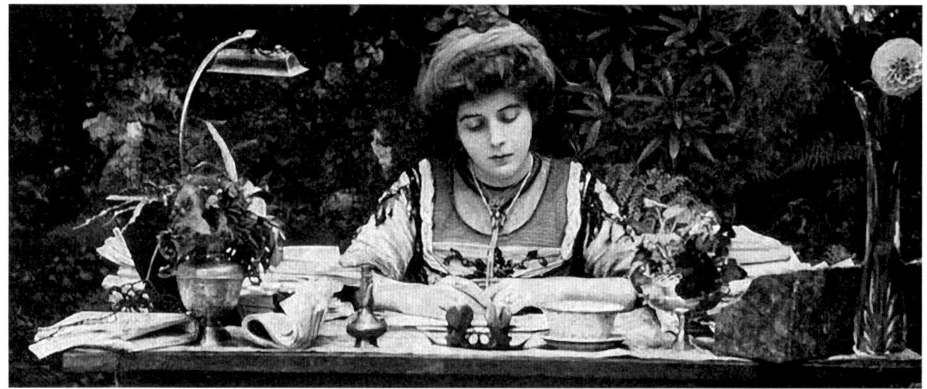

Claude Harris, *Marguerite Steinheil*, illustration from her book *My Memoirs*, 1912

ARTIST SLAIN IN PARIS HOME BY STRANGLERS

Murders that occurred as far away as France, when sufficiently lurid, drew the attention of American tabloid editors. On the night of May 30, 1908, the artist Adolphe Steinheil was garroted in his Paris home. The *New York World* reported a domestic servant "found the painter dead, resting on his knees, the body bent backward. He had been strangled by a whip-cord . . . his face was black and his lips were stiff." Even worse, the corpse of his suffocated mother-in-law was tied to a nearby bed frame. Steinheil's wife, Marguerite, was elsewhere in the building, bound and gagged, but alive.

She claimed that four cloaked intruders had tied her up then killed her husband and mother, but she soon changed her story and cast blame on her manservant and then on a housekeeper. Marguerite's tarnished past raised suspicion and investigators charged her with the double murder. Socially ambitious, Marguerite was the daughter of a wealthy provincial manufacturer and twenty years younger than her husband. Adolphe Steinheil descended from a lineage of successful stained-glass painters and had provided his bride entrée to fashionable Parisian society, where she'd hosted a popular salon. It came to light that Marguerite had been mistress to several powerful men, including French president Félix Faure, rumored to have died during an intimate tryst with her. The cuckolded artist Adolphe turned a blind eye to Marguerite's affairs

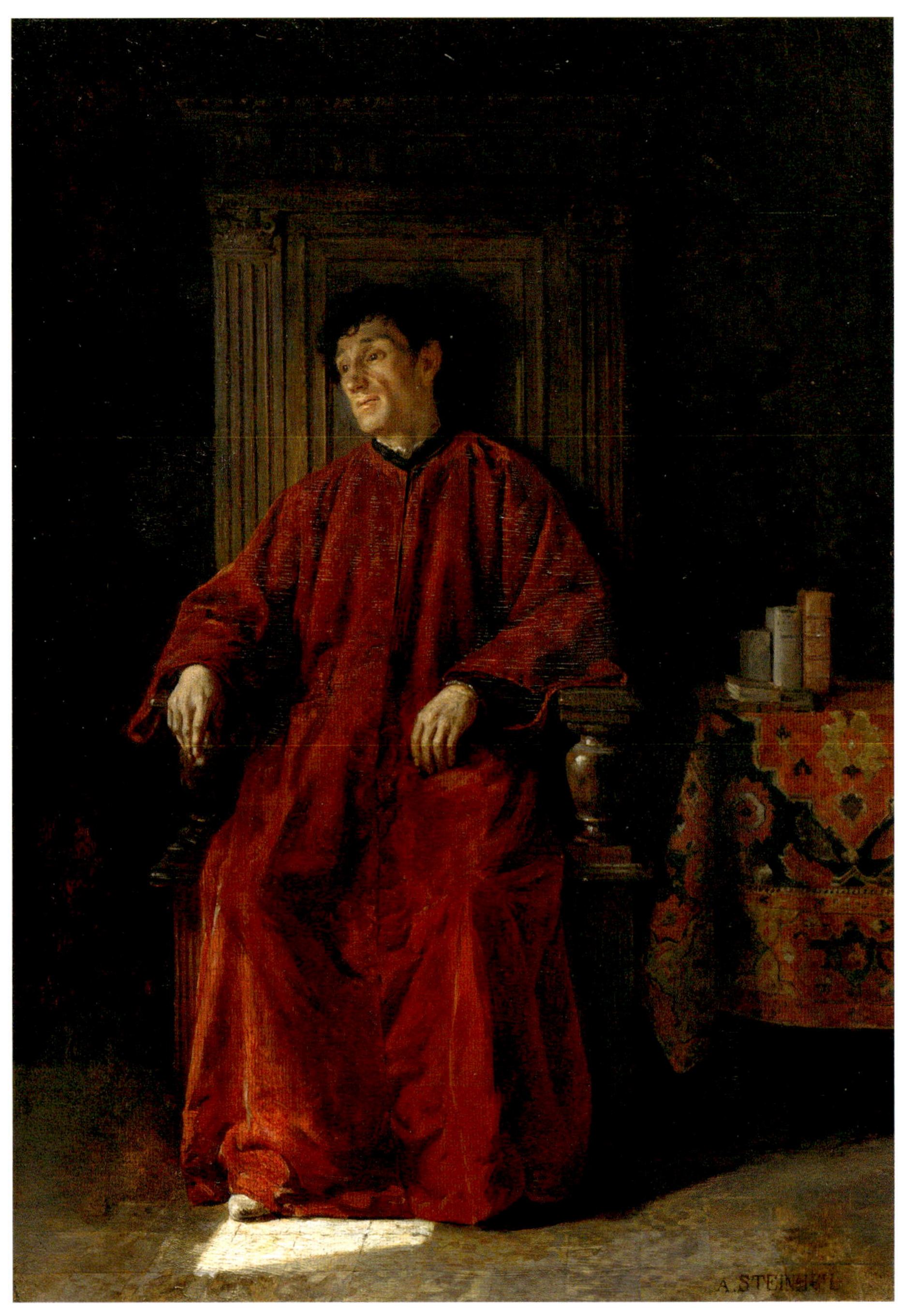

Adolphe Charles Edouard Steinheil, *Judge in a Red Robe*, ca. 1890. Cleveland Museum of Art, Gift in memory of Helen Borowitz 2013.260

and was compensated for his discretion with portrait commissions
from her paramours.

The press detailed every twist and turn of a buzzworthy trial
spiced with sexual intrigue and political scandal. The courtroom
was jammed with gawkers, including the writer Marcel Proust.
Prosecutors aired conflicting evidence and failed to present a
clear theory of motive. Marguerite was acquitted and decamped to
London, where she wrote an exculpatory memoir. She later married
an English baron, Robert Scarlett, prompting a nickname that
followed her to her death in 1954: the Scarlet Widow. The murders
of Adolphe Steinheil and Marguerite's mother were never solved.
A rare surviving example of Steinheil's portraiture, *Judge in a Red
Robe*, was acquired not long ago by the Cleveland Museum of Art.
Adolphe painted it around the time of his marriage to Marguerite.

In 1882 Arthur D'Hervilly experienced a tragedy of his own making
when he committed a serious crime that changed the course of his
life. After years of steady service at Morris, Tasker & Co. and a
recent promotion to manager, he was caught embezzling money from
the business. *The Philadelphia Inquirer* reported his arrest almost
sympathetically, leaving his name out of the initial account of the
crime and identifying him only as a "most respectably connected
young man . . . astray from the path of strict rectitude." D'Hervilly
was accused of pilfering "an amount large enough to cause the firm
to take short, sharp and decisive measures." Court records tallied the
theft at $15,000, an impressive sum for the time and the equivalent
of about $400,000 today. What he did with the money is anybody's
guess, though it must not have wound up in the hands of family or
friends. They were so slow to raise bail that he spent a week after
his arrest in county jail. He ultimately pled guilty and was sentenced
to a year of hard labor in Moyamensing Prison, nicknamed "the Jug"
by local toughs. His jailers assigned him his inmate number 12356
and jotted down a few intriguing points about D'Hervilly's physique
and habits in a Convict Description Docket filed away in the Philadelphia city archives. He was slight of stature, standing five feet five
inches tall and weighing just over one hundred pounds. He did not
drink alcohol and his "home influences were good."

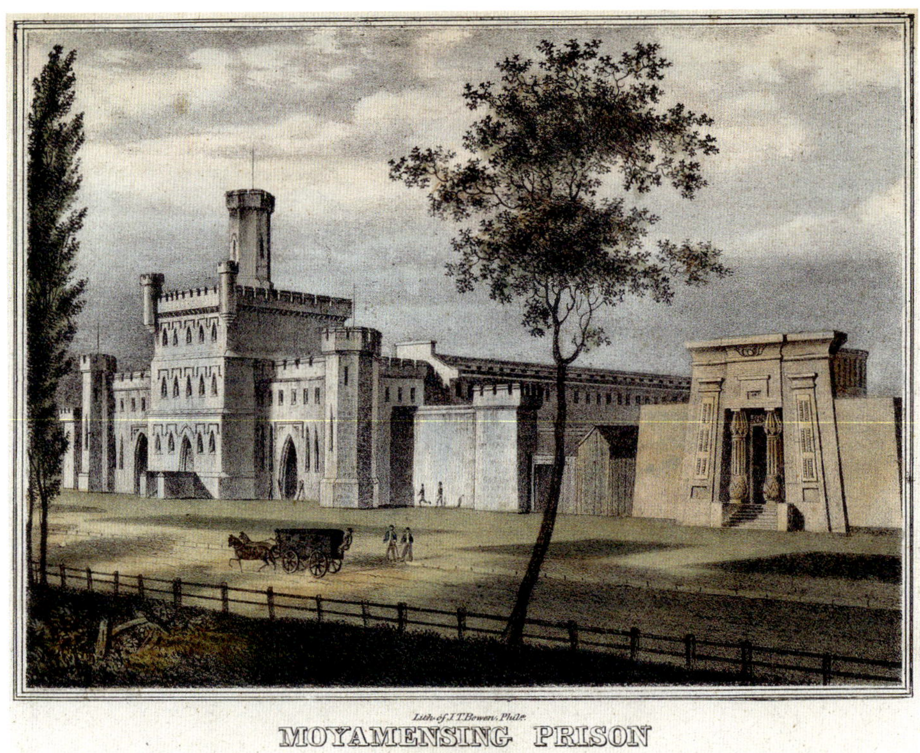

J. C. (John Caspar) Wild (artist) and J. T. Bowen (printer), *Moyamensing Prison*, ca. 1840–1848. Library Company of Philadelphia, Print Department, W241.4 [P.2097]

It is difficult to reconcile D'Hervilly's criminal past with the character he showed later in life. By the accounts of his professional colleagues at the Metropolitan Museum, he was a dedicated and trustworthy employee for twenty-five years. The embezzlement episode was a lamentable aberrance. D'Hervilly's long-term course suggests his heart and mind were focused not on a business career but on making art. It seems plausible that he schemed to escape office drudgery and have freedom to follow his muse full time. It is to D'Hervilly's credit that he confessed his wrongdoing, served his time, reflected upon his error, and realigned the scope of his ambition to fit his means. And it was fortunate for D'Hervilly that news stories that reported his transgression were not so unkindly sensationalized as the many obituaries involving crimes that he collected in The Met scrapbooks.

3. Your Obedient Servant

After Arthur D'Hervilly was released from Moyamensing Prison in February 1884, he found a place to live apart from the Chegaray Institute and was lucky to find a job as a clerk. But he and Ida soon left Philadelphia and bad memories behind to make a fresh start in New York, where they landed in East Harlem. By this time Arthur, in his mid-thirties, had cultivated an interest in art and learned to paint. He was talented enough to have a picture titled *Chasseur* (Hunter) exhibited at the prestigious National Academy of Design in 1887.

The academy was founded in 1825 to nurture homegrown American talent through a busy program of studio classes and annual exhibitions. Many top-notch artists of the day were members, and it was no small accomplishment for an unknown like D'Hervilly to have a picture accepted by its discerning selection committee. The jury for the 1887 show resolved to display "only the most worthy" objects and chose 503 pieces, down from a bloated checklist of 843 approved the year before. *Chasseur* was installed in the impressive National Academy building at 23rd Street and Park Avenue South, together with works by American masters Winslow Homer, Eastman Johnson, George Inness Jr., and Frederic Remington. Art by future Met curators Frank Edwin Elwell and George Henry Story was also on view. The opening reception must have been a heady experience for D'Hervilly, offering a glimpse of an artistic firmament he longed to join.

The title of D'Hervilly's entry echoed a theme favored by another Philadelphia painter, the great Thomas Eakins, who often visited New Jersey marshes to shoot waterfowl. Eakins made several pictures of fellow hunters with guns poised to fire, including a lovely example that was bought by The Met in 1916, the year the artist died.

Eakins and D'Hervilly both spent years in Philadelphia and were close in age. What's more, Thomas Eakins's father, Benjamin, of whom Thomas made a portrait, was a noted calligrapher who taught

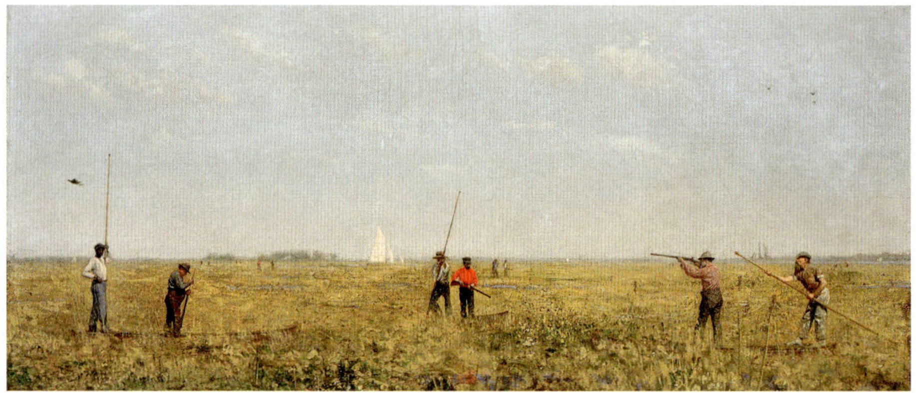

Thomas Eakins, *Pushing for Rail*, 1874. The Metropolitan Museum of Art, Arthur Hoppock Hearn Fund, 1916 (16.65)

the craft to aspiring office clerks. I can't help wondering if they knew each other—could D'Hervilly, so skilled in fine penmanship, have advanced his calligraphic technique under the tutelage of Benjamin Eakins? Thomas, like many of his generation, traveled to Europe to study at the École des Beaux-Arts and to absorb the influence of continental masterpieces. Might Arthur's desire to chase the same dream of an artist's life across the Atlantic have compelled his embezzlement? Of course we will never know.

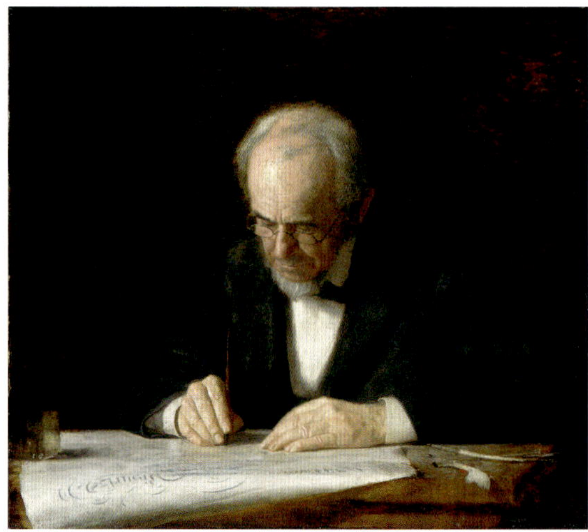

Thomas Eakins, *The Writing Master*, 1882.
The Metropolitan Museum of Art, John Stewart
Kennedy Fund, 1917 (17.173)

Likewise, we can't tell what D'Hervilly's painting looked like;
the National Academy of Design catalogue gave no details about
Chasseur, and the picture has disappeared.

In 1894, at age forty-three, D'Hervilly sent to The Metropolitan
Museum of Art a beautifully handwritten job application letter.

> Accompanying this is a favor I respectfully ask of the
> Directors of The Metropolitan Museum of Art.
>   Being unable to follow my profession, the Fine Arts, owing
> to inadequate means, I seek a position of some sort under your
> able management.
>   The petition I have "illuminated," that it might not remain
> in obscurity? Hoping for favorable result, I have the honor to
> remain, Sir,
>   Your obedient servant,
>   A. D'Hervilly

Seen in the light of D'Hervilly's sketchy past, his self-identification
as an artist, plea of poverty, and willingness to accept any role the
Museum offered are telling. He attached to his formal entreaty a
direct appeal in poetic verse to The Met's chief executive, Luigi
Palma di Cesnola, with whom, it seems, he'd been in contact before.

> Monsieur,
> As to when or how it came
> About (it matters little in this Connection)
> A certain Gent, the same,
> Promised to remember, to give
> Certain work of his selection.
>
> Must I fancy "it might have been"?
> Remembrance led astray?
> No? No harm to jostle that certain Gent's memory in
> A curious but respectful way.
>
> Monsieur, dites-moi, about
> Those presumably wanted things

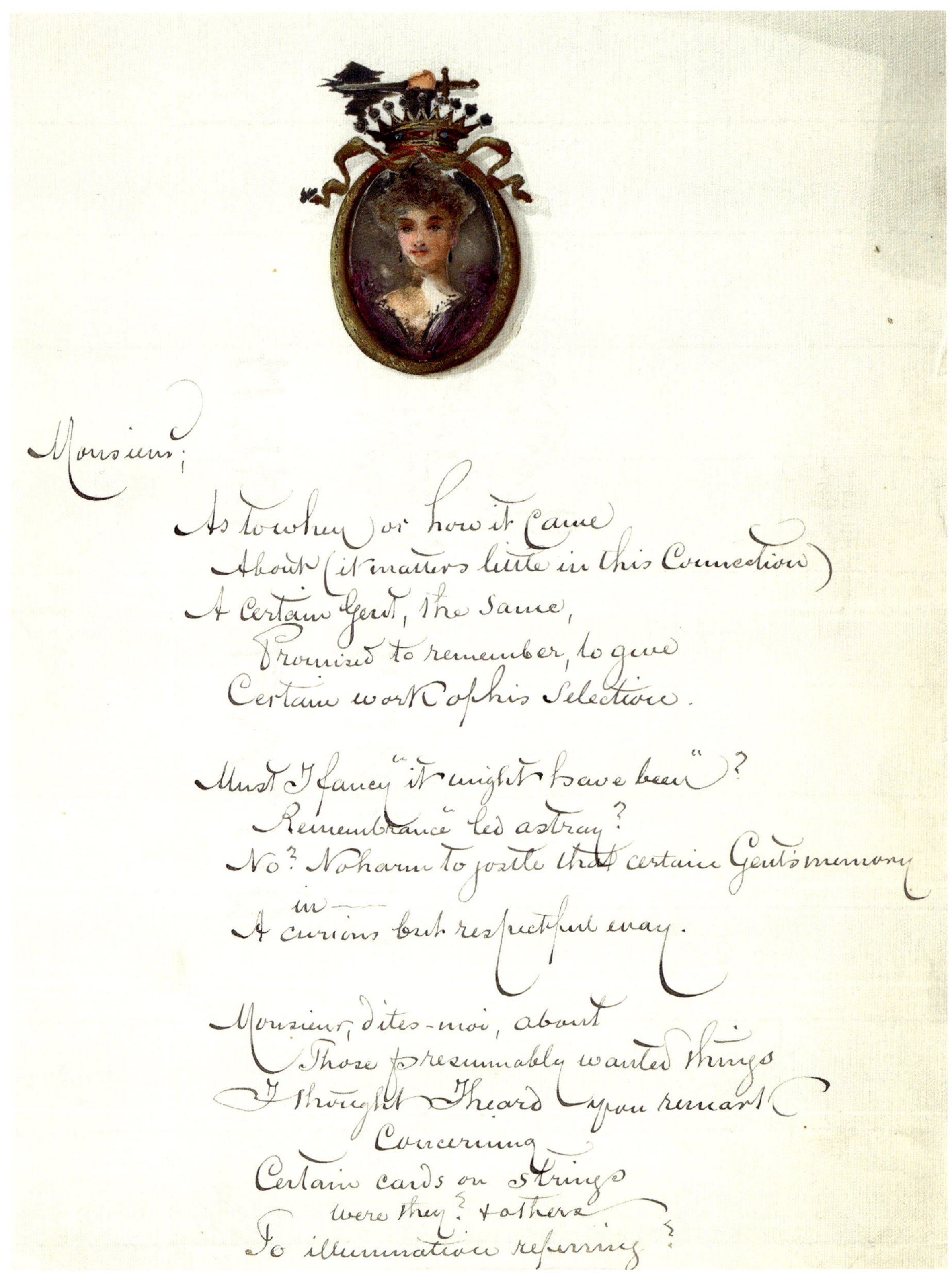

Arthur D'Hervilly to Luigi Palma di Cesnola, 1894. Arthur D'Hervilly file, Office of the Secretary Records, The Metropolitan Museum of Art Archives

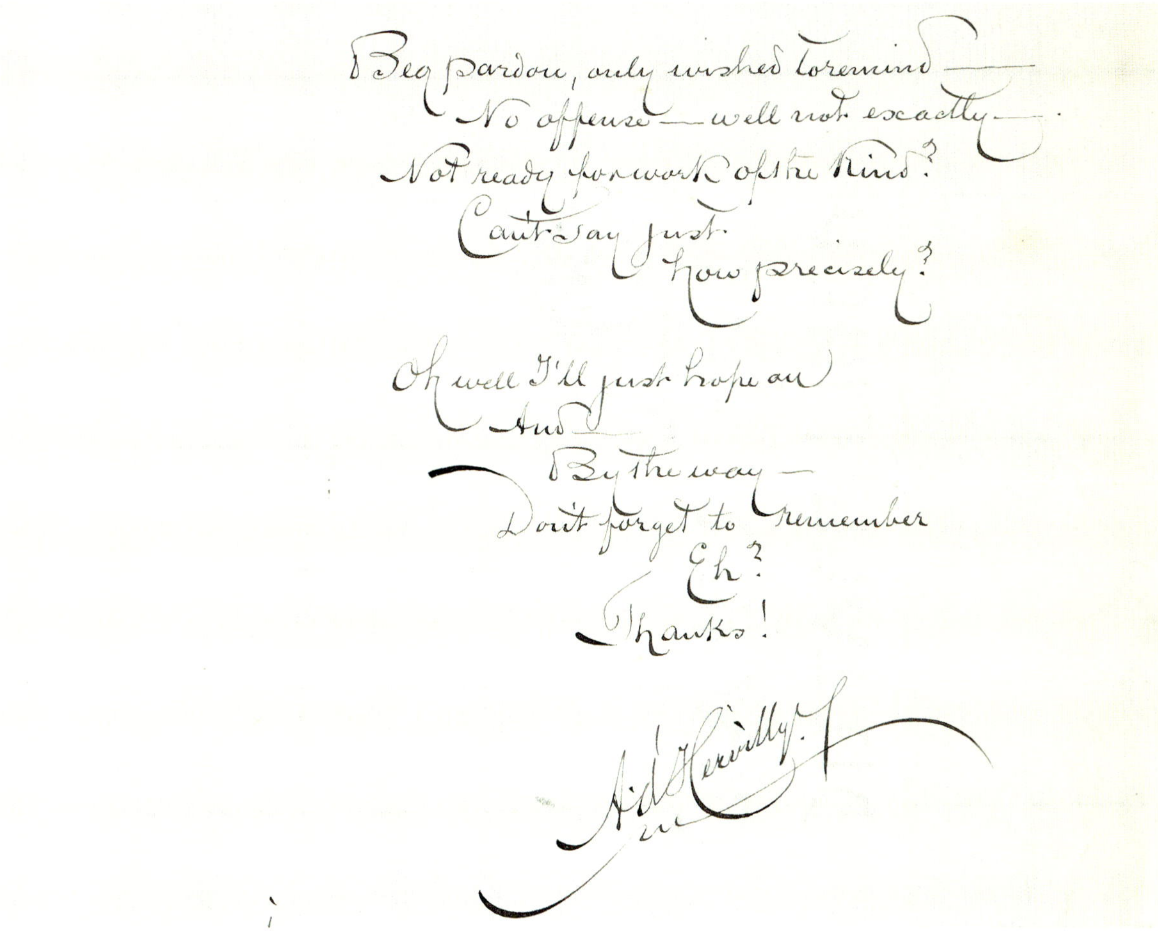

I thought I heard you remark
Concerning
Certain cards on strings
Were they? + others
To illumination referring?

Beg pardon, only wished to remind—
No offense—well not exactly—
Not ready for work of the kind?
Can't say just how precisely?

Oh well I'll just hope on
And
By the way—
Don't forget to remember
Eh?
Thanks!

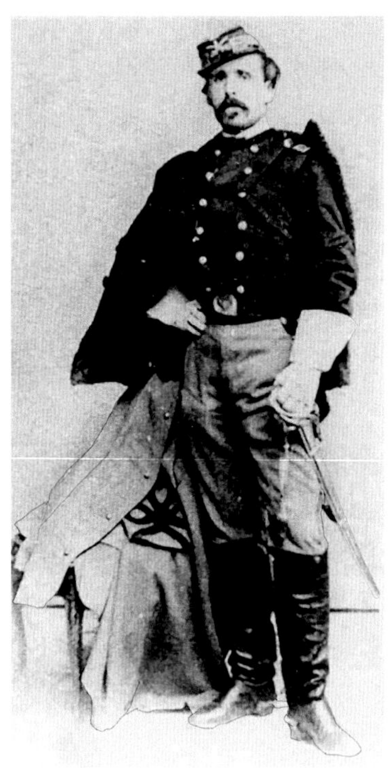

Luigi Palma di Cesnola, ca. 1863, photographer unknown

This rather coy missive, featuring eight question marks and decorated with a watercolor image of a portrait medallion, sought to refresh Cesnola's recollection of an offer of freelance work for D'Hervilly to create signage—or cards on strings—that they had discussed at an unknown earlier date. D'Hervilly's quirky pitch was perfectly aimed at The Met's colorful leader, an Italian American veteran of the U.S. Civil War who micromanaged staff, craved their respect, and prized loyalty.

Cesnola had served as Colonel of the 4th New York Cavalry and was awarded a Medal of Honor for leading a valorous charge in 1863 at the Battle of Aldie, where he was wounded and captured. He spent months in the decrepit Confederate Libby Prison and was eventually sprung in a prisoner swap. After the war, he claimed Abraham Lincoln had orally awarded him brevet brigadier general rank. Cesnola's many antagonists scoffed at his assumption of the title, but for the rest of his days he demanded to be addressed as "General." He next secured a diplomatic post as American consul in Cyprus, where he spent much of his time digging up archaeological antiquities. Cesnola formed a massive collection of ancient Cypriot stone sculptures, terra-cotta vessels, and glassware dating from prehistory to Roman times. He marketed this trove to museums around the world and eventually sold the bulk to The Met, only recently established in 1870 and still lacking substantial holdings of ancient art. As part of the deal the General came to New York and personally installed the artifacts. Museum trustees were suitably impressed by his pluck and acquisitive talent and appointed him to become the institution's first director in 1879.

Cesnola hired D'Hervilly in May 1894 and posted him as a gallery attendant, or guard. Arthur's new career began as the Museum

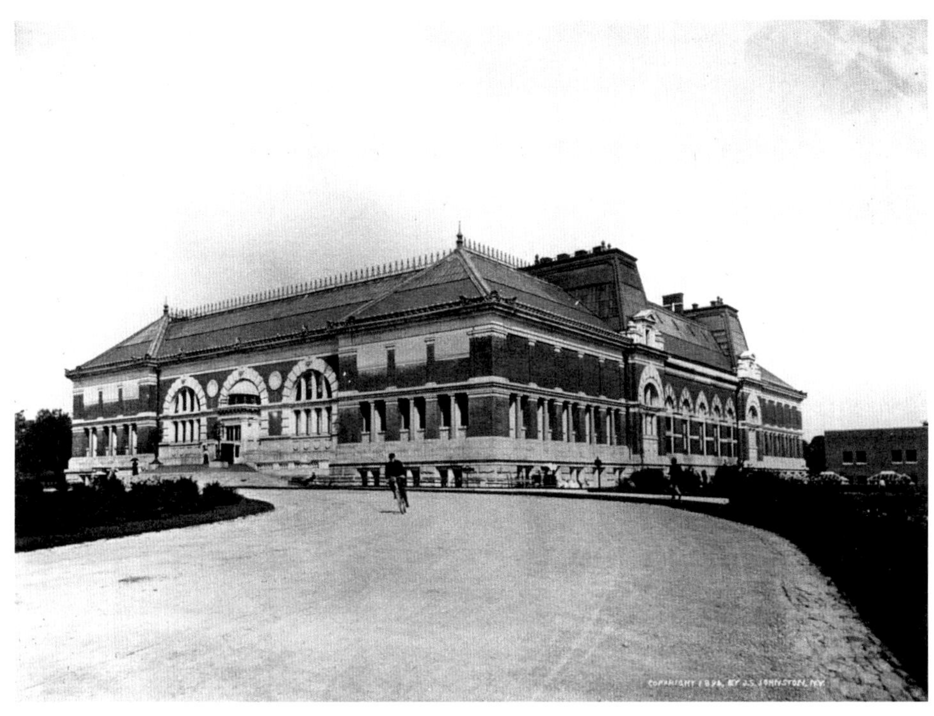

J. S. Johnston, *The Metropolitan Museum of Art*, south entrance, 1895. Watson Library Digital Collections, The Metropolitan Museum of Art (E116489)

unveiled a risqué new acquisition, a *Birth of Venus* by Alexandre Cabanel. The six-foot-wide canvas showed the recumbent goddess naked and floating upon a breaking wave beneath a squadron of putti. Later that year, the Museum achieved another milestone when it cut the ribbon for a new building wing that enlarged its still unassuming footprint in Central Park. The Met's massive and imposing Fifth Avenue facade and iconic entrance steps were not even in the design stage when D'Hervilly stood his first shift. There were only eighty other employees (as of 2024, there are more than 1,800), and compared to European powerhouses like the Louvre and British Museum, its art holdings were limited. Still, D'Hervilly must have felt privileged to spend his days in an atmosphere so fully charged with artistic inspiration.

Shortly after D'Hervilly joined The Met, museum trustees celebrated the opening of the Museum's new north wing with a formal dinner at the Waldorf-Astoria Hotel ballroom. Cesnola, tasked

with organizing the fête, recalled the fine penmanship and artistry
of D'Hervilly's job application. The General commissioned him to
letter and draw commemorative menus decorated with images of
Met artworks. Attendees and museum colleagues fondly recalled
these keepsakes decades later, though sadly none were saved for
the archives.

When D'Hervilly was hired at The Met, it may be that he hid his
criminal past—or perhaps he confessed it, convinced the General
of his reform, and the former Confederate prisoner of war sympa-
thized with another man who'd spent time behind bars. Whatever
the case, Cesnola appreciated not just D'Hervilly's calligraphy but
also his head for figures, and in January 1895 he pulled him into
the executive offices as assistant bookkeeper. He was entrusted
with increasing responsibilities under his mentor's watchful eye for
nearly a decade. D'Hervilly's personal affairs were apparently stable
in this period, and he lived in rented rooms in East Harlem with his
wife, Ida.

It's conceivable that D'Hervilly could have organized the obituaries
in his scrapbooks in a number of ways—by nationality, celebrity,
gender, or artistic practice, for example. His decision to place them
chronologically was the simplest approach, and the arrangement
has a leveling, egalitarian effect. The chance factor of death dates
results in well-known art celebrities being surrounded by relative
unknowns. Paul Cézanne, who died October 22, 1906, appeared
alongside the minor Hudson River School painter John D. Barrow
and Chicago newspaper illustrator Francis Brute Key. Claude
Monet's December 1926 obituary was placed beside that of Arthur
Jule Goodman, a Connecticut-born portraitist who once sold a
painting of Buffalo Bill Cody to Edward, Prince of Wales.

Some artists with no living relationship to one another were
paired *within* a single obituary only because they died around the
same time or from a similar cause. This was precisely how tabloids
framed the synchronous deaths of Robert Loftin Newman and
Louise Schofield.

NOTED PAINTER IS GONE.

Contemporary and Friend of Many Illustrious Americans Joins the Majority.

Funeral services for the late Ferdinand Lee Boyle, a noted painter and formerly professor of fine arts in the Brooklyn Institute of Arts and Sciences, will be held ten o'clock to-morrow at his late home,

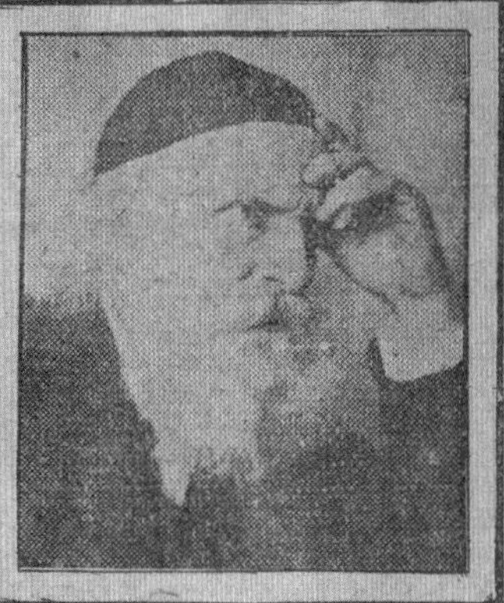

FERDINAND G LEE-BOYLE

102 Park place, Brooklyn. Professor Boyle, as told in yesterday's HERALD, died Sunday after an illness of four weeks of pneumonia.

He was eighty-seven years old. He had retired for many years from active life. In other days he was a friend and associate of Washington Irving, of General Grant, Samuel F. B. Morse, inventor of the telegraph; of B. Gratz Brown, Alexander McCullom, Charles Dickens, Archbishop Bailey, of New Jersey, and United States Senator Thomas H. Benton, of Missouri.

During the civil war he served as colonel of the Fourth Missouri Volunteers and was mustered out in 1865 as a brigadier general by brevet. He established and conducted the Western Academy of Art in St. Louis and was an associate in the National Academy of Design.

EDWIN DAVIS FRENCH.

Edwin Davis French, an engraver and designer, of Saranac Lake, N. Y., died in this city last Saturday. He was born fifty-five years ago at Newburgh, Mass. After some preparatory work went to the Connecticut Literary Institute at Suffield, Conn., and later was, for two years, a student at Brown University.

On leaving college he began the study of engraving under William Sartain, at the Art Students' League. His original vocation was that of an engraver of silver, but in 1894 he began the designing and etching of bookplates, and since that time had devoted himself to that kind of work almost exclusively. Among some of his plates are a series of New York Views" and the illustrations for "Journal." He was president of the Art Students' League of New York from 1889 to 1891 and member of the American Fine Arts Society. French was a member of several New York clubs. He leaves a wife, who was Miss Olivia of Enfield, Conn.

ART CRITIC DEAD.

SAN FRANCISCO, Dec. 14.—Miss Jane Gillespie, well-known California art critic, former president of Los Angeles, passed away here Wednesday. She has been an invalid for some time and her sister Helen devoted her time to her sister's care.

DEATHS OF A DAY

SAMUEL SARTAIN

He Won Fame by His Many Fine Etchings of Paintings.

Samuel Sartain, known as one of the most skilful steel engravers in this country, died at his residence, 212 West Logan square, yesterday, in his 76th year. He was a son of John Sartain, who introduced mezzotint engraving into this country, and was considered the foremost artist in that line of work in the world. Samuel Sartain was born

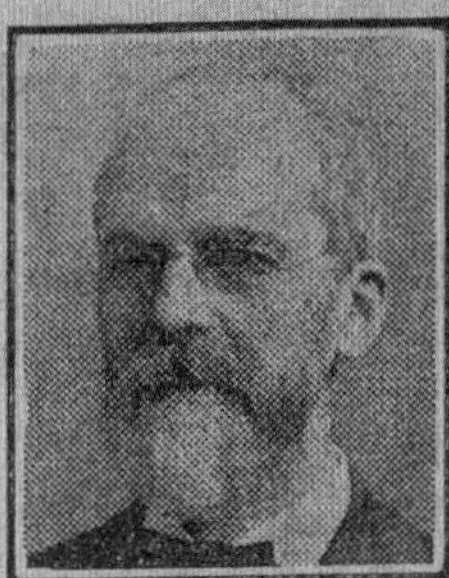

SAMUEL SARTAIN.

in this city, and early evinced artistic ability. Before he was 17 years of age he won fame among artists by an engraving of Harlow's portrait of Benjamin West. In mezzotint and line engraving he excelled, and his services were widely sought for the illustration of biographical works with portrait engravings because of his rare faculty in portraying striking likenesses.

Commissioned by the Art Union of Philadelphia in 1854 to engrave Schuessele's painting, "Clear the Track," the steel plate which he produced won for him a

OBITUARY.

The funeral of Francis Brute Key, formerly connected with the art departments of Chicago newspapers, took place yesterday afternoon at his old home at Hartland, Wis. He died in Chicago Sunday of heart failure, after returning from the West, where he spent four years in search of health.

John K. Clowry, 823 Spaulding avenue, one of the early settlers in Chicago and brother of Colonel R. S. Clowry, president of the

JOHN D. BARROW DEAD.

Skaneateles Loses a Well-known Landscape Painter.

SKANEATELES, Dec. 7.—John D. Barrow, aged 82 years, a well-known local landscape and portrait painter, died at his home in this village to-day.

WELL-KNOWN ARTIST OF OLD SCHOOL IS DEAD

PROF. FERDINAND THOMAS LEE BOYLE A VICTIM OF PNEUMONIA AT AGE OF 86.

Had Painted the Portraits of Many Distinguished Men in His Day—Conspicuous in Keeping the State of Missouri from Seceding in Civil War Time.

Prof. Ferdinand Thomas Lee Boyle, for many years professor of art in the Brooklyn Institute, and a teacher in the School of Art of Adelphi College, passed away yesterday at his home, 102 Park place, death being due to pneumonia, followed by heart failure, after an illness of four weeks. Prof. Boyle came to New York with his parents in 1828. He studied art under Henry Inman and was his favorite pupil from 1835 to 1837. In 1838 he entered the National Academy of Design, of which in 1850 he was elected an associate member. He moved to St. Louis, Mo., in 1855, where he organized and was Vice President of the Western Academy of Art in 1858. At the beginning of the Civil War he organized and was appointed Colonel of the Fifth Missouri Enrolled Militia, and was one of the men who, with the Blairs, was influential in keeping the State of Missouri from seceding. He was mustered out as a Brevet Brigadier General. While in Missouri he painted the portraits of Gov. B. Gratz Brown, of Missouri; Senator Thomas H. Menton, Gen. Frank P. Blair, jr.; Gov. Hamilton P. Gamble, of Missouri, and an ideal portrait "Young Missouri." He was a director of Fine Arts during the Mississippi Valley Sanitary Fair,

PAUL CÉZANNE.

There died a few weeks ago at his home in Aix, in Provence, France, the painter Paul Cézanne, an intimate friend of Emile Zola and a man of stubborn force and individuality. His passing away was hardly noticed outside of France, for he exhibited but little of late years, and his accession as chief of a school was of such recent date that it had hardly time to crystallize in the public mind before the man himself was dead. THE SUN's report of the autumn Salon at Paris, November, 1904, contained a condensed account of Cézanne's glorification by the more unruly element of the younger painters. Cézanne had the honor accorded him of a special room in which hung a few of his principal works—but only a few, for he began to paint industriously in 1866 and he had accumulated an enormous number of canvases during his long life. Even after the sterile eccentricities of the Odilon Redon room, after the violence displayed by many young fellows like Piot and others, the Cézanne exhibit was startling to the eye not accustomed to his drastic and unmodulated tonalities. But he was worshipped more than Carrière or Renoir, both of whom had special *salons*. The tide had set in toward Cézanne—the despised and rejected Cézanne—in a manner most unmistakable. At the time THE SUN remarked that in a few seasons another god might supplant Cézanne, which lightly

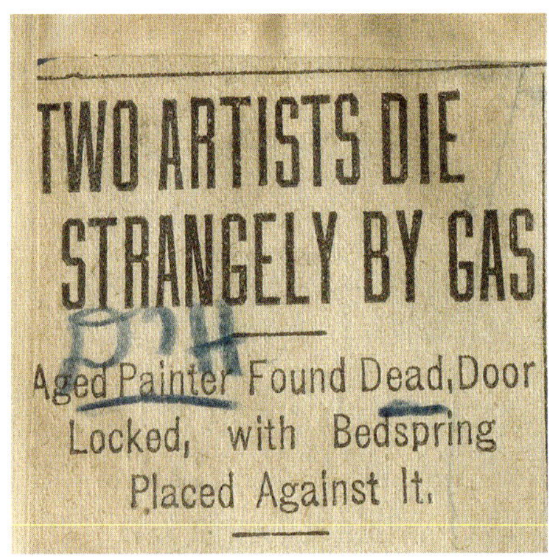

TWO ARTISTS DIE STRANGELY BY GAS

"There was a coincidence of deaths by gas yesterday in the field
of art when two painters, one a man and the other a woman, were
found dead in different parts of the city," announced a New York
paper on April 1, 1912. Newman, a reclusive octogenarian, had shut
himself in a newly rented room on Manhattan's east side, where he
perished by asphyxiation. His passing was ruled accidental, though
investigators noted a gas jet was turned wide open and a bed frame
was lodged against the door. The death of thirty-eight-year-old
Schofield occurred in her Harlem apartment and was blamed on a
faulty cooking stove.

Born in Virginia in 1827, Newman had trained in Paris with
history painter Thomas Couture. He fought in the Confederate army
in the Civil War. Postbellum, Newman tried his hand at portraiture,
taught art in Tennessee, and daubed signage in Baltimore. He later
moved to New York City, where he made small, intense oil paintings
of distorted human figures, some titled to suggest biblical inspiration,
such as a murky *Flight into Egypt* now in the Smithsonian American
Art Museum.

Newman toiled for decades at brooding pictures of this sort that
were acquired by connoisseurs but were seldom shown in public.
Exhibitions in 1894 at Knoedler Gallery and the Museum of Fine
Arts, Boston, marked his lifetime pinnacle of achievement. Rem-
nants of Newman's oeuvre rose to fresh prominence long after his

passing, when he was posthumously
favored with solo museum exhibitions, including a 1974 Smithsonian
show of more than one hundred
objects. The Metropolitan Museum
today owns three of his paintings. In
stark contrast, Louise Schofield went
largely unrecognized during her lifetime and no trace of her artwork has
since resurfaced.

The Newman-Schofield story
crossed the country and even circled
the globe through print syndication.
The proximity, timing, and causes of
their deaths intrigued editors near
and far and enticed them to embel-
lish a truth harsh enough on its own.
Details were changed and spuri-
ous facts introduced for dramatic

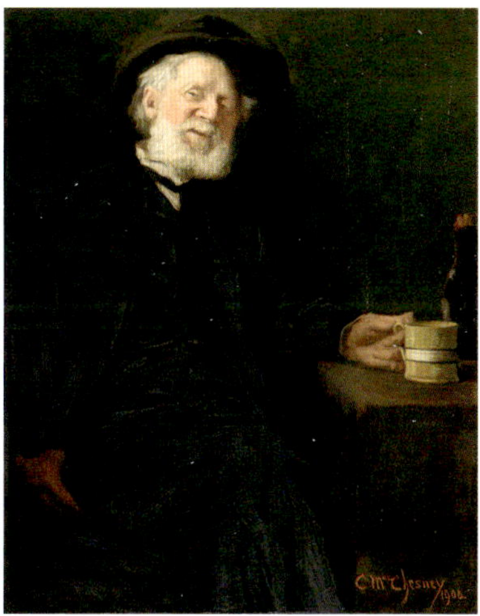

Clara Taggart MacChesney, *A Good
Story* (Portrait of Robert Loftin
Newman), 1900. Smithsonian
American Art Museum, Gift of
William T. Evans, 1914.6.1

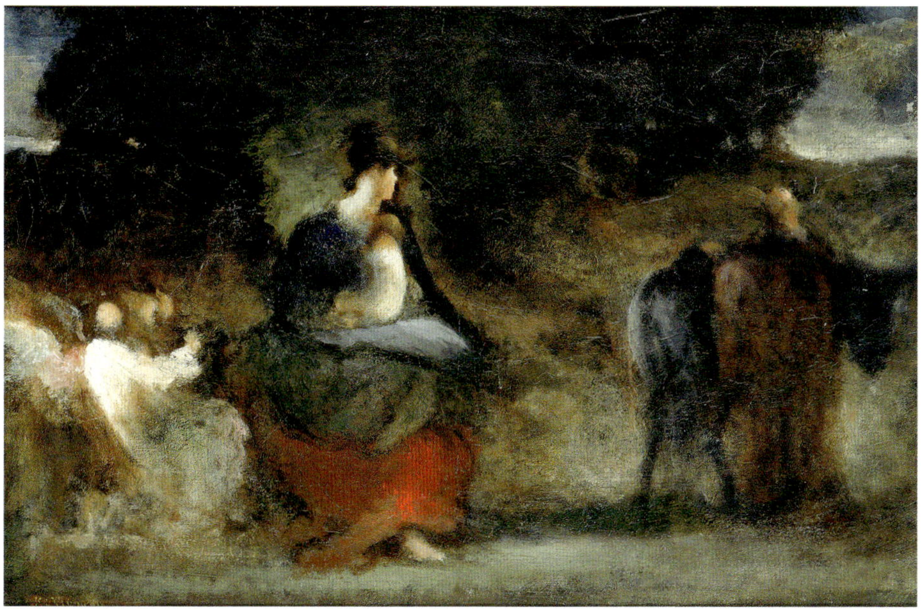

Robert Loftin Newman, *Flight into Egypt*, n.d. Smithsonian American Art Museum, Gift of
Mr. and Mrs. Donald Webster, 1975.57

effect. The Grand Forks, North Dakota, *Evening Times* misreported Newman's middle name, and—though he was childless—claimed his body was found by his son in a studio, though the tragedy unfolded in a newly leased apartment. The *East Oregonian* asserted Newman suffocated while "giving the finishing touches" to "a desert scene . . . conceived as his final effort."

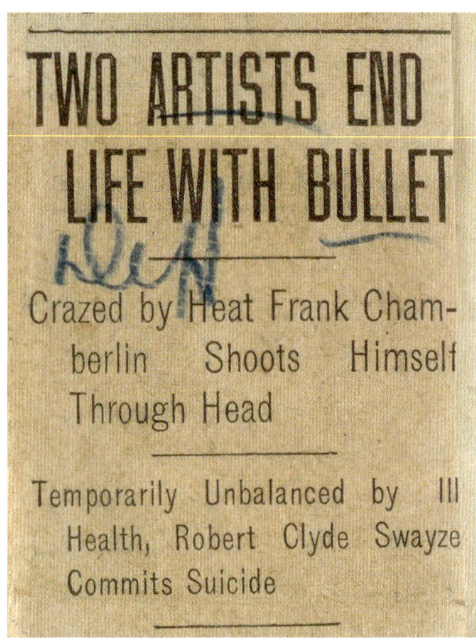

TWO ARTISTS END LIFE WITH BULLET

Another twin obituary, in the Monday, May 22, 1911, *Philadelphia Inquirer*, described the suicides of magazine illustrator Frank X. Chamberlain (whose surname the headline misspelled) and newspaper cartoonist Robert Clyde Swayze. Chamberlain, thirty-four, is reported to have frequently complained of the heat and shot himself in the head at 6 o'clock. Swayze, equally well known for his art in newspapers in San Francisco, New York, Philadelphia, and other cities, the story notes, shot himself at the exact same hour the Saturday before. Their pictures reached thousands of periodical readers in their time but today are difficult to trace. The scrapbooks are full of such misfortunate characters who died tragically and quickly faded into oblivion.

4. Press Intelligence

After the turn of the century, the largesse of benefactors Jacob S. Rogers, Henry Gurdon Marquand, and J. P. Morgan enabled the Metropolitan Museum to expand its galleries, raise an imposing Beaux-Arts facade along Fifth Avenue, hire more curators, and acquire spectacular works of art. New departments for Arms & Armor and Decorative Arts were established, and an ambitious excavation program was launched in Egypt. The long-serving Cesnola died in November 1904, prompting an organizational overhaul and reshuffling of responsibilities. Against this back-drop of frenzied institutional growth, Met management made a surprising move by appointing Arthur D'Hervilly—an executive office bookkeeper in his fifties with no formal art history educa-tion—second assistant curator of paintings in 1902 and assistant curator in 1907. He must have demonstrated an admirable work ethic and a fine sensitivity to pictures, but good timing, too, aided in his advancement.

In the early twentieth century, the professional qualifications for a curator were only vaguely defined, and many who held the title at The Met and other art institutions had little practical experience with the wide-ranging demands of the post. D'Hervilly's Paintings Depart-ment supervisors, George Henry Story, Roger Fry, and Bryson Burroughs, were by inclination and training artists rather than his-torians. They learned on the job to organize, catalogue, conserve, and exhibit the objects in their care. The vocational paths these men fol-lowed were more varied than is the norm today for a typical curator, so it is not completely surprising that D'Hervilly, a pen pusher with a smattering of art experience, landed a plum position at The Met. He also adroitly navigated his way when leadership of the Paintings Department rapidly turned over from Story to Fry to Burroughs.

In his new role as second assistant curator, D'Hervilly prepared a complete checklist of The Met's American pictures that was pub-lished in 1906, when Roger Fry was in charge. The formidable,

Cambridge-educated critic and practicing artist cared mostly about Old Masters and Post-Impressionists and spent much of his short tenure scouring Europe for such works to increase The Met's still-thin holdings. He bought several masterpieces, including an exquisite *Madonna and Child* by Giovanni Bellini. Focused on these lofty transactions, Fry was relieved to hand off to his humble factotum D'Hervilly the thankless task of inventorying hundreds of American canvases, which no doubt seemed provincial to the Englishman.

D'Hervilly was next assigned to aid a more ambitious effort—a revised and expanded catalogue of the Museum's entire painting collection, including European works. This book was finally published in 1914 under the direction of Fry's designated successor, the American artist Bryson Burroughs. D'Hervilly's precise duties were to measure each picture, pinpoint signatures, and update biographies of any painters still alive or recently deceased. As he gathered these facts, he interpolated them onto the margins of a well-thumbed prior edition of the catalogue. This working copy, abundantly annotated in D'Hervilly's distinctive script, remains to this day on a rare-books shelf in the Museum library.

D'Hervilly pasted a newspaper clipping on the inside cover of the book, probably culled from an edition of the New York *Evening Post* published before the updated Met catalogue appeared in 1914.

> I am sure that we often know too much to get the full value of
> our impressions . . . It is said that the most interesting writing
> is done by generally cultivated people concerning subjects
> that are new to them. The greatest enjoyment of nature often
> comes in the same way. It is quite possible to be "connoissered"
> out of one's senses.

The quotation is from *The Observations of Professor Maturin*, a text compiled—or authored entirely—by the literary scholar and educational administrator Clyde Bowman Furst, later published by Columbia University Press. This forgotten volume follows the form of *The Life of Samuel Johnson*, with Furst playing the part of a Boswell who records for posterity the philosophical musings and bon mots of the apocryphal gentleman scholar Bedelar Maturin.

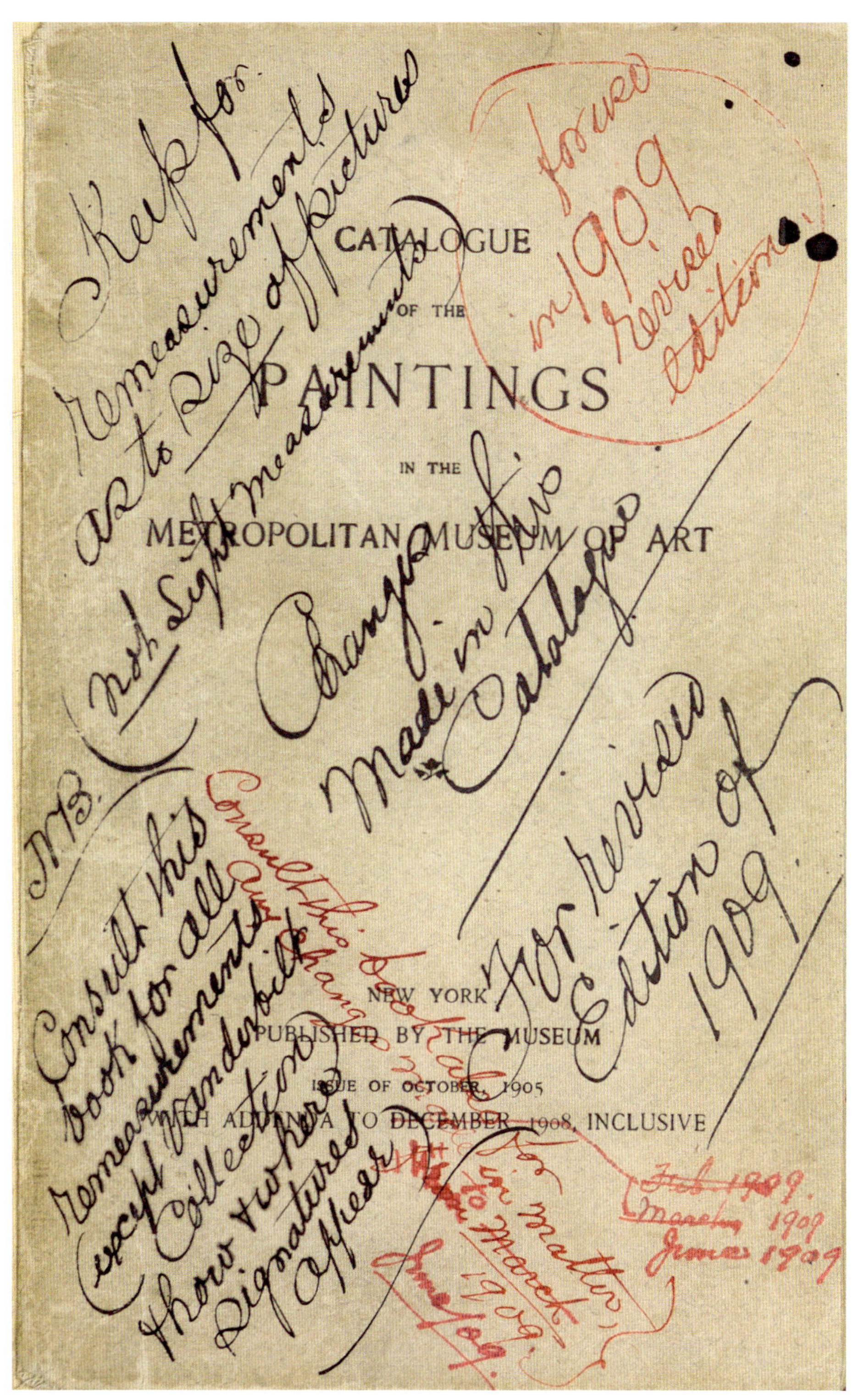

A. B. de St. M. D'Hervilly, *Catalogue of the paintings: brought down to [April 1912] by additions of monthly addenda for use in Revised Edition of 1909–1910–1911*, 1912. Thomas J. Watson Library, The Metropolitan Museum of Art

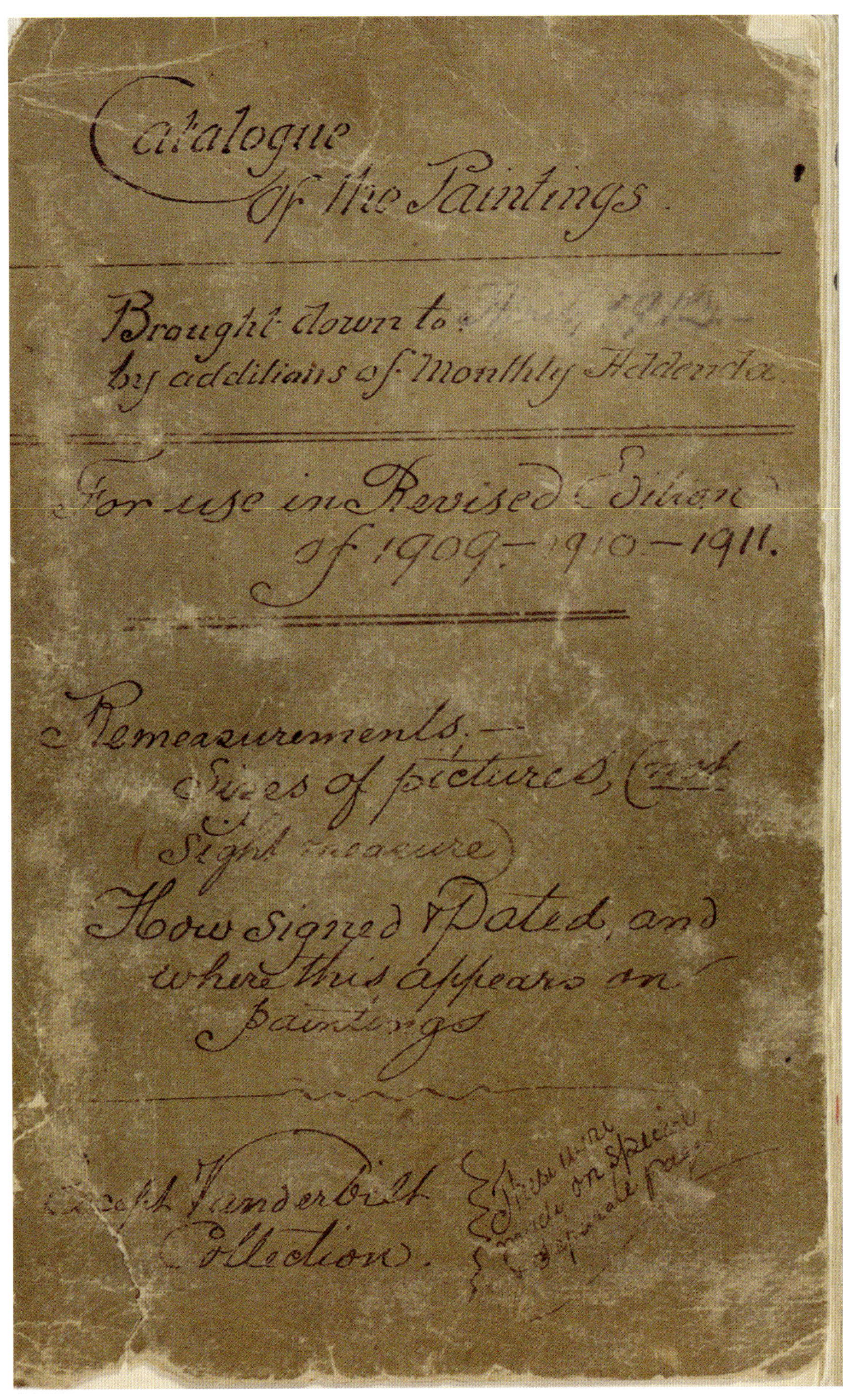

A. B. de St. M. D'Hervilly, *Catalogue of the paintings: brought down to [April 1912] by additions of monthly addenda for use in Revised Edition of 1909–1910–1911*, 1912. Thomas J. Watson Library, The Metropolitan Museum of Art

D'Hervilly's placement of the quote as an epigraph in his working copy slyly poked fun at belabored erudition, and the snobbery of the peripatetic Roger Fry. Seldom on hand in The Met galleries, Fry was acquainted with its treasures largely on authority rather than by intimate viewing, which probably irritated D'Hervilly.

It was around this time that D'Hervilly refashioned his name into a mysterious, elaborate new form. He appeared on a staff list published in the 1906 Met *Annual Report* as A. B. de St. M. D'Hervilly. A posthumous Met publication spelled out his abbreviations to "Arthuro Beraldo de Sancto Mauritio." No clues in his personal history explain why he altered and Latinized his name, although Sancto Mauritio probably alluded to an appearance of the appellation St. Maurice in his maternal genealogy.

The newly styled A. B. de St. M. occasionally served as a Met media officer, helping to host press previews of special exhibitions, including two 1909 blockbuster shows that highlighted Dutch Old Masters and colonial American furniture. Museum leaders aimed to entice an audience already primed for these oddly paired themes by the Hudson-Fulton Celebration, a citywide extravaganza marking the 300th anniversary of Henry Hudson's exploration of the river named in his honor and the centennial of navigation of the same waterway by Robert Fulton's paddle steamer *Clermont*. In addition to The Met exhibitions, festivities included a massive river flotilla, an air show by Wilbur Wright, and several elaborate parades.

ARTIST DIES AT HIS EASEL.

Some obituaries portray ambitious and diligent artists who perished as they put finishing touches to a potential pièce de résistance. The versatile, successful Swedish immigrant artist Bror Anders Wikstrom arrived in New Orleans in 1883, where he produced admirable paintings and illustrations and cofounded the Artists' Association of New Orleans. By 1885 he had cornered a specialty market designing fantastical Mardi Gras carnival floats.

In his youth Wikstrom had spent nearly a decade as a sailor; maritime and coastal landscape imagery are frequent subjects in

Brooklyn, N. [...]

... ... Wardell, ... Jason Pierce officiated at the services and the burial was in Cypress Hills Cemetery.

H. Girard Dusenbury.

H. Girard Dusenbury, who died on Wednesday at El Paso, Texas, where he had been staying for the past six months, was a young artist whose pictures had been published in magazines and newspapers. He was born in the Nineteenth Ward in 1885 and was the son of H. Girard and Jennie J. Dusenbury. He was a grandson of the late Edward Smith, the founder of the firm of Smith, Gray & Company. He was a graduate of Public School No. 16 and of the Erasmus High School and was a member of the Art Students' League of Manhattan. He leaves a brother, Warren E., and a sister, Marie Girard. The funeral services will be held at the residence of his brother, No. 361 Hancock street, on the arrival of the body in this borough.

New York Times
APR [...] 1909

ONLY SISTERS MOURN ONCE NOTED ARTIST

Ambrose Jackson, Whose Paintings Years Ago Were the Fashion, Dies in Poverty.

TEMPERAMENT HIS RUIN

While He Was Famous He and His Faithful Sisters Lived in Luxury— Now They Can't Bury Him.

Thirty-sixth Street was far uptown a quarter of a century or more ago, when Ambrose Jackson had his studio in a house just west of Broadway, but many of the city's wealthiest men and women frequently made the trip there, for the artist's fame was ripe; his pictures were well hung in the Academy, and invitations to the studio teas at which his sisters— Sarah Elizabeth, Bernice Maria, and Mary—received were much sought.

The circle of friends of the artist and his sisters was large, and in it were numbered some of the best known and most prominent of New York's residents. Mr. Jackson and the Misses Jackson, for the artist's sisters preferred keeping a home for him to marrying, attended St. George's Church and were enthusiastic church workers. All four had been confirmed there by Bishop Horatio Potter, uncle of the late Bishop Potter, who succeeded him.

The artist had more orders than he could fill, and for a time he made money rapidly until he was numbered among the wealthy, but in his good fortune Jack-

---

ARTIST DIES AT HIS EASEL.

B. A. Wikstrom, Designer of Hudson-Fulton Celebration Floats, Passes Away

B. A. Wikstrom, the artist, who was engaged by the Hudson-Fulton Celebration Commission to design the floats for the historical and carnival parades, died at work at his easel last night in his rooms, at 232 West Fifty-second Street. He had been very ill for four or five weeks with dropsy, but insisted upon continuing his work on the designs for floats. The design upon which he was at work last night when he passed away was that of a float of Die Lorelei, which was to be used by the Heinebund Society of this city in the carnival parade.

Mr. Wikstrom had finished fifty floats for the historical parade, about ten for the carnival parade, and roughly designed forty others for the carnival parade, so that it will be possible for the other artists in the employ of the Hudson-Fulton Celebration Commission to complete them. In this way all the floats in the two great parades will represent the work of Mr. Wikstrom.

For about thirty-five years Mr. Wikstrom designed the majority of the floats used in the Mardi Gras carnivals at New Orleans, and much of the reputation of those affairs is due to his artistic work. He handled a very wide range of subjects for these floats, and traveled all over the world to fit himself particularly for this special work.

He looked upon the Hudson-Fulton celebration as the master work of his life in the designing of floats, and it was his close application to that work which contributed largely to his illness.

Mr. Wikstrom was about 71 years old. He was born and educated in Sweden. He was graduated from the University at Stockholm and maintained a studio in Stockholm and owned a quaint home and large estate in the suburbs of that city.

Baltimore, Md., American Star
[...] 28 909

ARTIST FOUND DEAD ON FLOOR OF STUDIO

W. T. Wallace, Vice President of Alpha Co., Succumbs Suddenly to Apoplexy.

HAD BEEN IN FAILING HEALTH FOR SOME TIME

Believed to Have Gone to Offices About Midnight to Do Some Work.

Lying face downward upon the floor of his little artist's studio, Mr. William T. Wallace, 30 years old, vice president and head artist of the Alpha Photo-Engraving Company and son of Mr. Samuel S. Wallace, sales agent here for the Otis Elevator Company, was found dead at 8 o'clock this morning at the engraving company's place, northeast corner of Howard and Fayette streets.

Mr. Wallace had evidently fallen from his chair in an acute attack of illness, and Coroner Patrick F. Martin, of the Western district, after full investigation, gave a certificate of death from apoplexy.

[APR] 27 1909

BURIED

In a Pauper's Grave Was the Promising French Artist Who Lost in the Struggle With Fate.

Behind the death Saturday in the Betts Street Hospital and the burial of his body yesterday in potter's field is the story of the struggle that Leon Leetary, a French artist, made against fate, but lost in the race with the grim reaper.

Some few years ago Leetard, lured by the fact [...] nected with the engraving company since June, 1901. He was one of the best-known young artists in the city, having graduated at the head of his class from the Maryland Institute in 1896. He lived at 1009 North Fulton avenue.

The dead man's father and his brother, Mr. Lester Wallace, of the Drovers and Mechanics' National Bank, said that the young man had been [...] health for some time, and [...] when he called at the home of [...] 2341 Windsor avenue, Walbro[...] complained of nervous indigestion.

Mrs. Wallace, wife of [...] said that her husband had [...] yesterday morning feeling [...]

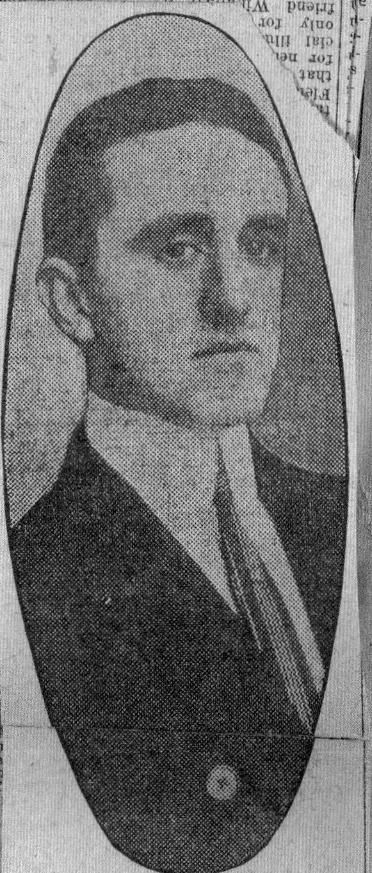

MR. W. T. WALLACE

[...] very ill and had died suddenly. Nothing was discovered by Coroner Martin, either in the studio or on Mr. Wallace's person to indicate that his death had occurred from other than natural causes.

After the examination by Coroner Martin [...] was removed to the Western [...]

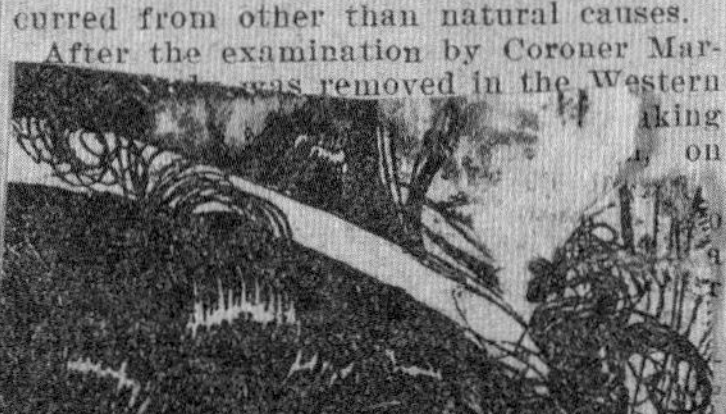

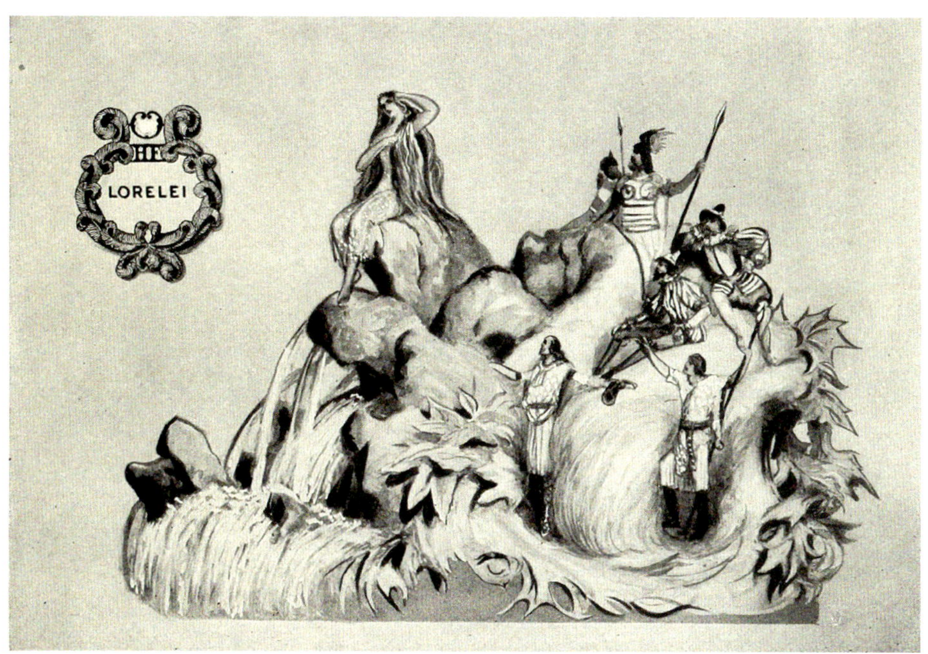

Bror Anders Wikstrom, *Lorelei*, 1909, in Hudson-Fulton Celebration Commission, *Official souvenir, Hudson-Fulton Celebration Carnival Pageant* (Redfield Bros., New York, 1909)

his paintings and designs. In 1909 he was invited to lead a project in New York planning mobile centerpieces for the Hudson-Fulton Celebration.

As he was touching up a Hudson-Fulton rendering for a float of the tale of the Lorelei siren, Wikstrom dropped dead. The imagery derived from a Heinrich Heine poem about a siren perched on a cliff along the Rhine River who so enchanted sailors with her beautiful song that they wrecked their ships on the steep rocks and drowned. *The New York Times* attributed Wikstrom's passing to "dropsy," an antiquated term for edema or a pooling of excess fluid in the body. "He looked upon the Hudson-Fulton celebration as the master work of his life in the designing of floats," noted the unusual front-page obit.

. . .

D'Hervilly understood the power of newspapers for publicity and tracked which reporters favorably reviewed important museum events. Popular publications were also valuable for institutional self-documentation. The Museum's practice of keeping a press archive of clippings about a wide array of Met happenings and pasting them into large scrapbooks dated to the institution's founding in 1870. By the turn of the century seven thick volumes were packed with news of art purchases, gallery improvements, and legacies of museum benefactors. This was the substantial Met-themed repository I had been searching through when I first stumbled on the anomalous scrapbooks of artists' deaths.

A few of these early Met history scrapbooks *did* contain artists' obituaries, but only for painters or sculptors directly affiliated with the Museum. The American painter John Frederick Kensett, a Hudson River School master, was a founding trustee of the Metropolitan Museum and a member of its powerful Executive Committee. In October 1872, soon after The Met first opened to the public, Kensett plunged into the cold water of Long Island Sound in a failed attempt to rescue a drowning friend. He soon fell ill with pneumonia and died some weeks later. News reports from this pre-tabloid era including a few in The Met press archive recounted the tragedy in a sober, dignified tone. One reprinted a lengthy proclamation by Met trustees that praised their fallen comrade as "a high-toned gentleman whose character and manners made him dear to the hearts

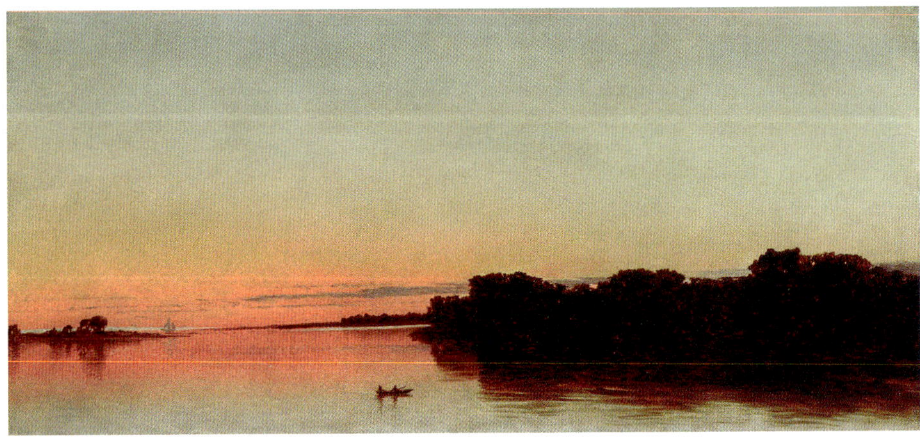

John Frederick Kensett, *Twilight on the Sound, Darien, Connecticut*, 1872. The Metropolitan Museum of Art, Gift of Thomas Kensett, 1874 (74.24)

of all who had the privilege of knowing him, and whose beautiful
landscapes faithfully reflect the peculiarities of our national scen-
ery." Two years after Kensett's death, his brother gave to The Met
a striking Kensett picture titled *Twilight on the Sound*. Kensett had
completed this transcendent scene of two boaters drifting toward a
murky shoreline a few months before his death, in a studio nearby
where he had entered the water.

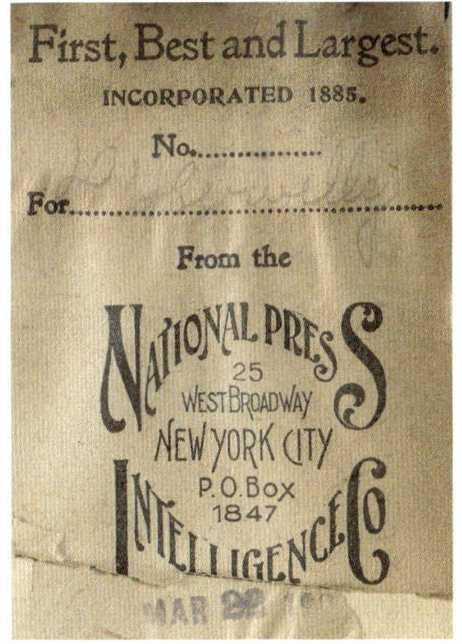

National Press Intelligence Co. advertisement,
The Collector and Art Critic vol. 4. no. 12,
October 1906

The National Press Intelligence Company was a fruitful source for
Met-themed newspaper clippings. Founded in New York in 1885, it
was one of many clippings bureaus that thrived a century ago. The
earliest of these businesses were established in Europe to cater to
actors, authors, and musicians eager to document their celebrity by
amassing glowing reviews of their work. Soon, the benefit of tapping
into deep wells of such reporting from around the globe was clear to
business leaders, politicians, and even museums.

Clippings bureaus employed readers—mostly women—to scour
hundreds of papers each day, bearing in mind a plethora of personal names, topical phrases, and concepts ordered by customers.
On encountering a target term, the reader underlined it with a bold

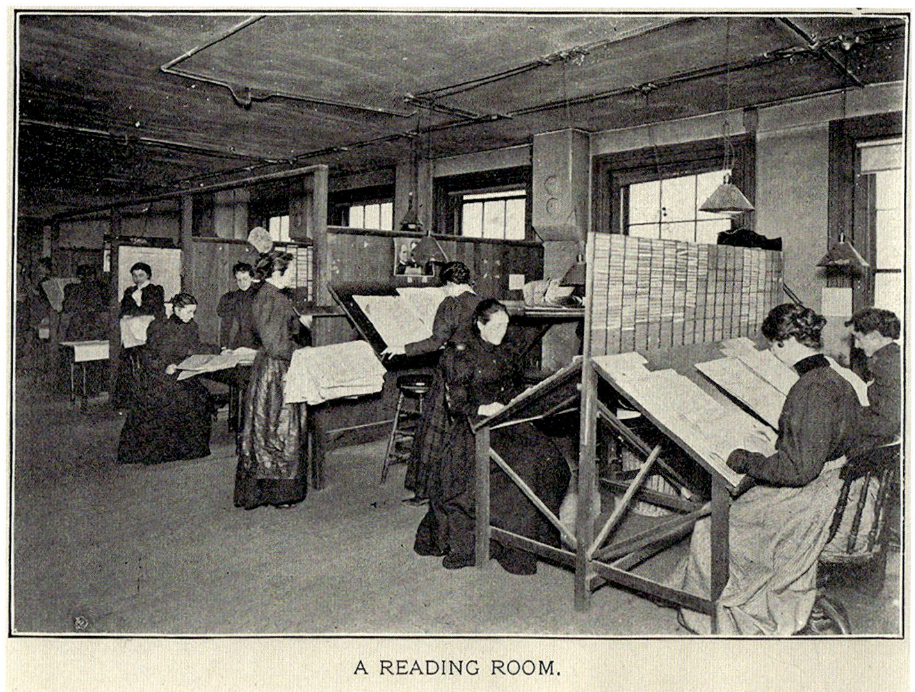

A Reading Room, ca. 1898, in Robert and Linn Luce, *The Press Clipping Bureau 1888–1898*, History Colorado (029.3 P926c), photographer unknown

stroke of colored pencil and scrawled the name of a client—like the distinctive blue "D'H" seen in The Met scrapbooks—or a patron code or number. Marked-up articles were clipped out and glued to header slips citing the name and date of the publication in which they had been found. The clippings were bundled and delivered to subscribers at a price of about five cents apiece. Batches prepared for The Met included mentions of the Museum by name and references to its trustees and staff, criteria that gleaned thousands of clippings over decades.

In the summer of 1906, shortly before his elevation to assistant curator, D'Hervilly ordered the National Press Intelligence to send him stories about deaths of artists. He probably expected these obituaries would prove helpful in his research of contemporary artists for the forthcoming paintings catalogue. Curiously, he did not request human-interest stories about still-living artists—only reports of the newly deceased were systematically harvested on D'Hervilly's watch. This odd search parameter garnered enough material to fill

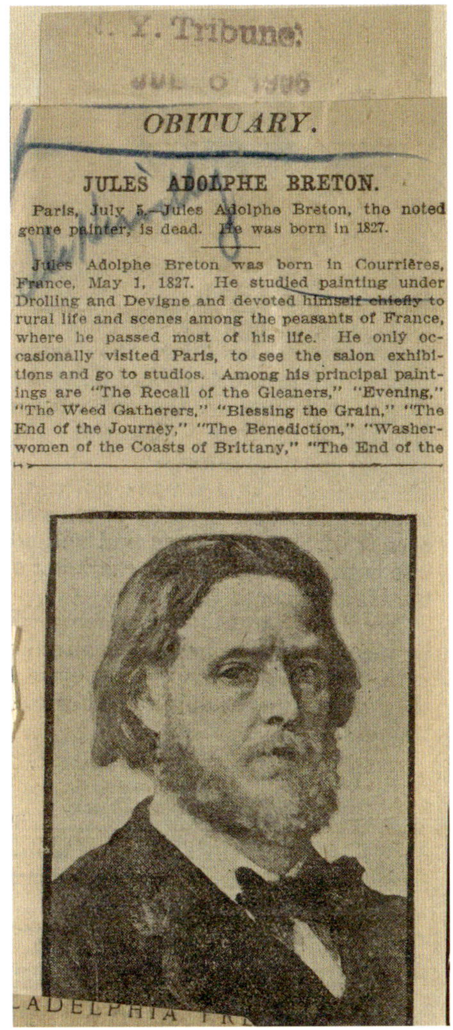

more than three hundred pages in the two overstuffed scrapbook volumes I found in the stacks a century later.

On page one of the first volume, Jules Breton, who died on July 5, 1906, is memorialized. D'Hervilly must have felt satisfied with the return on his small outlay when obituaries for this painter renowned for glowing scenes of French peasant life turned up in the very first packet he received from the National Press Intelligence. The Met then owned two works by Breton, whose entry in the paintings catalogue thus demanded a detailed curriculum vitae. The press clippings detail the artist's productive career but give little of the circumstances of

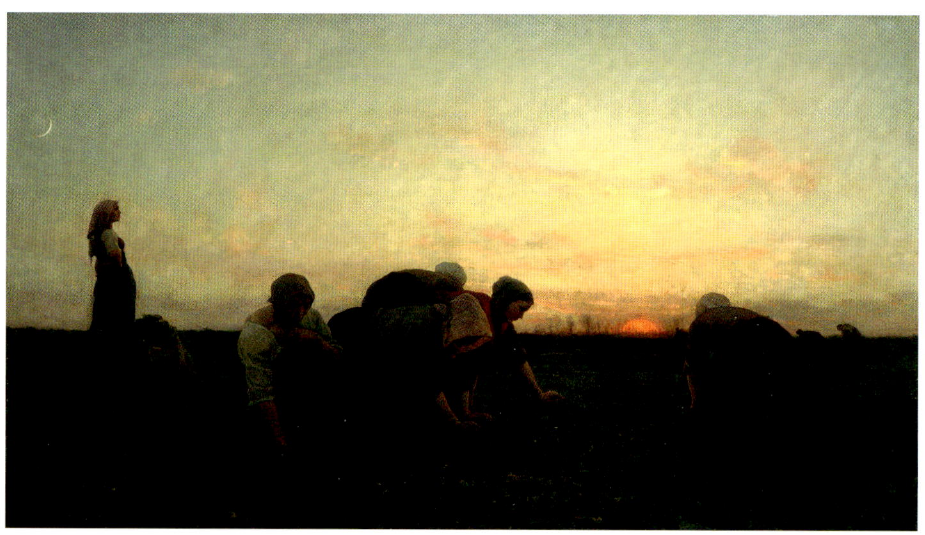

Jules Breton, *The Weeders*, 1868. The Metropolitan Museum of Art, Bequest of Collis P. Huntington, 1900 (25.110.66)

his passing at age seventy-nine. Breton enjoyed critical acclaim and financial reward in the nineteenth century, when he painted and sold hundreds of moody scenes of agrarian labor, religious ceremonies, and peasant studies. He was widely admired by his peers, including the shadowy outsider Vincent van Gogh, who in those days sold almost nothing. Meanwhile, pictures from Breton's studio in his native village in northern France were snapped up by collectors, including deep-pocketed Americans. Several Breton canvases that crossed the Atlantic in the nineteenth century were later donated to museums, including an evocative view of farm laborers bequeathed to The Met in 1900. Though Breton's reputation has since been eclipsed by that of van Gogh, his art remains prized. A Breton painting of a cluster of spectral figures wrapped in white dresses for a First Holy Communion ceremony, commissioned by a Met Museum founder, Samuel Putnam Avery, sold at auction in 2017 for $1.2 million dollars.

The scrapbooks tell the stories of many artists who were revered in their time, like Breton, but whose stars have since dimmed dramatically. There are four clippings in the first scrapbook about Charles Yardley "C. Y." Turner, born in Baltimore in 1850—the same year

Saturday, October 2?, 1918.

numbered 2,375, against 2,772 the day
before. Pneumonia cases decreased
from 699 to 500, and deaths from 307
to 241. Camp Dix, N. J., reported
only three cases yesterday, and the
quarantine there has been lifted.

A. B. Stelzer, Artist, Dies Of Pneumonia in France

Albert Bernard Stelzer, 26 years old,
of Washington, died of pneumonia on

Saturday, October 12, 1918.

PAINTER OF "SPIRIT OF '76" DIES

Archibald M. Williard Succumbs to Heart Disease at Age of 81

Cleveland, Oct. 12.—Archibald M. Willard, painter of the famous picture, "The
Spirit of '76," died yesterday at the age
of eighty-one, of heart disease.

Mr. Willard's painting was finished in
1876 and was exhibited at the Philadelphia Centennial, after which it was
bought by General U. H. Deveraux, of
Cleveland, who presented it to the town
of Marblehead, Mass., where it hangs
in Abbott Hall. General Deveraux's son,
Harry K. Deveraux, president of the
Grand Circuit, posed for the picture of
the boy in the painting.

Mr. Willard's father was the model
for the aged drummer. The fifer was
Hugh Mosier, a musician, in Cleveland.
Another picture which earned fame

Saturday, October 12, 1918.

NOTED PAINTER DIES.

A. M. Willard Succumbs to Heart Disease at 81.

CLEVELAND, Ohio, Oct. 12—Archibald M. Willard, painter of the famous
picture, "The Spirit of '76," died at his
home here yesterday, aged 81 years.
Death was due to heart disease.

Mr. Willard's painting was finished
in 1876 and was exhibited at the Philadelphia Centennial, after which it was
bought by General J. H. Deveraux, of
Cleveland, who presented it to the town

WAS ARTIST AND RUG CONNOISSEUR

Peter W. White Dies at His Home in This City.

LONG IN NEWSPAPER WORK

Made Name for Himself as Sketch
Artist, in Which Capacity He
Served for Several Years—Widely
Known as Judge of Oriental Rugs

Thursday, January 2, 1919.

Dance Shop Pupils.
This entertainment is planned under
the direction of Mrs. A. Lincoln Filene,
chairman of the central bureau of entertainment.

FAMOUS PAINTER DEAD

NEW YORK, Jan. 1.—The death in a
hospital here yesterday of Charles
Yeardley Turner of Baltimore, widely
known mural painter, was announced
tonight.

C. Y. Turner, Artist, Dies.

Charles Yardley Turner, the mural
painter, of 1,230 St. Paul Street, Baltimore, Md., died at the Presbyterian
Hospital in this city yesterday of Span-
ish influenza, after an illness of two
days. He was born in Baltimore on
Nov. 25, 1850, and studied at the National Academy of Design, helping to
found the Art Students' League of New
York. He studied also in Paris with
J. P. Laurens, L. Bonnat, and M.
Munkacsy.

Thursday, January 2, 1919.

CHARLES Y. TURNER, NOTED MURAL PAINTER, DIES

Influenza Victim, Who Lived in Baltimore, Was Visiting Friends Here When Stricken.

Charles Yardley Turner, noted mural
painter of No. 1230 St. Paul Block, Baltimore, died at the Presbyterian Hospital
in this city yesterday from influenza
after an illness of two days.

Mr. Turner, sixty-eight, came to New
York to visit friends. He was taken to
the hospital by Dr. W. F. Wright of No.
59 West 110th Street.

Born in Baltimore, Nov. 25, 1850. Mr.
Turner was graduated from the Maryland Institute and the National Academy of Design and studied at the Art
Students' League in this city. He was
instructed by J. P. Laurens and L. Bonnat in Paris from 1878 to 1881.

At the World's Columbian Exposition
1892 he was assistant director of decoration and was director of color at
the Pan-American Exposition. He won 19
medals at expositions here and abroad.

CHARLES Y. TURNER.

Charles Yardley Turner, painter and
mural decorator, died of influenza yesterday in the Presbyterian Hospital.
He lived in Baltimore, and was visiting friends here when he was taken
sick. He was born in Baltimore, November 25, 1850, was graduated from
the Art School of the Maryland Institute in 1870, came to New York
soon after, and founded the Art Students' League, of which he was afterward president. From 1881 to 1884 he
was professor of drawing and painting at the League.

In Paris Turner studied with Jean
Paul Laurens, M. Munkacsy, and L-

FRANK DUVENECK, ARTIST, DEAD

CINCINNATI, O., Jan. 3.—Frank Duveneck, internationally renowned artist,
died here to-day of a complication of
diseases after a six months' illness. He
was seventy-one years old, but up to the
time of his illness was an active figure
in American and European art circles.
He established studios and schools at
Munich and Florence, and was the re-
cipient of the Grand Medal of Honor of
the Panama-Pacific Exposition. The ex-
perts believe to be his best were "The
Whistling Boy," and "Portrait of Prof.
Loeffts" and "Girl and Forget-me-not."

FRANK DUVENECK, ARTIST, DEAD IN CINCINNATI

CINCINNATI, Jan. 3.—Frank Duveneck, artist, died here today at the age
of 71. He established studios at Munich
and Florence and received the grand
medal of honor of the Panama-Pacific
Exposition. Among his works were
"The Whistling Boy," "portrait of
Prof. Loeffts" and "Girl and Forget-Me-
Not."

EDWARD McNAMARA DIES OF GAS POISONING AT WEST END

Saturday, January 4, 1919.

Long Island polo and fox hunting
circles, is dead at the country home
of his sister, Mrs. Edward T. Cush-
ing, at East Williston, as a result of
an accident a month ago.

Mr. Roby was sixty-four years old
and the son of Mr. and Mrs. Eben
Roby of Boston. He was graduated
from Harvard in the class of 1877 and
later from the Columbia Law School.

Duveneck, Artist, Dead

Cincinnati, O., Jan. 4.—Frank Duveneck, internationally famous artist,
is dead here.

MR. F. DUVENECK, NOTED ARTIST, DIES

Was Known Internationally for His Portrait and Figure Paintings— Member of National Academy.

CINCINNATI, Ohio, Friday.—Mr. Frank
Duveneck, internationally renowned artist, died here to-day after a six months'
illness. He was seventy-one years old, but

FRANK DUVENECK DEAD.

Noted American Painter, Was Best Known for His "Whistling Boy."

CINCINNATI, Ohio, Jan. 3.—Frank
Duveneck, artist, died here today of a
complication of diseases, after a six
months' illness. He was 71 years old,
but up to the time of his illness was an
active figure in American and European
art circles.

Frank Duveneck was born in Coving-
ton, Ky., in 1848, the son of a lawyer,
and at an early age he was sent to a
monastery, near Pittsburg, to be educated. The monks discovered his won-
derful talents, encouraged and used
them by sending him all over the country to decorate churches of their order.
In many he painted huge pictures. One

JAMES CRAIG NICOLL, NOTED PAINTER, DIES

Founder and President of American Water Color Society Was Famous for His Marines.

Special to The New York Times.

NORWALK, Conn., July 26.—James
Craig Nicoll, a noted artist, President of
the American Water Color Society, of

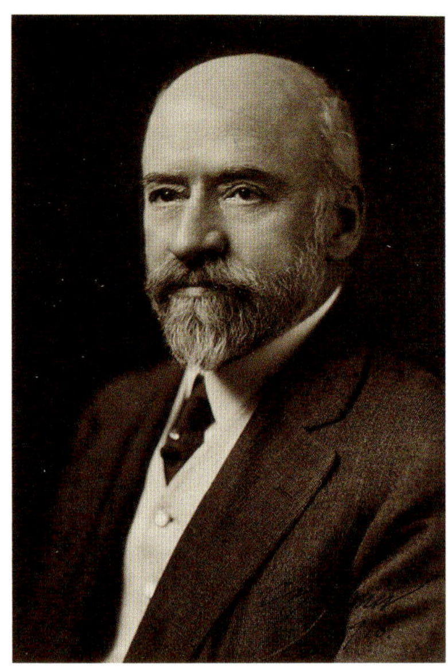

Janvier (Firm: Baltimore, MD), *Charles Yardley Turner*, 1916. Miscellaneous photographs collection, ca. 1845–1980, Archives of American Art, Smithsonian Institution

as D'Hervilly—who came to New York to study at the National Academy of Design and the Art Students League. After a European tour and tutelage by the French academician Léon Bonnat, he returned to America and won commissions for historically themed murals to adorn state courthouses and the Wisconsin State Capitol. Turner painted lunettes still on display today in the Hudson County, New Jersey, courthouse in Jersey City. He contributed to the visual design of the 1893 World's Columbian Exposition in Chicago and coordinated imagery for the 1901 Pan-American Exposition in Buffalo.

Several of Turner's oil on canvas paintings were collected by museums, including *The Bridal Procession* (1886), acquired by The Met in 1891. In time, however, this picture fell from curatorial favor, and it was deaccessioned and sold by the Museum in 1956. It resurfaced in 2013 and sold at auction for just $16,250. Like Turner's murals, its style is straightforwardly representational and reflects little engagement with pictorial innovations of the Post-Impressionist era. Turner's orderly compositions center on identifiable character types and easily legible narratives. Their muted and golden-brown hues allude to the past like scraps of old parchment. The venerable Turner was a safe choice for civic leaders privileged to commission artworks that were expected—and indeed have continued—to adorn grand public spaces for decades.

On New Year's Eve 1918, as a New York paper reported, Turner was "Visiting Friends Here When Stricken" and quickly succumbed to a deadly flu then epidemic. This understated account suggests even tabloid writers knew to tread lightly on the reputation of an establishment darling. Despite Turner's once lofty position on the

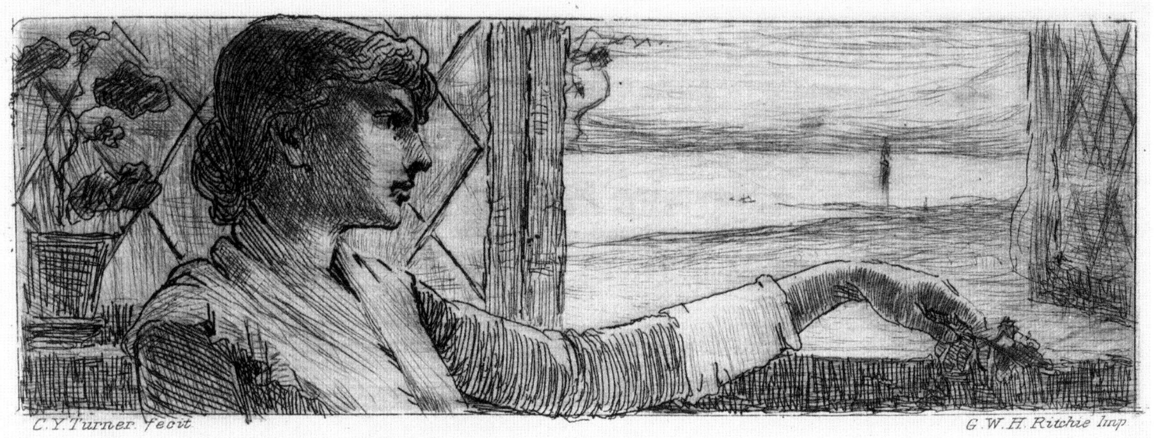

Charles Yardley Turner, ca. 1884, in New England Institute, *Art Yearbook 1884* (New York: Art Age Press, 1884), The Metropolitan Museum of Art, Rogers Fund, 1968 (68.513.7)

American art scene, only a few traces of his career remain in The Met today, including a tender etching of a woman's profile reproduced in a book tucked away in the Museum's Drawings and Prints Department.

The influenza epidemic of 1918 killed several other artists, including twenty-eight-year-old Egon Schiele and his mentor Gustav Klimt, age fifty-five, though obituaries for neither artist were added to the scrapbooks. Two years earlier a different strain of flu took the life of Edith Woodman Burroughs, a highly regarded sculptor and the spouse of Met curator Bryson Burroughs. It surely pained D'Hervilly to add to his collection several laudatory clippings about his boss's wife, who was only in her forties and the mother of their two children.

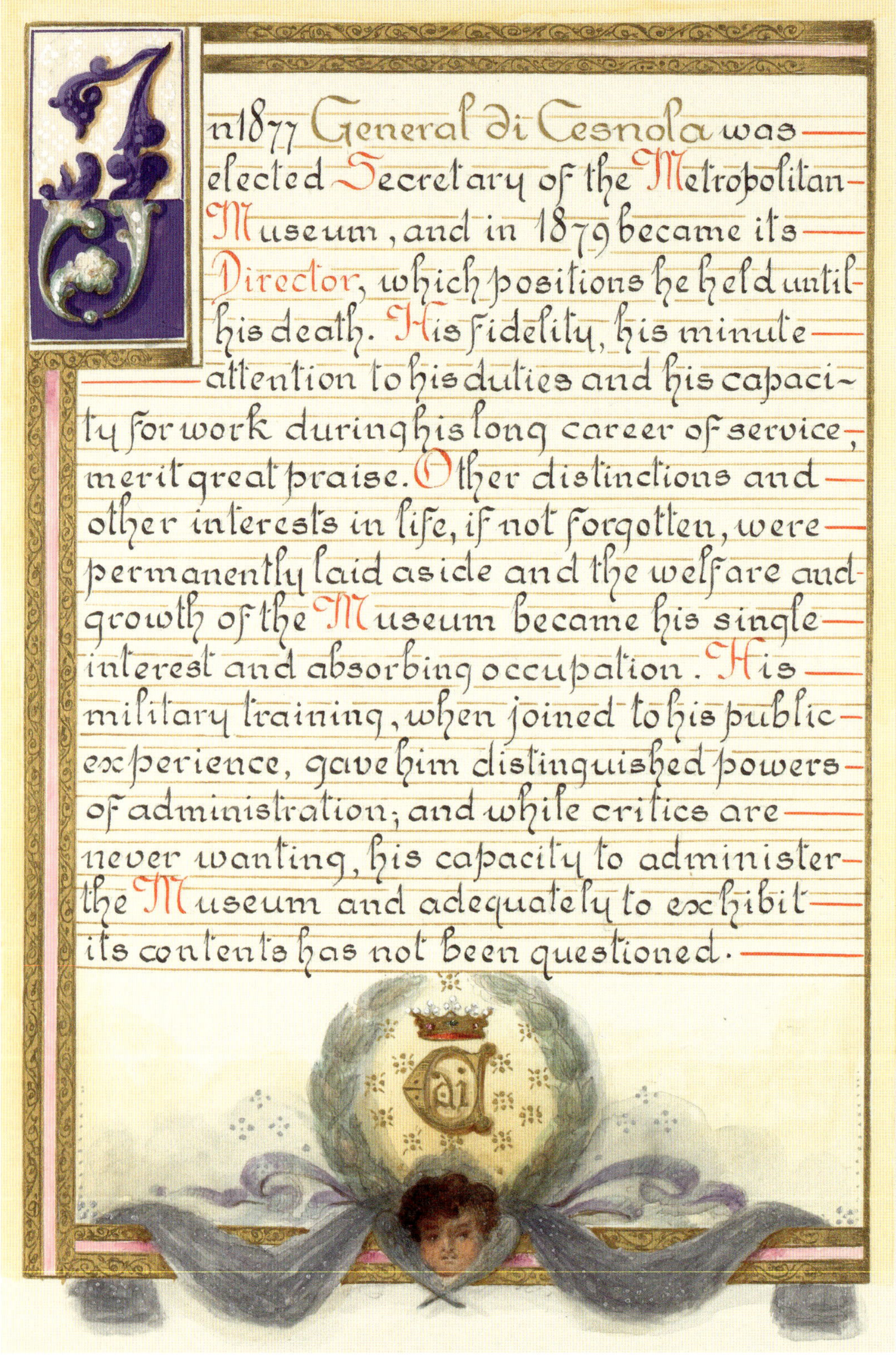

A. B. de St. M. D'Hervilly and Metropolitan Museum of Art Board of Trustees, Memorial resolution for General di Cesnola, 1904. Luigi Palma di Cesnola Collection, The Metropolitan Museum of Art Archives

5. The Privilege of Giving Help

Secure in his position at the Museum, D'Hervilly continued to make art—albeit at the behest of his employer. When Met benefactors died, museum trustees issued honorary proclamations hailing their service and extolling their virtues. On a few of these sad occasions D'Hervilly's creativity was called upon to draw sumptuous illuminated manuscript versions of eulogies for families of the deceased. One honored Frederic Rhinelander, a founding trustee who died in 1904 after serving briefly as Met president.

That same year, General Cesnola passed away at age seventy-two in a room at the Hotel Seymour on West 45th Street. D'Hervilly illustrated one sheet of his remembrance with the face of a cherubic young man topped by a "di C" monogram and a gem-studded crown, elevating the honoree from General to King.

Surprisingly, it seems that D'Hervilly produced no such elaborate memorialization for another museum leader, Francis Davis "Frank" Millet, an accomplished, award-winning painter and sculptor, who was elected a Met trustee in 1910. He perished under the most dramatic circumstances imaginable in 1912 as a passenger on the doomed ocean liner *Titanic* and is commemorated in a scrapbook with a full page of clippings.

Millet's adventurous life included service as a Union army drummer boy in the American Civil War, exotic travel as an international war correspondent, study at the Royal Academy of Fine Arts at Antwerp, and friendship with Mark Twain, who was a witness at Millet's wedding in Paris in 1879. Millet and his wife, Lily, had four children, subjects of portraits by John Singer Sargent. Later in life, Millet lived in a large mansion in Northwest, Washington, D.C., with Major Archibald Butt, a military officer and beloved aide to United States presidents Theodore Roosevelt and William Howard Taft. Butt referred to his companion as "Millet, my artist friend who lives with me." Historians have speculated their connection was romantic.

Returning to the U.S. from a vacation in
Europe, the two went down together on
the ill-fated ship.

Millet's successful creative practice
focused on painting genre and historical scenes similar to those of his occasional collaborator C. Y. Turner. Millet
was commissioned to ornament interiors of government buildings including the United States Customs House
at Baltimore and the Minnesota State
Capitol. His mural unveiled in 1905 in
the latter site, *Treaty of Traverse des Sioux*,
is a hagiographic tableau of settlers and
Native Americans shaking hands and
signing documents before a respectful
mixed audience, whitewashing a fraught political moment in 1851
when indigenous people on the Minnesota frontier were dispos-
sessed and defrauded.

In 1887 The Met had acquired Millet's painting *A Cosey Corner*,
which shows a young woman reading by the light of a cottage

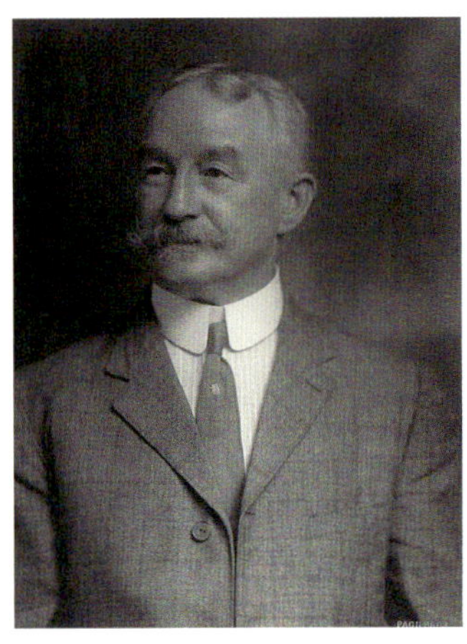

Pach Brothers, *Frank Millet*, ca. 1910. Staff and Trustee Photographs Collection, The Metropolitan Museum of Art Archives

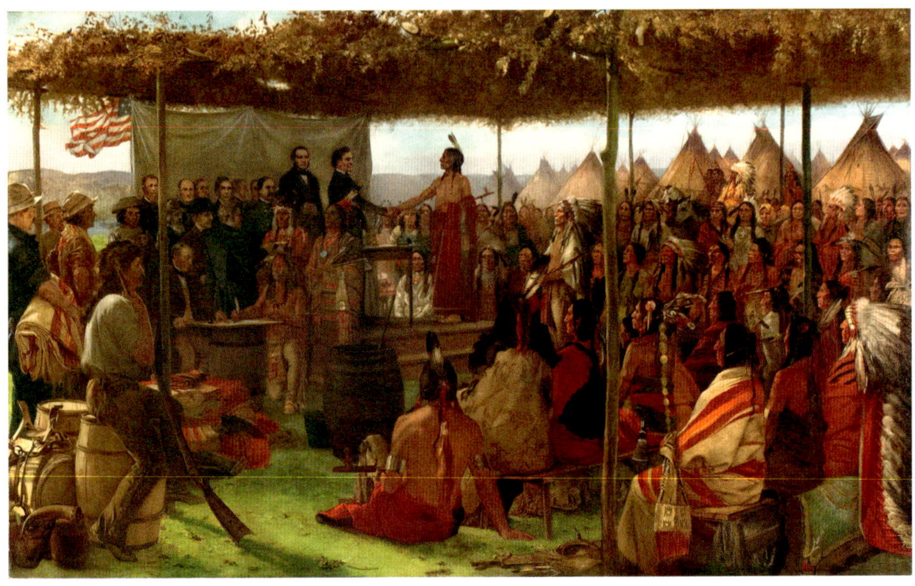

Francis Davis Millet, *Treaty of Traverse des Sioux*, 1905. Minnesota Historical Society

[...] POST [288?]

Wednesday, April 17, 1912.

[...]he Chester or the Salem.

[...]LLET WAS BRINGING DESIGNS.

Been Engaged to Decorate Walls of New Bedford Library.

NEW BEDFORD, Mass., April 17.—Frank [...]illet, the artist, who was aboard the [...]nic, and whose name does not appear [...]e list of survivors, had been engaged [...]int the mural decorations for the new [...]ic Library in this city.

[...]had notified the Library trustees that [...] sketches were complete and that he [...]d bring them back from Europe on [...] Titanic. The artist formerly lived in [...]apoisett, a few miles from New Bed-[...]

Wednesday, April 17, 1912.

[...]MILLET, ARTIST AND WRITER.

[...]hile Living Abroad He Kept in Touch With America.

Francis Davis Millet, the painter, was [...]rn in Mattapoisett, Mass., served in the [...]vil war as a drummer boy, was educated [...] Harvard and always identified himself [...]d his art with his native country, but [...]r years his home had been in England [...]cept when he was roving to odd parts [...] the earth, which was his recreation. [...]e lived with his wife in Broadway, [...]orcestershire, and was called the King of [...]e Worcestershire colony of writers and [...]tists, the Queen being Mary Anderson-[...]avarro. The Millet garden has been [...]ctured again and again in landscape [...] Royal Academicians.

[...]Millet was born in 1846. After his experience as a drummer boy he was for a [...]ar an assistant in the surgeons' corps. [...]om Harvard, which he entered at the [...]ose of the war, he went into newspaper [...]rk. He was on the Boston *Advertiser* [...]d the Boston *Saturday Evening Gazette* [...]d was city editor of the Boston *Courier*. [...]ing to the Royal Academy in Antwerp [...] 1871, he won a prize in his first year. [...]wo years later he became secretary to [...]arles Francis Adams, commissioner [...]om Massachusetts to the Vienna E[...] [...]sition. Millet reported the expositi[...] [...] New York newspapers, studied art a[...] [...]lped Mr. Adams at the same time. H[...] [...]urned to America in 1876 and assiste[...] [...]hn La Farge in decorating Trinity [...]urch, Boston. In 1877 he dropped into [...]urnalism again and went through the [...]sso-Turkish wars as correspondent for [...] New York paper and for the London [...]ily News. He accompanied his descriptions of battles with vivid sketches; [...]cidentally he got six decorations for [...]avery under fire.

[...]After the war Millet studied art in [...]ris. He was a member of the Fine Arts [...]y of the Paris Exposition in 1878. He [...]urned to Boston and was married. but[...]

[...]few years he was again wandering [...]urope and making pictures for *Har[...]s*. In the middle '80s he bought his [...] in Worcestershire.

[...]llet's face was known all over the [...]d. One day in Japan a friend said: [...]llet, at last we are in a place where [...]dy knows you." But at that moment [...] appeared a waiter who said: "Ah, [...] again, Mr. Millet."

[...]cently Mr. Millet had been in Italy [...]ead of the American Academy at [...]

[...]llet was director of decorations [...]e Chicago exposition, special correspondent of the London *Times* in the [...]

[...]ROOKLYN N.Y. EAGLE [288?]

Tuesday, April 16, 1912.

Field.

FRANK DAVIS MILLET.

Frank Davis Millet, artist, author and former newspaper correspondent, lived at 6 East Twenty-third street, Manhattan, and maintained a residence also on Broadway, Worcestershire, England. He was born in Mattapoisett, Mass., on November 3, 1846. He enlisted as a drummer in the Sixtieth Massachusetts Volunteers at the age of 18 years, and saw active service, within the year being promoted to acting assistant contract surgeon, Army of the Potomac.

After the war young Millet entered Harvard, where he was graduated in 1869, receiving an A.M. degree three years later. During the succeeding years he was secretary to the Massachusetts Commission to the Vienna Exposition, correspondent for the New York Herald, the London Daily News and the London Graphic during the Russo-Turkish war, director of decorations and then director of functions at the Chicago World's Fair, special correspondent of the London Times and Harper's Weekly at Manila during the Government's troubles in the Philippines; chairman of the United States Niagara Falls Commission, chairman of the advisory committee of the National Museum, secretary of the American Academy in Rome and of the American Federation of Arts, vice president of the Municipal Art Commission of this city, United States Commissioner-General to the Tokyo Exposition, and during his career received medals of honor from many societies and several Governments.

He was a member of the National Institute of Arts and Letters, the Society of Painters in Oil Colors, the G. A. R., honorary member of the American Institute of Architects. He was the author of one or two fiction books and of tales based upon his own adventures. He married Elizabeth Greeley Merrill of Boston, March 11, 1879.

[...]knowledged as one of the wealthiest [...]en in the city he interested himself in [...]litics. He worked for the election of [...]over Cleveland to the Presidency and [...]pported him in his second campaign. [...]terward he was elected as a Representative in Congress.

FRANK D. MILLET.

Few men had as wide a range of talent and experience as did Frank D. Millet, the artist and writer, who was born in Mattapoisett, Mass., in 1846. When a boy he enlisted as a drummer in the civil war and before the end of the struggle was promoted to be assistant in the surgeons' corps. After the war he entered Harvard, from which he was graduated to enter newspaper work. He served for a time as city editor of the Boston Courier. He gave up that field in 1871 to study art in the Royal Academy of Antwerp, where he quickly distinguished himself. His success commended him to Charles Francis Adams, who made him his secretary when he was appointed as Commissioner to the Vienna Exposition in 1873. Millet worked not only as secretary, but as correspondent for two New York papers and continued his art studies the while.

When he came back to America in 1876 he assisted John La Farge in the decoration of Trinity Church in Boston. A few years afterward he went to the Russo-Turkish War for the New York Herald, a conflict in which he earned six medals for bravery under fire. After that he went back to Paris to continue his art studies, returning to Boston to marry. After a few years he went to England, where he permanently made his home in Worcester. His canvases are hanging in the Metropolitan Museum of Art here, the Union League Club, the Detroit Museum, the Duquesne Club of Pittsburg and the National Gallery of New Zealand. His mural decorations are to be seen in many large public buildings.

N.Y. EVEN. SUN [288?]

Tuesday, April 16, 1912.

Knollwood Country clubs.

FRANK D. MILLET.

Artist and Correspondent a Missing Titanic Passenger.

Frank D. Millet, the artist and correspondent, who was born at Mattapoisett, Mass., in 1846, began his public career as a drummer boy in the Civil War. He was later promoted to be an assistant in the surgeon's corps, and before the conflict was over he saw a great deal of active service. After being graduated from Harvard he became a reporter on the Boston *Advertiser*, then city editor of the Boston *Courier* and head of the *Saturday Evening Gazette*.

Very soon after he took up the study of art at the Royal Academy in Antwerp he won a much-sought prize. His success brought him the position of secretary to Charles Francis Adams, when Mr. Adams became commissioner to the Vienna Exposition in 1873. Millet filled this place but kept up his art studies at the same time, and also covered the exposition as correspondent for two New York newspapers.

After serving as war correspondent for the New York *Herald* in the Russo-Turkish war of 1877, Millet went to Paris to devote himself to art and was chosen a member of the Fine Arts Jury of the Paris Exposition of 1878.

In his later years Millet was best known as a distinguished painter, and his canvases are to be found in almost every prominent city of the country. But he was a familiar figure at social functions of all kinds in New York, as well as in many other parts of the world, for Frank D. Millet was also one of the greatest travellers of his time.

[...]er of James Seligman, the banker, in 1894. Three children were born to them—Benira, Marguerite and Hazel.

Francis D. Millet.

Francis Davis Millet, the painter, was born in Mattapoisett, Mass., on November 3, 1846. When the Civil War began he enlisted as a drummer boy, and was soon made an assistant in the surgeons' corps. When the war was over he went home and entered Harvard College. From college he went to work for the Boston Advertiser as a reporter. Later he became city editor of the Boston Courier, and after this manager of the Saturday Evening Gazette.

In 1871 he went to Antwerp to study art at the Royal Academy and won a much coveted prize in his first year. In 18[...] Mr. Millet gave up painting in Paris to become special correspondent for the New York Herald in the Turkish war. His work attracted the attention of the London Daily News, who hired him to take the place of their regular correspondent, Archibald Forbes. During the campaigning he received the Rumanian Iron Cross, and on the field of battle the Russian military crosses of St. Stanislaus and St. [...]ne, and later the Russian and Rumanian war medals.

After the war Mr. Millet returned to Paris and served on the fine arts jury of the Paris Exposition in 1878. A year later he married Miss Elizabeth Greeley Merrill and came to America to live, first in Boston and later in New York. Among Mr. Millet's mural paintings is the big panel in the court house at Newark, N. J., representing the "Foreman of the Grand Jury Rebuking the Chief Justice of New Jersey" for submitting to the oppression of England in 1774. His decoration of the Baltimore Custom House is the most important of his work. His canvases are hanging in the Metropolitan Museum of Art, New York; also in the Detroit Museum, Union League Club of this city, the Duquesne Club of Pittsburgh and the National Gallery of New Zealand and in Brooklyn Institute.

NEW YORK N.Y. WORLD [288?]

Wednesday, April 17, 1912.

FRANCIS D. MILLET: ARTIST AND AUTHOR.

Francis David Millet, artist and author, was born in Mattapoisett, Mass., Nov. 3, 1846. He enlisted as drummer in the Sixteenth Massachusetts when eighteen years of age and served throughout the war.

After the war young Millet entered Harvard, where he was graduated in 1869. During the succeeding years he was Secretary to the Massachusetts Commission to the Vienna Exposition, correspondent for the New York Herald, the London Daily News and the London Graphic during the Russo-Turkish war, Director of Decorations and then Director of Functions at the Chicago World's Fair, special correspondent of the London Times and Harper's Weekly at Manila during the Government's troubles in the Philippines; Chairman of the United States Niagara Falls Commission, Chairman of the Advisory Committee of the National Museum, Secretary of the American Academy in Rome and of the American Federation of Arts, Vice-President of the Municipal Art Commission of this city, United States Commissioner-General to the Tokio Exposition, and during this career received medals of honor from many societies and several Governments.

He was a member of the National Institute of Arts and Letters, the Society of Painters in Oil Colors, the G. A. R., and honorary member of the American Institute of Architects. He was the author of one or two fiction books and of fact tales based upon his own adventures. He married Elizabeth Greeley Merrill of Boston, March 11, 1879. Their home was at No. 6 East Twenty-third street, this city.

In the last twenty years or so Mr. Millet became more and more widely known as an artist, and his work earned for him decorations from half a dozen countries. He was pre-eminently a painter of easel pictures, but also won distinction as a mural decorator and in other lines of artistic work. He was credited with having visited nearly every part of the globe, even the Arctic and the Antarctic. His last trip abroad had taken him to Italy, where he was the head of the American Academy at Rome. Among the institutions possessing canvases by Millet are the Metropolitan Museum of Art here, the Detroit Museum, the Union League Club, the Duquesne Club of Pittsburgh and the National Gallery of New Zealand. Of late he was engaged in making mural decorations for a number of public buildings, including the State Capitol at St. Paul, Minn., the Court House at Newark, the Custom House at Baltimore and the Federal Building at Cleveland.

Thursday, April 18, 1912.

[...]ore for the per[...] people than Taft."

Taft Asks About Butt And Artist F. D. Mille[t]

But Cruiser Salem, Wirelessing the President's Request to Carpathia, Gets No Reply.

The following wireless dispatch which was being sent from the scout cruiser Salem to the Carpathia, was read at the Brooklyn Navy Yard last night:

"President of the United States is very anxious to know if Major Butt, Mr. Millet and Mr. Moore are safe. Please inform me, so I can transmit to him."

(Signed) "CHANDLER."

Up to 10.30 o'clock the cruiser Salem had received no reply.

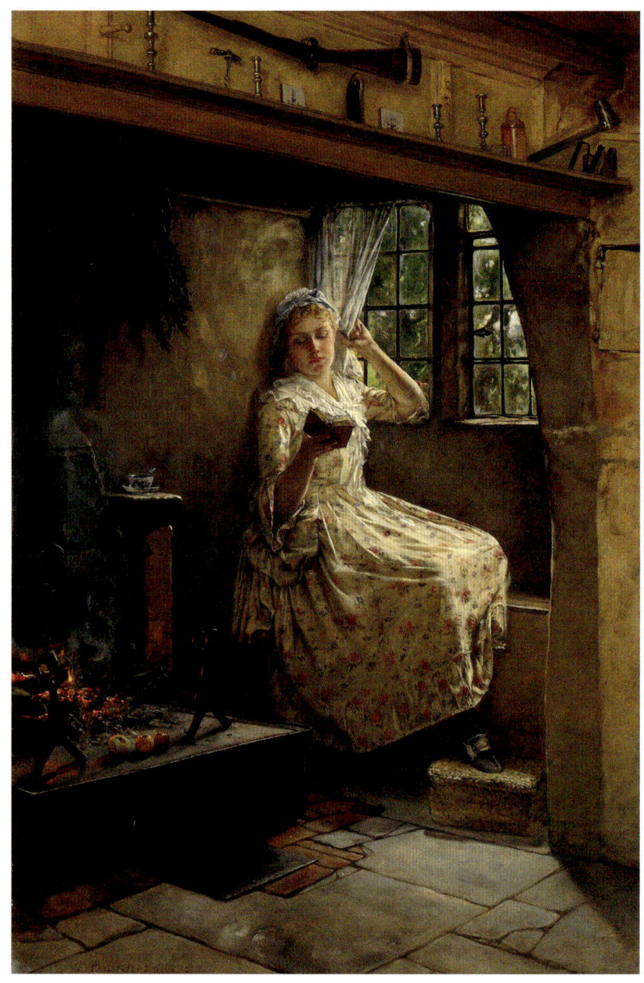

Francis Davis Millet, *A Cosey Corner*, 1884. The Metropolitan Museum of Art, Gift of George I. Seney, 1887 (87.8.3)

window. Beside the entry for this picture in D'Hervilly's working copy of the forthcoming Met paintings catalogue he penciled a note: *lost at sea April 15, 1912 on SS 'Titanic.'*

Accounts of Millet's death lauded his heroism, noting that *Titanic* survivors witnessed him help fellow passengers aboard lifeboats. Despite the horrific drama of his life's ending, which surely piqued the interest of tabloid writers, the headlines of their stories were restrained and composed in diminutive type. Their decorous tone suggested that an artist of Millet's magnitude, intimately linked with

America's top political office, was not fair game for sensationalist treatment. His body was recovered and buried in his native Massachusetts. Archibald Butt's corpse was never found. A public monument to both, designed by Thomas Hastings and Daniel Chester French, was installed in Washington, D.C., in 1913. The Met saluted Frank Millet on the cover of its June 1912 *Bulletin*, reproducing an image of a bronze relief portrait of the artist made by his friend Augustus Saint-Gaudens.

D'Hervilly took keen interest in workaday New York artists, including many who honed their talent by rigorously duplicating Old Masters in The Met galleries. Through faithful copying, he opined in the Museum *Bulletin*, "the secrets of the masters are learned. . . . Every great painter has copied and been copied. There is no good reason why the galleries of the Museum should not be filled with copyists." In 1906 he surveyed European art institutions' policies regarding copyists and discovered they were warmly welcomed at the Louvre, the National Gallery in London, and the Hermitage. He advocated for their more courteous treatment by The Met, removing an arbitrary size limit of their canvases, expanding their hours of access, and upgrading a locker room where they stored supplies and works in progress. D'Hervilly closely monitored this space and posted hand-lettered signs with specific rules he insisted the copyists follow, as though in return for the privileges he'd won for them.

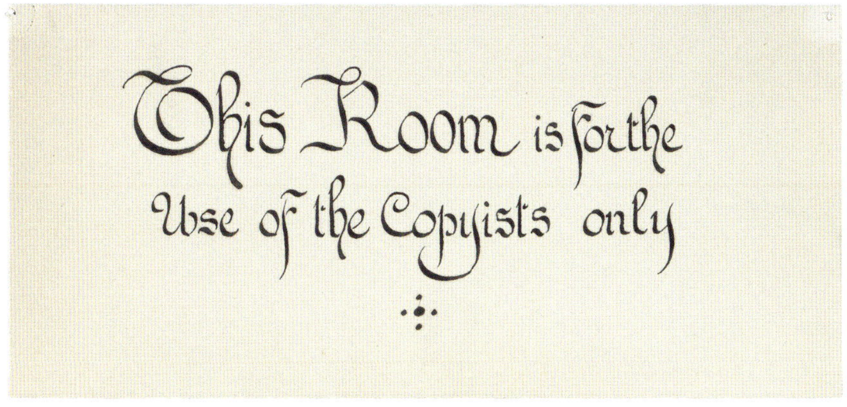

This Room is for the use of the Copyists only

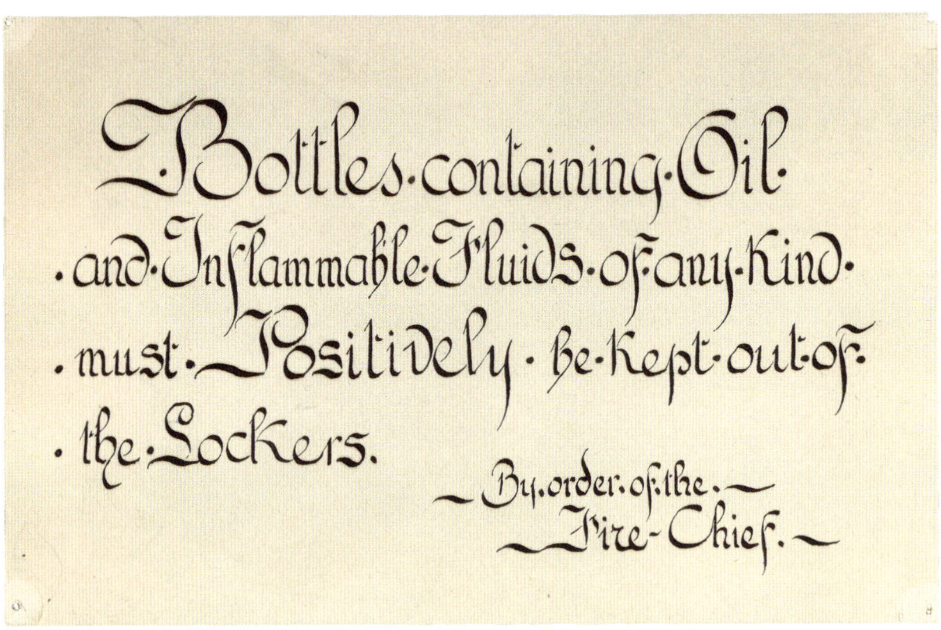

Bottles containing Oil and Inflammable Fluids of any Kind
must Positively Be Kept out of the Lockers. By order of the
Fire-Chief.

Rags and Paper must not be put in lockers but must be put in
the Can which is in this room for that purpose

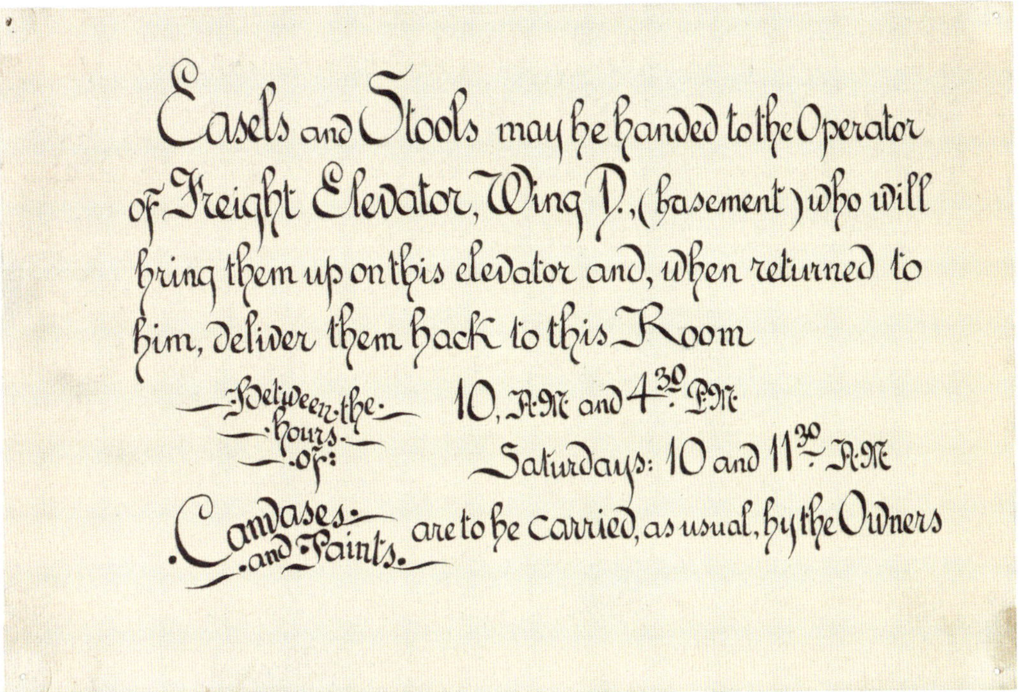

Easels and Stools may be handed to the Operator of Freight
Elevator, Wing D., (basement) who will bring them up on this
elevator and, when returned to him, deliver them back to this
Room Between the hours of: 10 A.M. and 4:30 P.M. Saturdays:
10 and 11:30 A.M. Canvases and Paints are to be carried, as
usual, by the Owners

He recorded in a notebook summaries and assessments of their
projects.

"Sculptor Rondoni made a copy in plasterline of Houdon's bust
of Franklin, from the cast of which he has made a copy in
marble. This is one of the best copies made in any department;
a very beautiful piece of work doing full credit to the sculptor
who was eagerly watched by hundreds as he worked at his
plasterline head."

Romolo Rondoni is listed in New York City directories of his
time as a sculptor but left behind virtually no other trace. Few of

the copyists D'Hervilly named in his reports of their visits can be
identified today with certainty. His gallery notes, like the obituary
scrapbooks, form a kind of index of an underground artistic frater-
nity of which D'Hervilly considered himself a member. In the same
directory that names Rondoni, Arthur D'Hervilly appears with his
profession given as "artist," not curator.

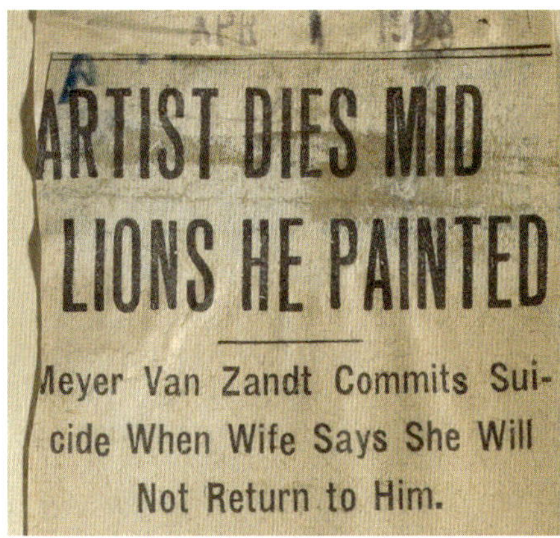

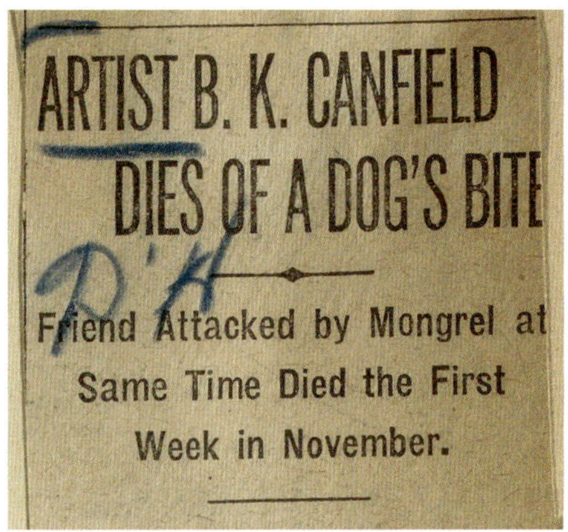

Another great New York institution, the Bronx Zoo, likewise made
special provisions for visiting artists. Soon after the zoo opened to the
public in 1899, its first director, William Temple Hornaday, oversaw
construction in the Lion House of an artists' studio where big cats,
orangutans, and other beasts were lured to pose before painters and
sculptors who specialized in the animal kingdom. Works by a few of
them, such as the esteemed sculptors Anna Hyatt Huntington and
Alexander Phimester Proctor, were installed elsewhere on the zoo
grounds and remain in situ to this day.

Two lesser-known artists who painted big cats at the zoo appear
in The Met clippings scrapbooks. Meyer Van Zandt, brooding over the
end of his marriage, took his own life in 1908 by gas inhalation, in
an apartment crammed with portraits of Bronx Zoo lions. William
Henry Drake, who illustrated a popular edition of *The Jungle Book* by
Rudyard Kipling, also focused on felines and committed suicide in
1926 by the same method as Van Zandt. Tragic animal encounters are
a recurring motif in the scrapbooks. Louise Frederici was killed in
Los Angeles in 1911 while trying to rescue her cat from a house fire.

ARTIST DIES FOR HER CAT IN FIRE

Miss Louise B. Frederici, of New York, Rushes Back in Flames at Los Angeles.

[SPECIAL DESPATCH TO THE HERALD.]

Los Angeles, Cal., Monday.—Returning to a burning structure to try to rescue an Angora cat and three kittens, Miss Louise B. Frederici, thirty years old, an artist of New York, lost her life early to-day in a fire which destroyed three houses in Thorne avenue. The young woman was caught beneath a falling roof and incinerated. Another pet cat was responsible for saving eleven lives.

Mrs. Nellie S. Drane, of No. 233 Thorne avenue, had arisen just before five o'clock and lighted the heater in the kitchen. She had returned to bed and fallen asleep. She was awakened some time later by the actions of a pet cat, which had discovered the flames. The cat ran to her room and started to claw the clothing from her bed. This awakened Mrs. Drane, who, smelling smoke, rushed into the kitchen to find the rear of her home ablaze. She gave the alarm and the other eleven occupants of the house, including Miss Frederici, barely escaped from the burning structure in their night clothes.

Miss Frederici after gaining the street remembered that her pet cat, which was nursing three kittens in a basket in her bedchamber, had been overlooked. Ignoring the protests of her friends, she dashed back through the smoke and flames. She had no sooner disappeared into the doomed structure than spectators were horrified to see the roof give way and crash to the first floor.

PAUL DE LONGPRE DEAD.

Famous Painter of Flowers Passes Away at His Home in California.

Los Angeles, June 29.—Paul de Longpre, the painter of flowers, died in his home in Hollywood late this evening after a long illness. Nearly a year ago he underwent an operation for mastoiditis. After he recovered he was attacked by rheumatism.

Paul De Longpré's "Yard of Roses" and yards of various other flowers are known throughout the country because so many of his paintings and water color drawings have been reproduced and sold for framing by lithograph houses. He began to paint pictures of flowers on fans in 1867 in Paris, or twelve years after his birth at Lyons, France, in 1855.

He attended the Paris public schools until 12 years old, but gave up school work temporarily after he had met with some slight success with his paintings on fans. In 1874 he was married to Josephine Estievenard in Paris. Two years later his first oil paintings were accepted by the Paris Salon.

The savings which he had got together during a busy life were wiped out when his Paris bank failed. Financially ruined, he decided to try America and came here in 1890. Six years later he gave his first exhibition in America, when he showed a number of paintings, all of flowers, at the American Art Galleries in Twenty-third street. He has exhibited in American cities annually since then.

De Longpre moved to Los Angeles in 1899. There he found that he had so far recovered from his financial losses as to be able to build a residence. Hollywood which ever since has been a showplace for tourists. Three acres planted with brilliant hued flowers surround the house.

REV. B. H. NEIBED.

ARTIST'S SUDDEN DEATH

CHALKLEY WILSON FOUND A CORPSE BY HIS WIFE.

Shortly after 5 o'clock last evening Chalkley Wilson, a well-known portrait painter and pastel artist was found dead in an outbuilding at his residence, 302 North Front street. Mr. Wilson was 55 years of age. He was apparently in the best of health yesterday and his sudden death was

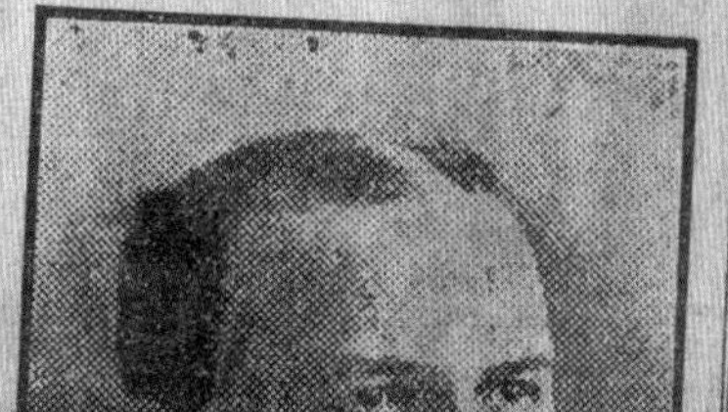

9

ARTIST ENDS LIFE IN HOTEL

Emil H. F. Speinkrauf Fires Bullet Into His Temple— No Reason Known.

Emil H. F. Speinkrauf, an artist, forty years old, committed suicide by shooting himself in the right temple. He lived in a small hotel, at 2789 Fulton street. It is thought by the guests of the hotel that Speinkrauf killed himself Tuesday night. He was found yesterday afternoon by Mrs. Anna Mein, the propereitoress. She said that she knew of no reason why the artist took his life, and that she could not say when the act was committed, as no shot was heard in the hotel. However, several of the guests claimed that on Tuesday about midnight they thought they heard a suppressed sound, resembling the muffled report of a pistol. This they attributed to an exploding battle, and thought no more of the matter.

The following day when Mrs. Mein attempted to arouse Speinkrauf there was no response. She entered his room by means of a passkey and found him dressed, lying upon the bed. The weapon was still clutched in his hand. Speinkrauf was an artist, and also a drawing instructor, a designer, and gave lessons in painting. The room in which he died was decorated with oil and water colors, and several portrait paintings of his friends and family. He had lived at the hotel for a year and a half.

Mr. Speinkrauf was from Berlin and was a man of good education. He studied art for years in the Latin quarter of Paris, where he later had a studio. He came to this country about ten years ago.

Mrs. Buehler's relatives from Racine visited her at the Meyers Hotel last night trying to encourage her in the belief that the girl would eventually return, but they were unsuccessful. Mrs. Buehler now says she is certain that Violet is dead.

MRS. ULLRICH, ARTIST, IS DEAD

Painting, 'Knitting for Grandmother,' Is Her Best Known Work.

Mrs. Hattie Edsall Thorp Ullrich, an artist whose miniatures and canvases have several times been accorded high honors at the Chicago Art Institute, died at her home, 932 Judson avenue, Evanston, yesterday afternoon. She was 40 years old.

Mrs. Ullrich was a painter both of miniatures and large canvases. Her picture, "Knitting for Grandmother," is the best known of her larger pictures. It was exhibited at the Art Institute several years ago and was considered to be the best picture of its kind exhibited there.

Mrs. Ullrich was a pupil of the late Martha Baker, who died a few days ago. Mrs. Baker said that Mrs. Ullrich was one of the most brilliant of her pupils. Her husband, Albert Ullrich, also well known in local art circles, and two daughters, Dorothy and Beatrice, survive her.

Funeral services will be held from St. Luke's Episcopal Church at Evanston, Tuesday afternoon, at 2:30 o'clock. The body will be cremated at Graceland Cemetery.

Miss E. A. Rockwell.

Miss E. A. Rockwell, the well known artist formerly of this city, died at the home of her nephew, Mr. Louis R. Cole, at Los Angeles, Cal., December 21. For some years she was associated with Mr. A. Francois in the portrait business in Albany. She is survived by her brother, J. R. Rockwell, of Albany.

NEW YORK TIMES

Sunday, Oct. 12, 1913

FIND ARTIST DEAD
A SUICIDE BY GAS

Bacon in Brief Will Leaves Pictures and Possessions to His Wife.

HAD WORKED TO THE LAST

Unfinished Portrait on an Easel in His Studio—Daughter Says He Was Victim of Despondency.

Charles R. Bacon, an artist about 55 years old, was found dead in his studio at 152 West Fifty-fifth Street, known as the Holbien Studios, late yesterday afternoon. Gas was escaping from two light jets and a small stove. All of the windows and doors in the studio were closed. The man was lying partly dressed on a small couch in one corner, and probably had been dead

BOSTON (MASS.) TRANSCRIPT

Thursday, Oct. 9, 1913.

his wife and two sons.

FREDERICK T. STUART, ARTIST

Following Service in the Civil War, He Became Well Known as a Steel Engraver and Painter of Watercolors

Frederick T. Stuart, a veteran Boston artist whose home was in Newton Centre, and well known in his profession, died last night at a hospital in Brookline. Mr. Stuart, who was seventy-six years of age, had been in ill health for several years, yet he was at times around and about, when temporarily better. He served in the Civil War and was a topographical draughtsman, and his reminiscences of stirring scenes which he witnessed, especialy during the battle of Gettysburg, were of thrilling interest

After the war he occupied himself with steel engraving and became especially well-known in portrait work, and he also did etching on copper plate. One of the finest examples of Mr. Stuart's portrait engraving was a picture of Lincoln, which artists have pronounced exceptionally good. He also was a painter in water colors, and his works have been exhibited in various cities. Mr. Stuart was formerly a member of the Boston Art Club and of the Boston Society of Water Color Painters. He was a widower and is survived by a daughter, Mrs. E. A. Cutler, and a son, Morton Stuart, both of Newton Centre.

The Weekly Folk Press, Aberdeen, Scotland, Oct. 4, 1913

J. CAMPBELL NOBLE, R.S.A.

Mr James Campbell Noble, R.S.A., died suddenly last week. For some time past Mr Campbell Noble had been in poor health, and the unexpected death of his son last year was a heavy blow which fell with the more severity upon his impaired constitution, though in the end his death, after three days' illness at Ledaig, Argyllshire, where he had been sojourning and sketching, came with surprising suddenness from heart failure.

Mr Campbell Noble was born in Edinburgh sixty-seven years ago. At the age of fifteen he entered the employment of J. O. Brown, lithographic draughtsman, George Street, a nephew of David Bryce, R.S.A. As an apprentice he was engaged for about four years chiefly upon architectural drawings, and when Mr Brown gave up business, would at once have been introduced to a more particular study of colour work in London had it not been that his parents opposed this step on account of his youth. Continuing, therefore, to pursue his vocation in Edinburgh, he undertook several commissions for the trade, illustrating books on anatomy for several of the University Professors. His works were almost entirely landscapes and sea pieces. He was first known when, in 1870, he exhibited in the Royal Scottish Academy's Galleries as a figure painter. He was elected an Associate in 1879, in which year his principal exhibition picture was "The Duet."

He painted a good deal in the vicinity of Gogar, while a visit to Holland later was productive of a brilliant series of pictures of Dutch landscape and shipping subjects. For many years, indeed, Mr Campbell Noble had been recognized as one of the most skilled and poetic exponents of the quaint waterways of Holland and elsewhere. At a later period he devoted much time to the Highlands, and chose his subjects mostly in the valley of the Dulnain in Nairn, and amid the scenic beauties of the Trossachs. His pictures were always marked by a fine poetic conception, and were worked out in a superb quality of colour. At the previous Royal Scottish Academy exhibition his quarry subject formed another outstanding exhibit of the year.

JOURNAL, ITHACA 9-29-13

ailments. He was [illegible] years old. The funeral services will be held on Wednesday at 2 p. m. and the Rev. E. L. Myers will be the officiating clergyman. The interment will be in the Groton Rural Cemetery.

Edward Jerome Goodrich

Services for Edward Jerome Goodrich, 62 years old, who died Saturday at the home of his daughter, Mrs. I. M. France, at Syracuse, were held at her home last night. The body was brought to Ithaca today.

Mr. Goodrich, who had been in poor health for many years, came to Syracuse four years ago. He was an artist, sculptor and violinist. For years he was a scene painter for many of the famous actors of a past generation, and acted in the same capacity with the Barnum & Bailey show. In the early seventies he served as a scout with Colonel William F. Cody. The two had a long visit the last time Colonel Cody was in Syracuse.

BROOKLYN N. Y. CITIZEN (19)

Wednesday, Dec. 3, 1913

WANTED BODY FED TO DOGS.

Artist Kills Self by Gas in Studio—Leaves Strange Note.

Alexander Bock, an artist, committed suicide in the two-room studio at No. 519 East Fifteenth street after writing a note in which he asked that his body be fed to the homeless dogs and cats of the city.

It is believed to-day that Bock was made morbid by reading the works of Schopenhauer and Emma Goldman. A well-thumbed copy of "On the Fourth Root of the Principle of Sufficient Reason," written by the German philosopher, was found on a table.

Lying on top of the book was found the following note, evidently scrawled by Bock just before he turned on the gas: "I do not believe in any kind of religion or in any God. I am the most radical atheist that ever can be. I don't want any religious or charitable society to take any interest in my burial. The authorities of this city may feed my body to the homeless dogs and cats." He then directed that his furniture be turned over to Carl Gross, of No. 330 East Ninety-first street. Bock was grieved by the manner in which he felt Gross had treated him, "after receiving favors."

DR. PECK WELL AGAIN

Ike Morgan, illustrator and newspaper artist, is dead at his late home, 100 Columbia Heights, Brooklyn. He was born on June 28, 1871, in Grand Tower, Ill. He was educated in the public schools of St. Louis, and studied drawing and painting in the St. Louis School of Fine Arts. He did his first illustrative work for The St. Louis Republic. Mr. Morgan was later connected with The Chicago Record-Herald, and with several New York newspapers. He was the creator of "Kids of Many Colors," and had drawn illustrations for a number of children's books.

N. Y. MORNING WORLD (82)

Monday, Nov. 24, 1913

JOHN DE WOLF, LANDSCAPE ARCHITECT, IS DEAD.

Worked on the Parks of Greater New York—Was Descended from Rhode Island Pioneers.

BRISTOL, R. I., Nov. 23.—John De Wolf, sixty-four, first person to hold the position of landscape architect of the parks of Greater New York, died today at the home of his brother-in-law, Nathaniel Greene Herreshoff, the yacht builder. Mr. De Wolf was born here in 1850. He studied landscape gardening abroad and laid out the grounds of the Villa Maria on Lake Como, Italy. From 1871 to 1878 he was with the United States Coast and Geodetic Survey.

In 1892 Mr. De Wolf was appointed Superintendent of Brooklyn parks, under Mayor Boody, a Democrat. A subsequent Republican administration dropped him out. Robert A. Van Wyck, first Mayor of Greater New York, appointed him general landscape gardener of all the parks, and he served until early in 1902, when he was transferred to his old post of Superintendent of Brooklyn Parks. After a few months there he was dismissed by Commissioner Young. Several days later Mr. De Wolf was found unconscious from opium in the Imperial Hotel, New York. A doctor

The same year, Bert K. Canfield, a painter who often depicted animals, succumbed to rabies after being bitten by a dog. In an odd twist on the canine theme, Alexander Bock committed suicide in 1913 and left a note that denounced organized religion and demanded his corpse be fed to stray dogs. *The Washington Herald* suggested "Bock was made morbid by reading the books of Schopenhauer." The German philosopher advocated ethical treatment of animals and spent his last years mostly in the company of his beloved pet poodles.

D'Hervilly was gratified to observe that not only fine artists but also furniture and textile designers, theater and film producers, and others engaged in business-driven creative work routinely studied objects in the Museum galleries. In a 1915 Met *Bulletin* essay he rhapsodized over "the supreme importance of the decorative arts in connection with the nation's manufactures," noting that design professionals and students benefited from "intelligent observation" of Met pieces. By making its holdings easily accessible to people who made sofas, wallpaper, rugs, and other household products, "the Museum has lived up to its privilege of giving useful and definite help." His attention to this audience segment was consistent with a fresh trend at museums in general that aimed to forge connections to modern industry.

D'Hervilly tallied these task-oriented visitors and wrote anecdotes describing their endeavors. He once encountered a pair of puppeteers sketching a harpsichord that they planned to replicate in miniature for the stage. "The Museum even helps Marionettes," he quipped. On a more somber note, he recorded the work of a visiting designer who in 1914 drew "subjects for reproduction in automobile hearses." The same year, he assisted employees of Presbrey-Coykendall Company, a maker of funeral monuments and mausoleums, as they examined The Met's full-size plaster cast replica of the Cross of Muiredach, a 19-foot tall, elaborately carved stone high cross that has presided over a medieval Irish monastic ruin for more than a thousand years.

Another form of commercial art, magazine and book illustration, proliferated in D'Hervilly's lifetime; 1850 to 1925 is a period known as the Golden Age of Illustration, thanks to new engraving and printing techniques. When D'Hervilly received a clipping headlined ARTIST WHO IS ILL KILLS HIMSELF TO FREE HIS FIANCEE, reporting the tragic death of Léon Guipon, he may have known his work from such popular publications as *The Century Magazine*, *Collier's*, and the like, which sometimes featured Guipon's work on their covers.

Born in Paris around 1873, Guipon immigrated to America as a child, and by the turn of the century he supported himself making pictures to accompany short stories in *Scribner's* and *Harper's* magazines and mass-market romance novels. In 1910 he was affianced to Agnes Foster, but then came a shocking diagnosis of heart disease that doctors warned might soon kill him. "Realizing that he was living in the shadow of death," his chronicler wrote, "and wishing to spare the grief of widowhood to the girl he had promised to marry," he chose to take his own life. To ensure financial security for his betrothed, Guipon mailed her a bank check for his life savings of nearly $7,300, then shot himself in his studio on Manhattan's west side. The public administrator of New York City, however, stopped payment on the check and claimed his residuary estate because Foster was not yet his wife and he left no survivors.

Guipon was also a writer and had published a short story in the May 1904 *Century* that augured his death in the studio by gunshot. "The Last of the Crocabiches" is set in the Paris atelier of two American expatriates. One night, as they boisterously toss about a life-size artist's mannequin, an alarmed

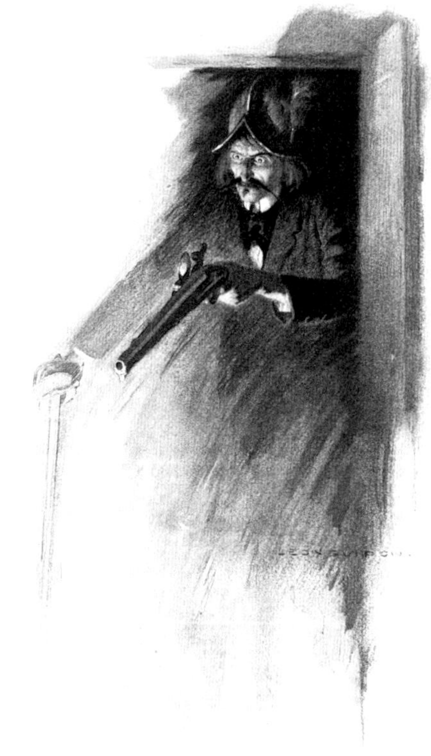

Léon Guipon, "The Last of the Croca-biches," *Century Illustrated Monthly Magazine*, May 1904

WEDNESDAY, JUNE 15, 1910

ARTIST WHO IS ILL KILLS HIMSELF TO FREE HIS FIANCEE

Knew His Heart Was Failing and Wanted to Save Her from Widowhood.

SENT $7,292 CHECK; WILL IN HER FAVOR

Leon Guipon, Whose Work Appeared in Leading Magazines, Found in Studio Lifeless from Bullet.

NOTIFIED HIS BEST FRIEND

Wrote a Letter Telling of His Intention—
He Used a Mirror to Make His
Aim Certain.

Realizing that he was living in the shadow of death and wishing to spare the grief of widowhood to the girl he had promised to marry, Leon Guipon, who had won distinction as an artist, mailed to her a check for $7,292. Then he made a will disposing of his effects and, asking that his body be cremated and the ashes cast to the four winds, he sat at his easel and marked in faint outline the profile of a woman's face. Then he fired a bullet through his head and died yesterday in his studio, No. 360 West Twenty-second street.

He had written two letters, one to Miss Agnes Foster, daughter of A. J. Foster, president of the People's National Bank at Roxbury, Mass., and the other to H. C.

of pictures to magazines, including the Century, Harper's and Scribner's. There also was a key to a safe deposit box in a trust company's vaults … done. It …

… himself, I will kill myself."

… financial affairs …

Breull was born in Germany and was a graduate of the Royal Academy of Munich. He leaves a wife and three children.

…AY, JUNE 15, 1910.

FRIEND OF INDIANS DIES IN STAMFORD

Consumptive Artist, Known to the Navajos as the Fearless Rider, Came from the East.

WON TRIBE BY SNAKE DANCE

Contemporary of Parrish and Glackens Lived Among the Indians and Followed Their Customs.

Just at sunset on Monday afternoon Frank P. Sauerwen, friend and painter of Indians, died in Stamford, Conn., in the

SATURDAY, AUGUST 20, 1910.

MR. FRANK FOWLER, ARTIST, IS DEAD

Well Known Portrait Painter and Writer Had Been Honored by Many Societies.

Frank Fowler, the well known portrait painter and writer on art topics, died early on Thursday at the home of his

MONDAY, AUGUST 1, 1910.

…body will be taken to the Cypress Hill Cemetery, Brooklyn, for interment, which will be to-morrow. Mr. Bishop was fifty years old.

C. M. BANKS, ARTIST AND DESIGNER, DIES

Following an illness of about seven months, Charles M. Banks, an artist and designer, died at his home, 699 Hunterdon street, early yesterday morning. Pulmonary trouble, complicated with cirrhosis of the liver, was the cause. He was in his forty-third year.

It was in December of last year that failing health forced Mr. Banks temporarily to lay aside his brush and, while from time to time he resumed his work, the encroachment of the malady finally forced him to abandon active employment. Three weeks ago his condition took a change for the worse and complications set in. For the last three days he had been in a state of coma and although the attending physician was hopeful of his recovery, he died without regaining consciousness.

Born in New Philadelphia, O., September 11, 1867, Mr. Banks, when but six months old was taken by his parents to New Brunswick, where his father, Rev. Charles Banks, began a pastorate extending over thirty-six years at the German Reformed Church. He received his education in the public schools of that place and when a lad of but fifteen began the study of designing. He made a specialty of wallpaper designing and for several years was employed in the Moss Engraving Company. During that period he served a term as chief of the fire department. Four years ago to-day he joined the art staff of the News and held a position in that department up to the time of his death.

Mr. Banks, twelve years ago, married Mrs. Mary H. Welch, of New Brunswick. She and a daughter, Katherine, ten years old, survive him. Funeral services will be held at his late home Wednesday afternoon at 1 o'clock. Interment will follow in Elmwood Cemetery, New Brunswick.

SATURDAY, JULY 23, 191…

…covered is a mystery.

WOMAN ARTIST DIES ENVELOPED IN FLAMES

Mrs. Gustav Faber Victim of Gasoline Stove

SAN BERNARDINO, July 22.—Mrs. Gustav Faber, a well known artist, was burned to death this afternoon as a result of trying to fill a gasoline stove while it was lighted. She was instantly enveloped in flames, and, running from the house, was a human torch and beyond relief when aid arrived. She died a few hours later. The home was destroyed. Mrs. Faber was an artist of rare talent, her pictures having been awarded prizes at many art exhibits.

neighbor, believing they are accosting a female model, pushes open their door. The would-be hero brandishes a flintlock pistol, which luckily misfires. Guipon illustrated this yarn with an image of the man leveling his enormous weapon. The engraver who rendered the picture for publication, H. C. Merrill, was a fellow commercial artist and the friend fated to discover Guipon's lifeless body after his lovelorn suicide.

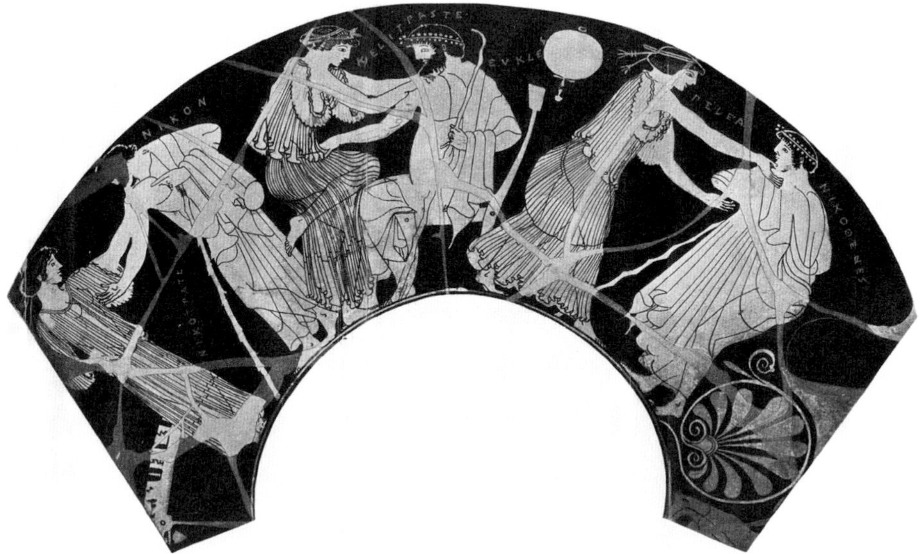

Gisela M. A. Richter, "Two Vases Signed by Hieron in The Metropolitan Museum of Art." *American Journal of Archaeology*, vol. 21, no. 1, 1917

D'Hervilly remained affiliated with the Paintings Department for the rest of his career after 1902, but he was always congenial with colleagues elsewhere in the Museum. Gisela Richter was a Greek antiquities specialist and among the first women appointed curator at The Met. In the 1910s she published scholarly articles about ancient vases for which D'Hervilly made photographic collages to accompany her text. These creative compositions enabled viewers to see, in a single glance, complete figural scenes that encircle the objects. To create his conic projections, D'Hervilly probably cut apart and glued together prints made by the Museum photo lab.

Technical aspects of photography and motion pictures fascinated him, and he made detailed notes about practitioners of these arts whenever they turned up in Met galleries. "Someday perhaps," he presciently wrote in 1915, "motion picture views of events in the Museum such as classes with their instructors moving about may be taken for record-of-events use and stored away to be thrown upon the screen at will."

It was still a question of serious debate at the time whether photography was an art at all. Alfred Stieglitz, a pioneer creator and collector of the medium, had argued the case with Met director Cesnola as early as 1902. He urged the General to acquire for the Museum an outstanding set of photographic prints and later recalled Cesnola's shocked reply: "Why, Mr. Stieglitz, you won't insist that a photograph can possibly be a work of art . . . you are a fanatic!" A set of masterful photos gathered by Stieglitz was finally shepherded into The Met in 1928 by its broad-minded print curator William Ivins. By then, the argument had already been settled outside museum walls. Even tabloids, it seems, had begun to identify photographers as artists, although perhaps more for their attitude about their work than for their images.

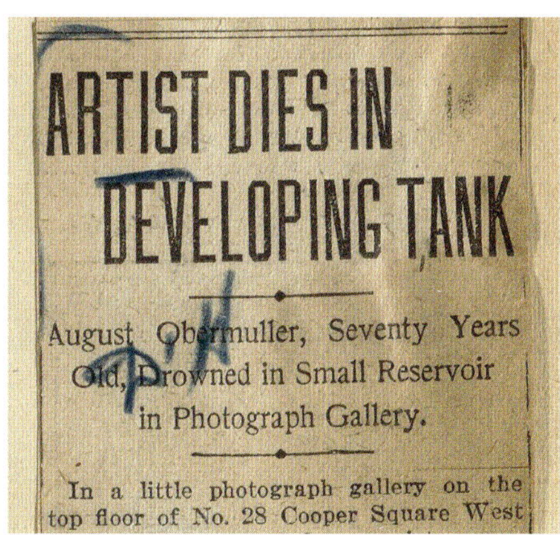

ARTIST DIES IN DEVELOPING TANK

In November 1910, when the seventy-year-old photographer August Obermüller drowned in a vat of photo chemicals, *The New York Herald* made the case for his artistic identity by invoking his stereotypical "habit of caring little for money and much for the merit of his pictures." Obermüller specialized in cabinet card portraits of circus and sideshow performers like the Rubber-skin Man and Krao Farini, a Laotian woman born with hypertrichosis, which causes abnormally excessive hair growth. His photographs place his studio in the late 1890s at 388 Bowery, and in the early 1900s at 28 Cooper Square, which converges with the Bowery, then a rough-and-tumble strip lined with dime museums and playhouses where these entertainers performed. Obermüller's pictures anticipated those Diane Arbus made decades later a few miles north around Times Square.

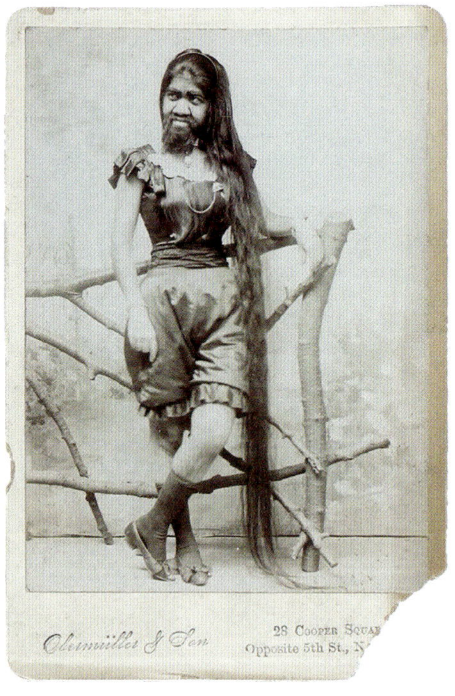

Obermüller & Son, *Krao Farini*, ca. 1890

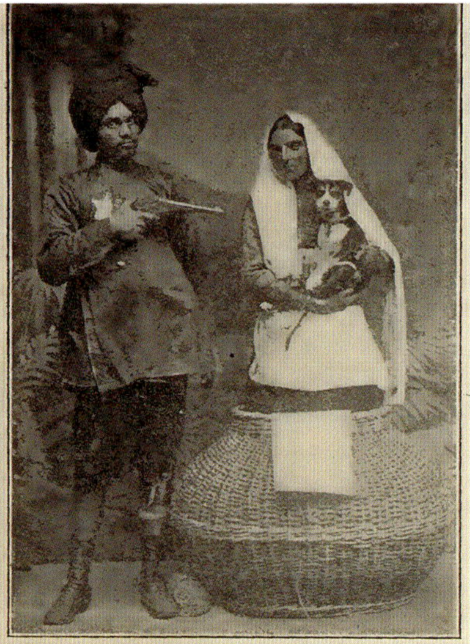

A Hindoo and wife, who have escaped from a Regular Hindoo Troupe and are "fooling 'em" alone on their own responsibility.
Photograph by Obermuller & Son, New York.

Obermüller & Son, *A Hindoo and wife*, ca. 1906, in Harry Houdini, "Unknown Facts Concerning Robert Houdin," *Conjurer's Monthly Magazine*, vol. 1, no.3, November 1906, Harry Houdini Collection, Library of Congress

.   .   .

On a mission to study early American painters John Singleton
Copley and Gilbert Stuart, the artist and critic James Britton visited
The Met in July 1918. Unable to find a portrait of George Washington
that he wanted to see, Britton thought to ask his acquaintance
D'Hervilly for help. Britton summarized their conversation in
his diary.

> Stop in to see D'Hervilly and have a long talk with him. He is
> much interested in my book and agrees Copley is much finer
> than Stuart among the Americans. Seems surprised when I
> say that The Met turned down a fine Copley that they could
> have bought, that they want them and are very anxious to
> get good ones as Boston is so much ahead of them in that
> matter. Says any that are for sale should be offered. They want
> them badly.

Twelve years after publishing his survey of American paintings,
D'Hervilly remained engaged with the genre. But his nonplussed
reaction to news that the Museum had passed up a proffered Copley
suggests his boss Bryson Burroughs kept him out of the loop on
important acquisition decisions, just as connoisseur Roger Fry had
done. Despite D'Hervilly's years of curatorial experience and aware-
ness of embarrassing gaps in The Met's holdings, his peers narrowly
circumscribed his duties and sidelined him from any serious role
in collection development. In the twilight of his career he made the
best of the hand he was dealt and focused on helping people from all
walks of life to draw inspiration from great artworks for their own
creative purposes.

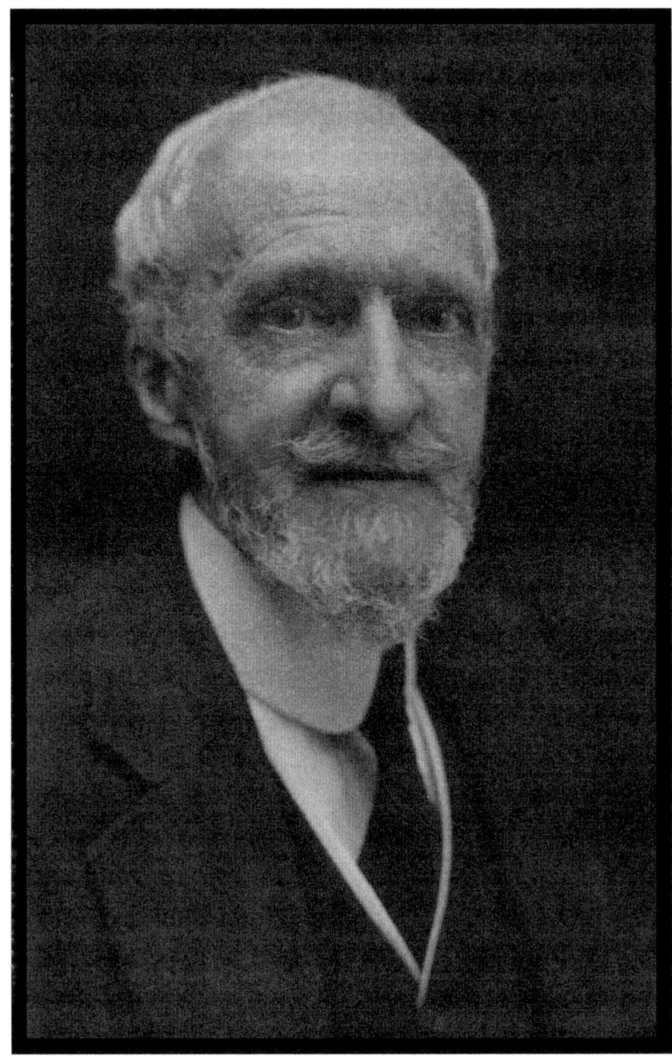

R. Liebig, *A. B. de St. M. D'Hervilly*, ca. 1915. The Metropolitan
Museum of Art Archives

6. Slave of Duty

Arthur D'Hervilly died on April 7, 1919. A few newspapers printed
brief obituaries, misspelling his name in a variety of ways, though
all agreed his heart gave out as he prepared to commute to The Met.
One headline called him a SLAVE OF DUTY AT ART MUSEUM
who never took vacation and always ate lunch at his desk. *The New
York Times* offered mild praise, declaring him "a man with a charm-
ing feeling for art, and a quaint sense of humor."

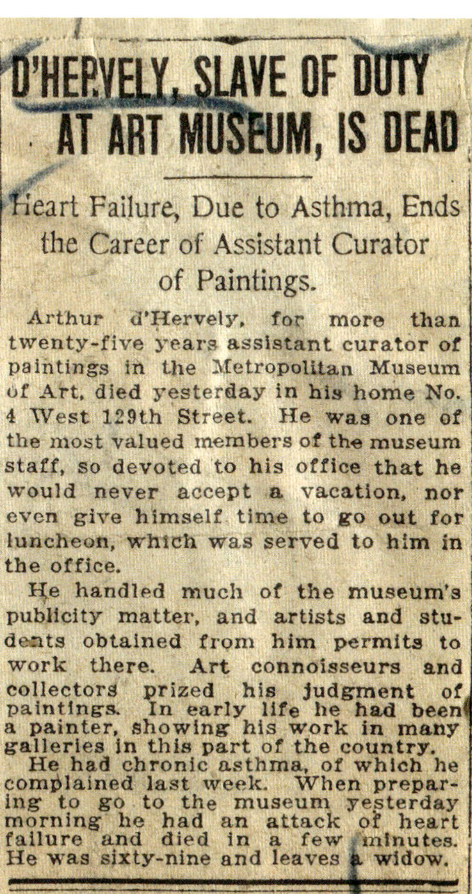

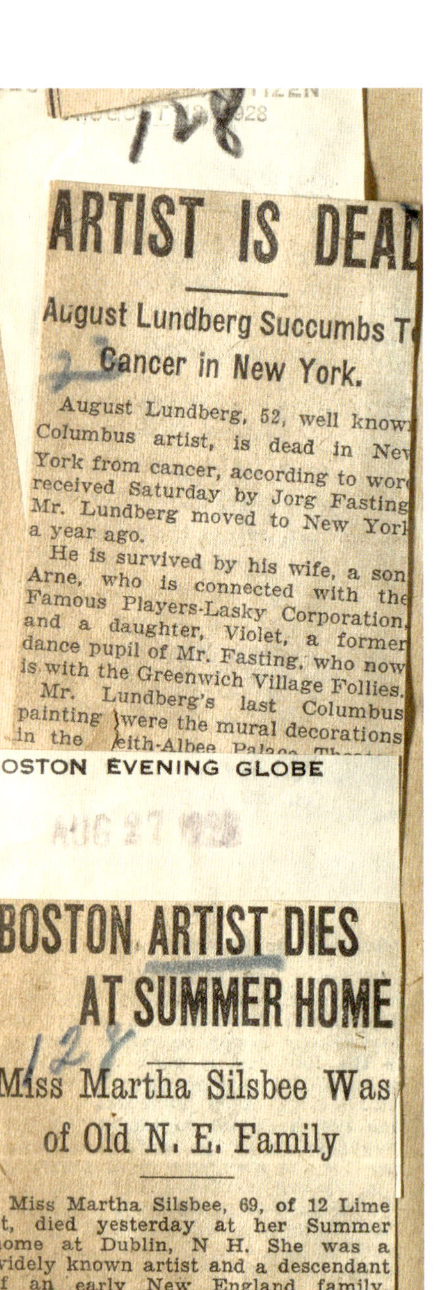

ARTIST IS DEAD

August Lundberg Succumbs To Cancer in New York.

August Lundberg, 52, well known Columbus artist, is dead in New York from cancer, according to word received Saturday by Jorg Fasting. Mr. Lundberg moved to New York a year ago.

He is survived by his wife, a son Arne, who is connected with the Famous Players-Lasky Corporation, and a daughter, Violet, a former dance pupil of Mr. Fasting, who now is with the Greenwich Village Follies.

Mr. Lundberg's last Columbus painting were the mural decorations in the Keith-Albee Palace Thea...

BOSTON ARTIST DIES AT SUMMER HOME

Miss Martha Silsbee Was of Old N. E. Family

Miss Martha Silsbee, 69, of 12 Lime st, died yesterday at her Summer home at Dublin, N. H. She was a widely known artist and a descendant of an early New England family, which passes with her death.

Miss Silsbee was a descendant of Capt Nathaniel Silsbee of Salem, one of the famous sea captains of that port, who later became United States Senator from Massachusetts.

Miss Silsbee was a member of Mayflower Club, the Water Co's and the Chilton Club, and was time prominent in the Echer association of Boston...

ARTIST IS DEAD

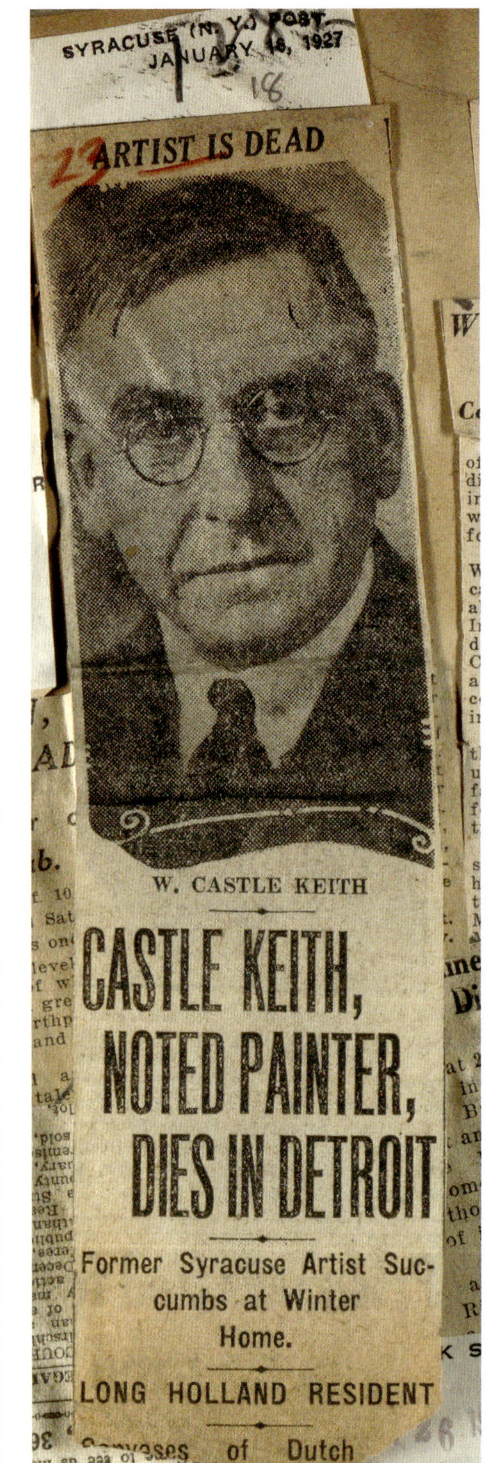

W. CASTLE KEITH

CASTLE KEITH, NOTED PAINTER, DIES IN DETROIT

Former Syracuse Artist Succumbs at Winter Home.

LONG HOLLAND RESIDENT

Canvases of Dutch

SPEAKMAN, ARTIST AND AUTHOR, TAKES LIFE AT BELLEVUE

Tells Taxi Driver of Date With "Man on White Horse" at Hospital

HAD BEEN IN ILL-HEALTH, IS WIFE'S EXPLANATION

Wrote Books of Travel on China, Ireland and the Mississippi River

Harold Speakman traveled in many foreign lands the better to write books about those he encountered and to illustrate his books with sketches of the things he saw. Yesterday he embarked on another journey and of this one there will be no record. If death is what he expected it to be, he is voyaging into the unknown astride a white horse behind a phantom rider.

"Quick," he told Frank McGlynn, a taxicab driver whom he hailed at the corner of 83d Street and Broadway at 5.05 o' ... morning, "take me to ... "Mr. Speakman," Mrs. Speakman said, "has been ill a long time. He was operated on several times for an internal trouble. At the end of his Trip through China, on which he wrote "Beyond Shanghai" in 1921, he was operated on in Shanghai. He has undergone operations several times since. His illness probably upset his mind.

"He arose early this morning and went out. There was nothing unusual in that—he often walked along Riverside Drive in the early morning—and he usually did not waken me."

In addition to the book on China, Speakman, who was thirty-nine, was the author of "Here's Ireland," published in 1925 and of "Mostly Mississippi," published in 1927. He had just returned from a trip through India, on which he was writing a book. He drew the illustrations for his own books. He and Mrs. Speakman drifted down the Mississippi in a houseboat gathering material for that book, and its illustrations were by both of them.

His Met colleagues dutifully gathered five of these clippings and pasted them into a scrapbook. Furthermore, for a decade after his passing they continued to honor D'Hervilly's documentary impulse by amassing hundreds more artists' death tales and adding them to the trove. But distracted, no doubt, by the amusements of the Roaring Twenties, their gluing technique became sloppier and they folded clippings more and more tightly to cram dozens onto each page, rendering them difficult to open and view without causing damage. Finally, in the autumn of 1929, they canceled D'Hervilly's standing order with the clippings bureau. It could have been a cost-saving decision motivated by the October stock market crash— as in the rest of the country, belt-tightening measures were taken everywhere in the Museum.

There had been a subtle shift by the end of the 1920s in the way some newspapers reported artists' deaths. Obituaries were generally less lurid than those of the 1900s and 1910s and focused on the lives and accomplishments of their subjects rather than particularities of their mode of death. They began to resemble obituaries typical of our own time, simply presenting the name, occurrence, location, and matters of fairly indisputable fact.

Still, the sad occurrence of suicide continued to tempt some editors to revert to yellow journalism and share untoward details. Among clippings haphazardly attached to the tattered final page of the scrapbooks is one concerning Edmond Thomas Quinn, a Philadelphia-born sculptor who had been a pupil of Thomas Eakins. Quinn was critically acclaimed and several of his bronze portraits found permanent homes in outdoor spaces around New York, including a life-size monument to actor Edwin Booth in Gramercy Park and a bust of composer Victor Herbert in Central Park. Quinn's body was found floating in New York Harbor on September 12, 1929, and he was presumed a suicide. *The New York Times* described the appearance of his corpse in the city morgue as "clean shaven and of fair complexion" and noted he had failed to kill himself a few months earlier by swallowing "oxalic acid salts dissolved in wood alcohol."

. . .

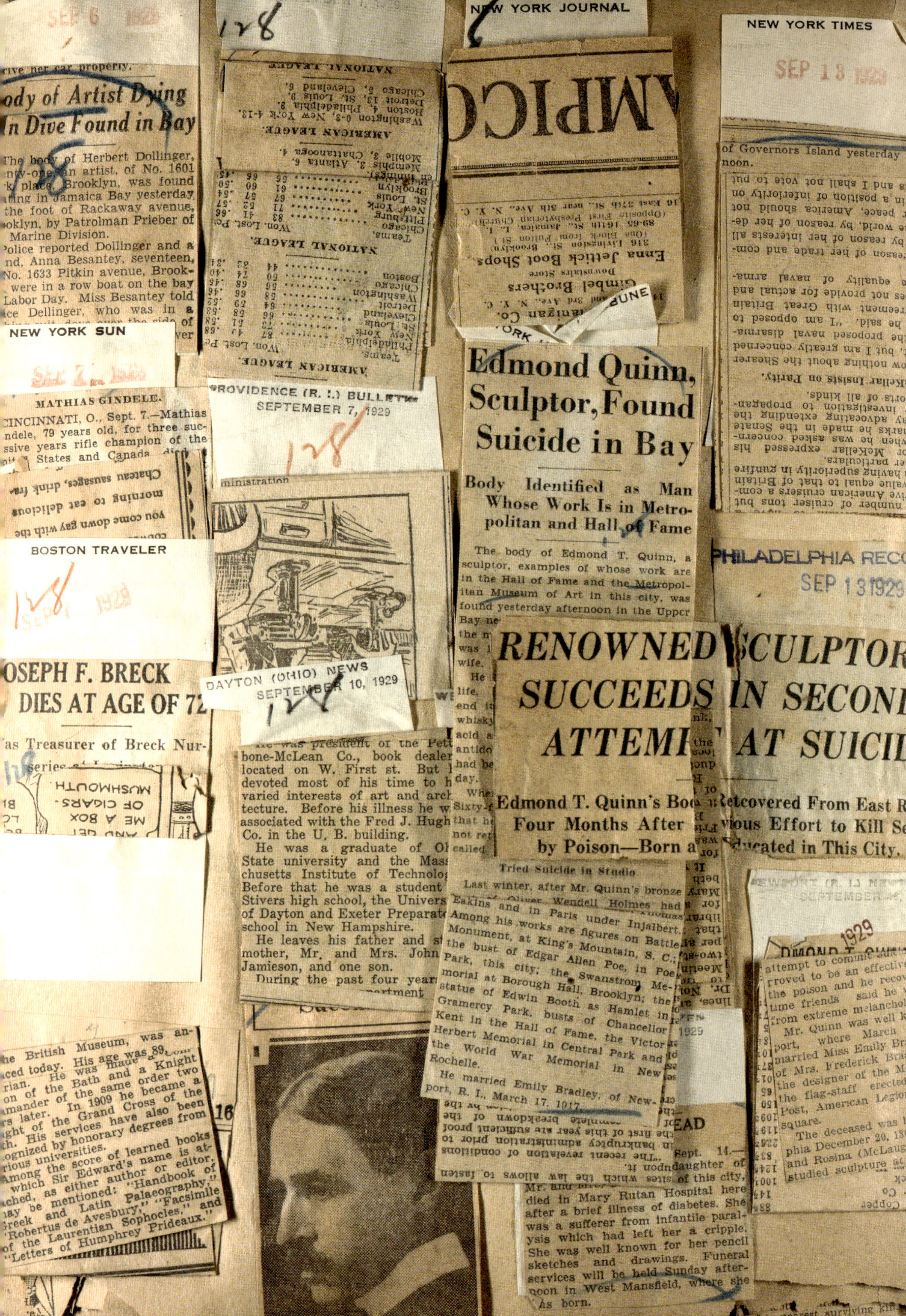

128

...rive her car property.

ody of Artist Dying
In Dive Found in Bay

The body of Herbert Dollinger, [twe]nty-one, an artist, of No. 1601 [Par]k place, Brooklyn, was found [float]ing in Jamaica Bay yesterday. [at] the foot of Rackaway avenue, [Bro]oklyn, by Patrolman Prieber of [the] Marine Division.

Police reported Dollinger and a [frie]nd, Anna Besantey, seventeen, [of] No. 1633 Pitkin avenue, Brook[lyn] were in a row boat on the bay [on] Labor Day. Miss Besantey told [poli]ce Dellinger, who was in a [bath]ing suit, dove over the side of...

MATHIAS GINDELE.

CINCINNATI, O., Sept. 7.—Mathias [Gi]ndele, 79 years old, for three suc[ce]ssive years rifle champion of the [United] States and Canada, died...

128 SEPT 1929

OSEPH F. BRECK
DIES AT AGE OF 72

[w]as Treasurer of Breck Nur[series of Lexington...]

AMPICO

Enna Jettick Boot Shops

Gimbel Brothers

of Governors Island yesterday a noon.

...as and I shall not vote to put [Americ]a in a position of inferiority on [f]or peace, America should not [in] the world, by reason of her de[fense] by reason of her interests all [by] reason of her trade and com[merce] to equality of naval arma[ment.]

"...[do]es not provide for actual and [a]greement with Great Britain," he said. "I am opposed to [the] proposed naval disarma[ment,] but I am greatly concerned [k]now nothing about the Shearer [it,]

McKellar Insists on Parity.

[ef]forts of all kinds.

[an] investigation to propagan[da,] lay advocating extending the [re]marks he made in the Senate when he was asked concern[ing] [Sena]tor McKellar expressed his [fo]r particulars.

...h having superiority in gunfire value equal to that of Britain [g]ive American cruisers a com[bat] number of cruiser tons but

Edmond Quinn, Sculptor, Found Suicide in Bay

Body Identified as Man Whose Work Is in Metropolitan and Hall of Fame

The body of Edmond T. Quinn, a sculptor, examples of whose work are in the Hall of Fame and the Metropolitan Museum of Art in this city, was found yesterday afternoon in the Upper Bay ne[ar]...

RENOWNED SCULPTOR SUCCEEDS IN SECOND ATTEMPT AT SUICIDE

Edmond T. Quinn's Bod[y Re]covered From East R[iver] Four Months After [Pre]vious Effort to Kill Se[lf] by Poison—Born a[nd Ed]ucated in This City.

Tried Suicide in Studio

Last winter, after Mr. Quinn's bronze [statue of] Oliver Wendell Holmes had [been made,]...

Among his works are figures on Battle [Abbey] Monument, at King's Mountain, S. C.; the bust of Edgar Allen Poe, in Poe [Park,] Park, this city; the Swanstrom Memorial at Borough Hall, Brooklyn; the statue of Edwin Booth as Hamlet in Gramercy Park, busts of Chancellor Kent in the Hall of Fame, the Victor Herbert Memorial in Central Park and the World War Memorial in New Rochelle.

He married Emily Bradley, of New[port], R. I., March 17, 1917.

[H]e was president of the Petti[bone]-McLean Co., book dealer[s] located on W. First st. But [he] devoted most of his time to h[is] varied interests of art and arch[i]tecture. Before his illness he w[as] associated with the Fred J. Hugh[es] Co. in the U. B. building.

He was a graduate of O[hio] State university and the Massa[chusetts] Institute of Technolog[y.] Before that he was a student [at] Stivers high school, the Univers[ity] of Dayton and Exeter Preparat[ory] school in New Hampshire.

He leaves his father and st[ep]mother, Mr. and Mrs. John [H.] Jamieson, and one son.

During the past four year[s...] [de]partment

1929

DMOND T. QUINN

attempt to commit suic[ide] [p]roved to be an effective [dose of] the poison and he recov[ered.] time friends said he w[as suffering] from extreme melancholi[a.]

Mr. Quinn was well k[nown in New]port, where March [17, 1917, he] married Miss Emily Bra[dley, daughter] of Mrs. Frederick Brad[ley,] the designer of the Me[morial] the flag-staff erected [at] Post, American Legion square.

The deceased was b[orn in Philadel]phia December 20, 186[4, son of] and Rosina (McLaug[hlin) Quinn. He] studied sculpture at...

the British Museum, was an[nounced] today. His age was 89. [He was made libra]rian. He was made a Knight [Commander] of the Bath and a Knight [Command]er of the same order two [years] later. In 1909 he became a [Kni]ght of the Grand Cross of the [Bath.] His services have also been [rec]ognized by honorary degrees from [va]rious universities.

Among the score of learned books [with] which Sir Edward's name is at[ta]ched, as either author or editor, [may] be mentioned: "Handbook of [G]reek and Latin Palaeography," ["]Robertus de Avesbury," "Facsimile [of] the Laurentian Sophocles," and ["]Letters of Humphrey Prideaux," [and...]

Illness Fatal

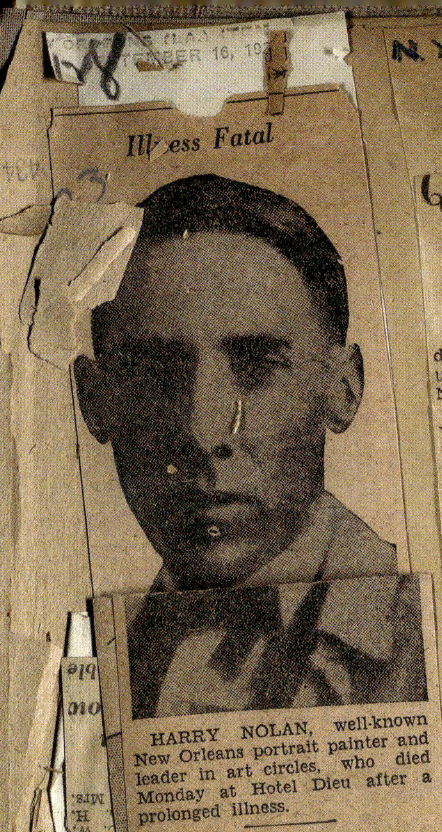

HARRY NOLAN, well-known New Orleans portrait painter and leader in art circles, who died Monday at Hotel Dieu after a prolonged illness.

Harry Nolan, Artist, Dies

Illness Fatal To Well-Known Portrait

Mystery Shot Kills F. R. Whiteside, Artist

PHILADELPHIA, Sept. 19 (AP) —Frank Reed Whiteside, sixty-three-year-old Philadelphia landscape artist, instructor and author, was shot to death under mysterious circumstances as he stood on the doorstep of his home tonight.

his life. Last May he took poison, but was revived.

Quinn achieved fame as a sculptor. Examples of his work are in the Metropolitan Museum of Art, the New York University Hall of Fame, and in numerous parks and museums throughout the country.

Was Active Worker.

He was actively at work, despite his physician's orders, up to the day of his death. He had just com-

Quinn, Noted Artist, a Suicide

When fame palled. He tried to die. His first attempt was a failure. That was four months ago. Now he has apparently succeeded.

A body found floating in New York Bay, off Governor's Island, is believed to be that of Edmond T. Quinn, noted American sculptor, of No. 207 East Sixty-first street.

With his work in the Metropolitan Museum, New York University's Hall of Fame, and museums in other American cities, the sixty-year-old sculptor wished to die.

MISTAKE SAVED HIM.

Four months ago, he mixed oxalic acid salts with whiskey, and drank the potion. A mistake saved his life.

He had mixed the poison with its most effective antidote.

Last Monday he went to the

QUINN, NOTED ARTIST, A SUICIDE

Continued from First Page.

bank and never returned. The search ended with the finding of the body.

At the Morgue the body is reported as having been identified by the attorney for his wife, Mrs. Emily Bradley Quinn. Melancholia, explained his friends, and a long period of despondency caused the vigorous sculptor to attempt

With his work in the Metropolitan Museum, New York University's Hall of Fame, and museums in other American cities, the sixty-year-old sculptor wished to die.

MISTAKE SAVED HIM.

Four months ago, he mixed oxalic acid salts with whiskey, and drank the potion. A mistake saved his life.

He had mixed the poison with its most effective antidote.

Last Monday he went to the bank and never returned. The search ended with the finding of the body.

The bust of Edgar Allen Poe in Poe Park, the Statue of Hamlet in Gramercy Park, the bust of Oliver Wendell Holmes at the Hall of Fame, are among his works.

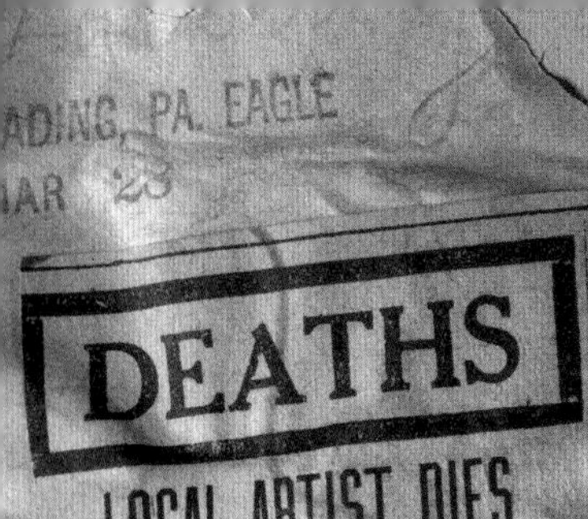

DEATHS

LOCAL ARTIST DIES

EUGENE S. REESER'S WORK KNOWN IN THIS AND OTHER STATES AND IN FOREIGN COUNTRIES.

Eugene S. Reeser, art goods dealer and one of Reading's best-known artists, passed away at 3 o'clock this...

Veteran Was Well Correspondent and as Painter for Many Years.

... The death of ... in the Civil war, and was noted as a painter. He commanded the troops that guarded the White House during President Lincoln's second inauguration.

At the time of the Lincoln centennial Mr. Hartshorn sent The Union an interesting account of his life.

Arthur Walton, one of the best-known artists of Scotland. He died on March 20 in his home in Edinburgh. He was born in Renfrewshire and was 61 years of age.

Mr. Walton was president of the Royal ...

EAGLE CRITIC, DIES

Hamilton Easter Field, president of the Brooklyn Society of Artists, art editor of The Brooklyn Eagle, and a recognized leader of the modernist school of art in New York City, died last night of pneumonia at his home, 106 Columbia Heights, after a three weeks illness. He was 49 years old. The funeral services will be held at the home tomorrow afternoon at 2 o'clock and burial will be privately in the Friends Cemetery, in Prospect Park.

Mr. Field achieved a reputation for himself, not only as an artist of genius, but as a critic and an insurgent against the false and the unreal.

eral Grant to Be Unveiled in Washington April 27.

A LABOR OF TWELVE YEARS

Artist Never Took a Lesson in Painting and Modeling, but Met

life at a homestead in Hamilton Ave., where he had a studio. Some of his works hang in homes of prominent Columbus persons and his landscapes can be seen also in the governor's mansion.

... buried tomorrow from ... son, Max Mitchell, at 808 South Allison street. He did a number of portraits in city hall and some of the capitol friezes at Harrisburg.

tended by Many.

Delegations From Many Organizations and Hosts of Friends Attended Fun...

MISS MARY GALT, A NOTED ARTIST DIES

Artist Who Graduated With the High Institute and the Julian Academy and the Winning of the Grand Prize — Come Home This Month Answer

Jack Huotari of Belt, one of the most talented young art students of Paris, died in the American hospital, Paris, France, this morning, according to a cablegram received here by deputy sheriff Fred Huotari here. Fred and Hans Huotari, the latter fireman on the Great Northern, left at noon for the home of their mother on a ranch near Geyser, and funeral arrangements will be made after she and other relatives have been con...

ARTIST, BROKE, ENDS HIS LIFE

Art did not bring money for Carl Lugo, believed to have held a national reputation for his designs, to purchase food and pay his rent. So yesterday he ended his career in a gas filled room at 3611 Twenty-third street.

Lugo is said to have found no sale for his creations and to have done no work for five weeks. Among his ...

LOS ANGELES, Sept. 6.—His life a sacrifice to what he called the pursuit of spiritual beauty, E. M. Manigault, a Los Angeles artist, died today from self-imposed starvation in San Francisco, according to word received from that city. Manigault dropped in the street. According to Dr. S. T. Pope of San Francisco, Manigault ... fasting ...

ARTIST IS DEAD

JOHN KARST OF SULLIVAN COUNTY GREAT TEXTBOOK ILLUSTRATOR.

TROY, N. Y.—With the death of John Karst at his country home in ... ing at 611 East Franklin street. His funeral will take place from the home ...

Sir Thomas Brock

Sir Thomas Brock, the sculptor, died yesterday in London at the age of seventy-five years. Born in Worcester, England, he was knighted in 1911. He was educated under the ... Foley, and among his important ... the Chicago Art Institute yesterday and shot himself through the head. Tuesday Undaras paid his last financial debt, for which he had given an ...

WAYNE PAYS TRIBUTE TO PAXSON, ARTIST

Missoula Man Speaks Before Society of Montana Pioneers in Session.

Tribute was paid to the memory of ... S. Paxson, artist, pioneer and trailblazer ... by attorney William ...

Swiss ... months ago at the ... colony, are making inquiry regarding his supposed estate ... letter was received yesterday ... Captain Dick Ghost, of the B... of Charities, from Paul ...

ART DAWSON

Art... Dawson, well known ... of Arde... and well known in ... lage, who has lived in R... Virginia, for more than a y... at his residence in Richmond ... night, August 28, in his six... year His wife, two sons, Ha... John, and two daughters, Mr... rence and Mrs. Parrott, surviv... Dawson had been ill for about ... months and his ...

Hugo and Thiers

PARIS Sept. 8.—Leon Bonnat ... tor of the French School of Fi... died to-day. M. Bonnat was ... ninetieth year, having been b... Bayonne on June 20, 1833. ... president of the French Soc...

L. Heudle, 54, for nine years ... of Memorial Art Gallery, died la... at his home here. He was a me... the Association of Art Museum ... tors, and an artist who exhibited ... Pennsylvania Art Society exh... Corcoran Art Gallery, Washingt... tional Academy of Design and ot... tionally known exhibits.

J. Bell Dies at 105; His Widow

DIES AT B...

Henry J. Frey, who ... home of his daughter, ... to pay a fine of $10 and ... prosecution.

NOTED ARTIST D...

Henry J. Frey, aged 8... prominent portrait and ... painter, died on Sunday at ... of his daughter, Mrs. George ... 522 Avenue C, West Bethle... 86 years. He was a native of ...

William M. J. Ric... Noted American Portrait...

William Morton Jac... noted American portr... and landscape artist, di... late on Friday in his st... 15 West Sixty-seventh st... was due to heart ... disease, from which Mr. Rice ... had been a suf... for some ...

The most intensively pleated clippings in the scrapbooks are impossible to read without causing them irreparable harm. Frustrated, I began to look for intact versions of these stories in online databases of historical newspapers. A test query for the phrase ARTIST LEAPS returned the full text of a fold-hidden February 1921 clipping about commercial illustrator Wilson C. Dexter. But the words also appeared in the headline of an August 1926 obituary in *The Bismark Tribune* of North Dakota for sculptor Gaëtan Ardisson, which was not among The Met clippings.

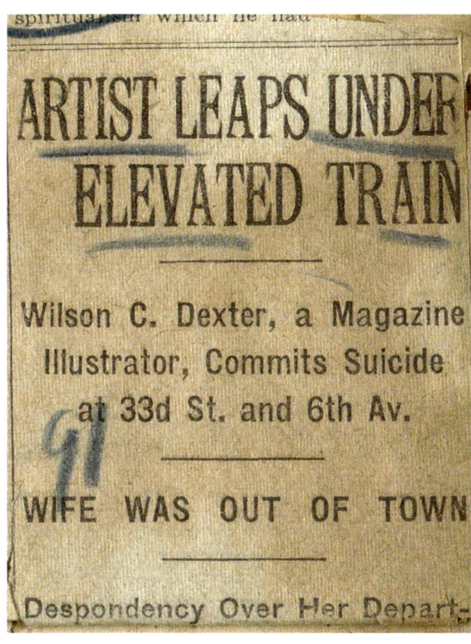

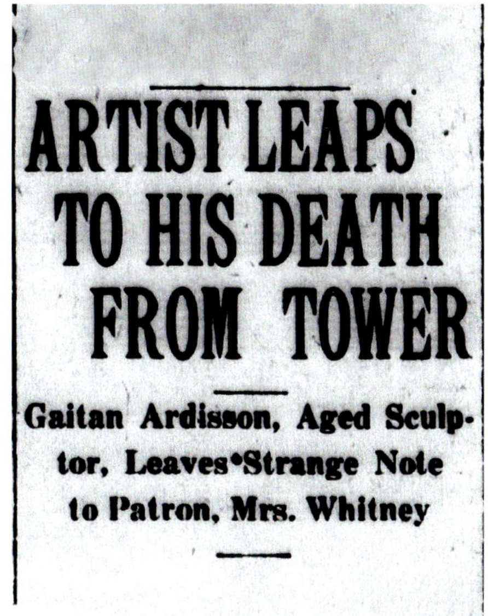

I suddenly realized that the National Press Intelligence had not snipped for D'Hervilly and his successors *every* artist's death story published at the time—the scrapbooks contain only a part of an unknown whole. But with patient use of twenty-first-century technology, many that were missed at the time could now be retrieved, and the search could be extended beyond American borders to find examples from English-language newspapers published as far away as Australia. Following D'Hervilly's lead, I zealously began to gather dozens more artist death stories into a virtual scrapbook of my own.

. . .

MINDSHROUDED

WITH GLOOMY AND DARK FOREBODINGS

New York Artist Ended Life in Bath Room.

STRANGLED WAS THE NOTED ARTIST

LUCKLESS WOMAN HUMAN TORCH

Well Known California Artist Burned to Death in Trying to Fill Gasoline Stove While Lighted.

STARVES TO DEATH PAINTING OWN FACE TO BECOME FAMOUS

Artist Succumbs Before Mirror After Struggle

ARTIST, SOLDIER, REAPER VICTIM

Noted Painter of Missoula Succumbs After Long Illness.

GIRL ARTIST WAS STRANGLED

FOUND IN ROOM THAT HAD BEEN OCCUPIED BY A MAN, SHE WAS COLD IN DEATH.

Los Angeles Murder Mystery in Puzzling the Police—Woman companion Being Held.

BABY ON HER ARM, GIRL KILLS ARTIST BLAMED FOR WOES

"You Ruined My Home," Screams Young Woman as She Shoots Brooklyn Man.

's Sensation

ARTIST OF NOTE PASSES AWAY IN POVERTY

His Wife and Model Exhausted After Nursing Pneumonia Victim

ARTIST WAS NOTED FOR INDEPENDENCE

Had 10-Foot Fence Around Home and Arose at 4:30 to Walk in Dew

SAD RESULTS OF A SPREE

Salt Lake Artist Commits Suicide by Choking Himself with Handkerchief

STARVATION REWARD OF ARTIST

Artist Perishes On Burning Couch In Her Apartment

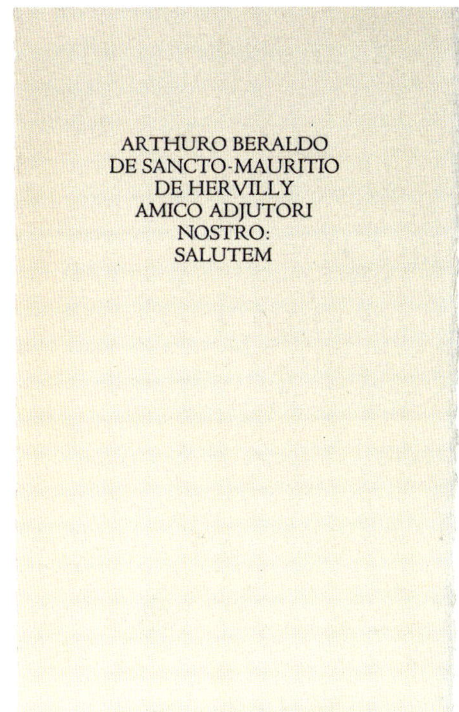

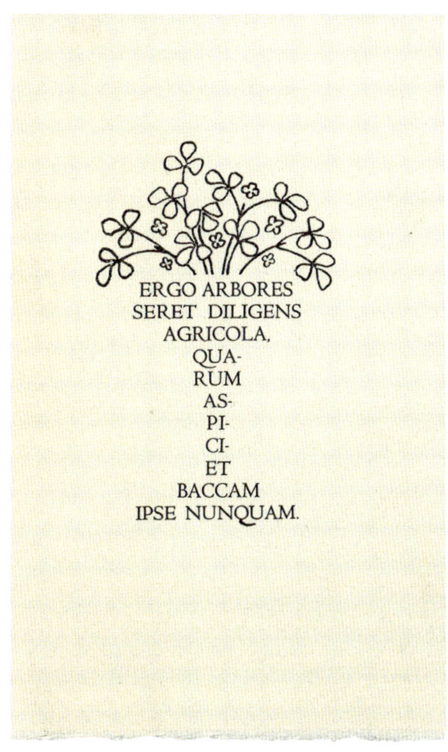

Memorial leaflet for A. B. de St. M. D'Hervilly, 1919. Arthur D'Hervilly file, Office of the Secretary Records, The Metropolitan Museum of Art Archives

Upon his death The Met eulogized D'Hervilly, printing a small leaflet, composed in Latin, which saluted "our friend and helper" who, like the "diligent farmer" praised by Roman statesman Cicero, "plants trees of which he himself will never see the fruit." D'Hervilly was buried in Kensico Cemetery in Valhalla, New York. His grave has no headstone, and there is no record of who paid for the funeral; he likely had little money to his name. His bereft widow, Ida, lived out her days on a scanty pension from the Museum employees association that was secretly supplemented by Robert W. DeForest, president of The Met board of trustees. She died in 1930 and was buried beside her husband. Their unmarked graves are a few hundred yards away from that of General Cesnola, which is topped by an imposing monument and Medal of Honor plaque commemorating his military valor.

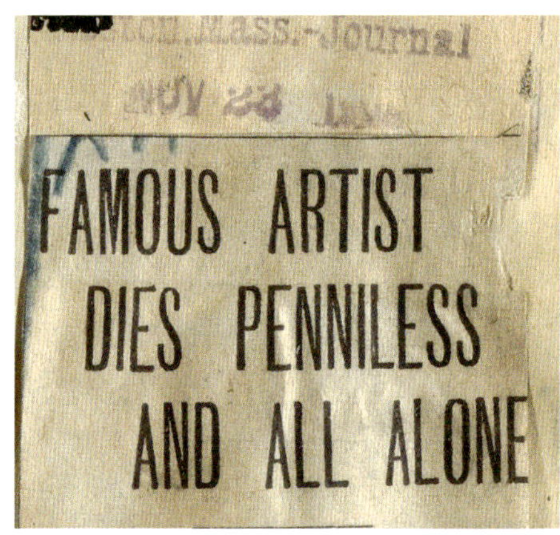

FAMOUS ARTIST DIES PENNILESS AND ALL ALONE

It was this 1908 obituary of Imogene Robinson Morrell that had fixed my gaze when I first opened the scrapbooks. The grim poetry of its headline compelled me to read on, as it was crafted to do, and I was intrigued by the celebrity attributed to an artist unknown to me. I explored the whole story of Morrell's life and death. She launched me on a long journey of discovery about an artistic generation whose fates were bound together on the pages of the D'Hervilly volumes.

Born in Massachusetts around 1830, Morrell was one of a pioneering group of American women who lived by their art in the Victorian era and blazed a trail to Europe, where they found mentorship and camaraderie. In her twenties, she studied in the Düsseldorf atelier of Wilhelm Camphausen, who specialized in grandiose battle scenes. She also absorbed the influence of Emanuel Leutze, the famed painter of *Washington Crossing the Delaware* (1851), a treasure of the Metropolitan Museum since its acquisition in 1897. Morrell spent more than a decade in France, copying in the Louvre, comanaging a busy studio with compatriot Elizabeth Jane Gardner, and selling pictures to a vibrant community of American expatriates.

She eventually married and returned to the United States, where she made a splash with a large painting of the arrival of the Puritans on the Massachusetts coast. Her composition derived from a rendition of the story by the American poet Henry Wadsworth

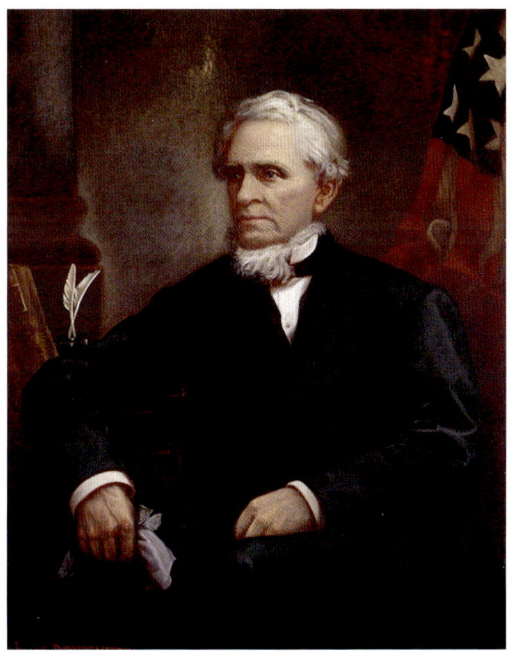

Imogene Robinson Morrell, *John Adams Dix*,
1883. U.S. Senate Collection (32.00014.000)

Longfellow. It shows Miles Standish, the commanding military
leader of the European colony, lording over the fallen bodies of
two indigenous men after a skirmish. Propagandistic imagery of
encounters between Native Americans and European colonizers
was prevalent in post–Civil War America, and contemporary critics
celebrated Morrell's achievement in this vein. The picture won a
prize medal at the 1876 Centennial Exposition in Philadelphia.

Morrell settled with her husband in Washington, D.C., where she
taught students and fulfilled portrait commissions from political
dignitaries. Her painting of Senator John Adams Dix, also secretary of the treasury and a Union army major general, remains in
the U.S. Senate collection and is one of few surviving works by her
hand. But at the end of the nineteenth century Morrell's popularity
waned and she suffered one misfortune after another. Much of her
unsold oeuvre of hundreds of paintings on canvas was destroyed in
a cataclysmic warehouse fire. Despite her mastery of large paintings
on historical themes, she never managed to tap public funds then

pouring forth to endow patriotic murals for government buildings. In August 1901 she could not make the rent and was forced from her home by a flinty landlord, an indignity trumpeted by a Washington newspaper under the headline AGED ARTIST EVICTED. Seven years later, Morrell's long, eventful life ended when she had a stroke in a boardinghouse where her corpse was "Found Amid Scenes of Squalor and Neglect."

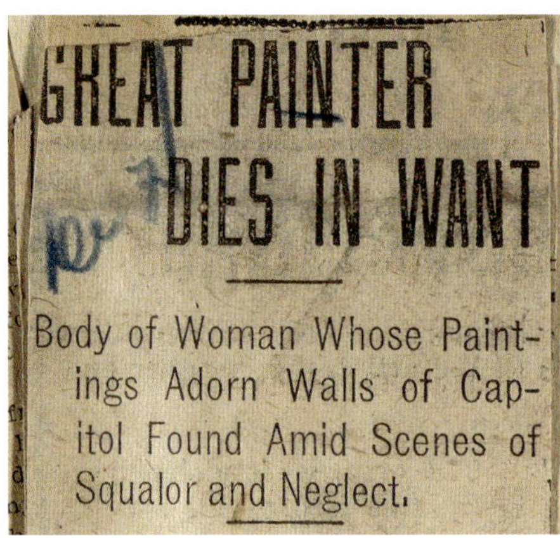

Arthur D'Hervilly's presumed intention, when he first began gathering artist obituaries in 1906, was for the National Press Intelligence to provide him with useful biographical information about contemporary artists he was researching for the new Met paintings catalogue. Over time, he saw that most obituaries described artists who were not then, and likely never would be, featured in The Met.

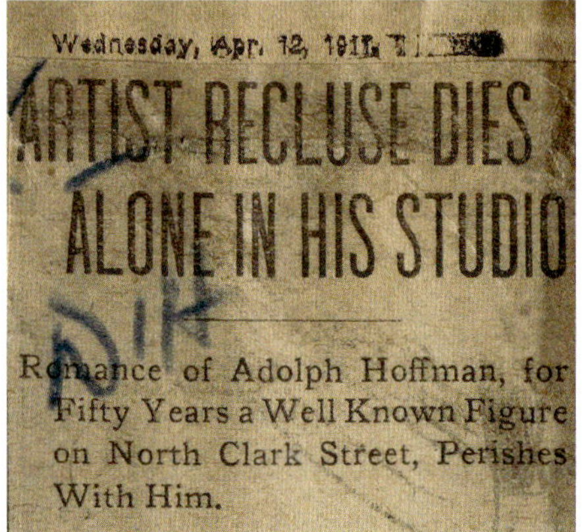

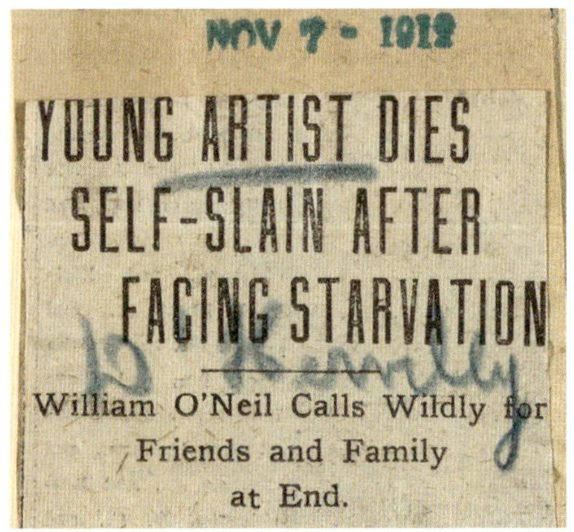

Robert Loftin Newman and Amedeo Modigliani are exceptional cases of artists whose death stories were acquired by The Met long before examples of their art found a place in the Museum. The clippings turned out to be of slim value for D'Hervilly's cataloguing duties, yet he continued to pay the National Press Intelligence to deliver them to him month after month, even after the updated catalogue was published in 1914. By then, his massive, collage-like death chronicle had assumed a different purpose.

When, late in his career, D'Hervilly's responsibilities shifted away from curation of art objects and toward engagement with special contingents of museum visitors, he painstakingly recorded for posterity the names and accomplishments of the copyists, commercial illustrators, and design professionals who came to The Met to study famous masterpieces. Meanwhile, he continued to paste into his scrapbooks death notices of people equally as anonymous as those humble copyists right alongside obituaries of celebrated

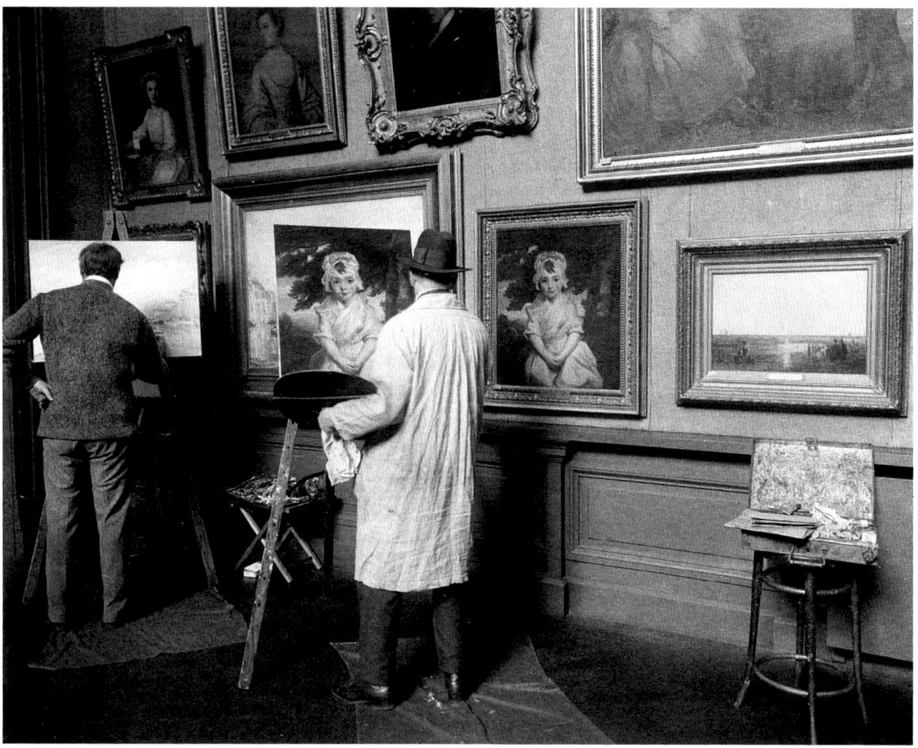

Copyists at work in the paintings galleries, 1920. The Metropolitan Museum of Art, photographer unknown

NEW BEDFORD [MASS.] STANDARD

Thursday, Apr. 20, 1911.

MARION ARTIST DEAD.

WAS IN TURN WHALEMAN, DECORATOR, AND PAINTER.

George F. Handy, a Veteran of Civil War—Was Twice Wrecked on One Voyage—Was Standard Subscriber for Over 35 Years.

George F. Handy, of Marion, in turn seaman, decorator, house painter and amateur artist, died in that town late Wednesday afternoon. Mr. Handy was born in Marion in 1847, and was 63 years of age. He had just recovered from a long attack of pneumonia, when he was stricken with appendicitis.

In 1864 Mr. Handy enlisted and was a member of the G. A. R., in Sons of Veterans, took a great interest in the Pythagorean lodge, A. F. & A. M. Besides a widow, he leaves three sisters, Miss Cynthia Handy and Mrs. Russell Gray of Marion, and Mrs. George F. Healey of Rochester.

SAN FRANCISCO, CAL., POST

Thursday, Apr. 13, 1911.

ARTIST WM. KE...
AS HIS WIFE REA...

N. Y. PRESS

Friday, Apr. 28, 1911.

REJECTION OF HER ART WORK FATAL

Friends Believe Disappointment Killed Mrs. Matthews.

MODEL WAS ACCEPTED

Afterward, However, Committee Withdrew Commission to Make Bronze Bust of Taft.

Friends of Mrs. Elizabeth St. John Matthews, painter and sculptor, whose sudden death from heart disease occurred in Hahnemann Hospital, Park avenue and Sixty-seventh street, on last Wednesday night, were positive in their assertions yesterday her end had been hastened by grief and disappointment due to the rejection of a plaster bust of President Taft she had made, which first had been accepted as a fine likeness.

It is said Mrs. Matthews was directed by a committee of prominent New Yorkers to make a bronze bust of the President and was to have received $5,000 for it. The stipulation was she first should make a plaster cast and if the verdict of the com-

---

CHICAGO, ILL., Record-Herald

Tuesday, June 27, 1911.

widow and three sons, V. P. Harvey of Wheat, Philip Harvey of Boston and Harry Harvey Chicago.

MRS. EVELYN B. BEACHEY, teacher ceramic painting and design at the Art Institute, was buried Sunday after funeral services held her home, 206 West Forty-sixth street. She died Saturday from the effects of burns which she had received in the effort to rescue her mother, Mrs. Mary A. Brackett, who was severely burned June 14. Mrs. Brackett died at the Chicago Hospital soon after the accident.

WASHINGTON, D. C., POST

Tuesday, Dec. 5, 1911.

...the president general.

Portrait Artist Buried.

Charles Armor, the well-known portrait artist, who died suddenly at his residence, 615 North Carolina avenue southeast, was buried yesterday afternoon Rock Creek Cemetery. He is survived by a wife and three daughters.

PHILADELPHIA, PA., PRESS

Thursday, Apr. 27, 1906.

M. Tait officiating.

JOHN J. BOYLE, ARTIST

John J. Boyle, widely known as a painter of religious subjects, a former prize winner at the Pennsylvania Academy of the Fine Arts, died of pneumonia yesterday at his farm at Ocean View, N. J.

Mr. Boyle had a studio at 1305 Arch Street and was widely known among artists. He labored under great physical difficulties, having been for years afflicted with curvature of the spine. His last local work of size was the mural decorations for the parish school of St. Francis of Assisi. He also has large works in various churches in this city, Baltimore and Washington.

BALTIMORE, MD., SUN 1906

Thursday, Apr. 27, 1906.

FAMOUS MURAL ARTIST

John J. Boyle Passes Away—Paintings In Baltimore Churches.

[Special Dispatch to the Baltimore Sun.]

Philadelphia, April 26.—John J. Boyle, a former pupil and prize winner of the Pennsylvania Academy of Fine Arts and a well-known mural painter whose pictures, dealing with religious subjects, adorn a number of Catholic churches in Philadelphia, Baltimore, Washington and other cities, died of pneumonia yesterday at his farm at Ocean View, N. J.

While studying in Paris Mr. Boyle became afflicted with curvature of the spine and underwent heroic treatment. He continued his studies and worked harder than many men enjoying perfect health.

One of the last orders which Mr. Boyle filled was for a picture which was sent to Italy, where it will be copied in mosaic for a Catholic church in this country. While a pupil at the Pennsylvania Academy of Fine Arts he won two scholarships which enabled him twice to travel and study in Europe.

men like Auguste Rodin and Claude Monet. He aspired, like
Giorgio Vasari, to preserve "in the memory of the living" hundreds
of unsung artists whose creative achievements would otherwise
become "the prey of death and oblivion." D'Hervilly had probably
long since dropped any ambition of his own to make a great artwork. Still, he created and saved within the Museum's sturdy walls
a powerful, poignant, and lasting memorial to the lives and struggles
of hundreds of little-known artists of his time.

REJECTION OF HER ART WORK FATAL

Elizabeth St. John Matthews died in a hospital of heart disease in
April 1911. Her husband and her physician both asserted the sculptor's
end was "hastened by grief and disappointment due to the rejection
of a plaster bust of President Taft she had made." Matthews had been
commissioned by prominent associates of the Yale Club to make a portrait honoring the twenty-seventh U.S. president, for which she would
be paid $5,000. But upon viewing her maquette they reneged and can-
celed their order for a bronze edition. Matthews had won the deal on
the strength of her 1902 bas-relief *The Martyr Presidents*, a triple profile
of the three American leaders who, up to that time, had been assassi-
nated: Abraham Lincoln, James Garfield, and William McKinley.

NOTED SCULPTOR WHO DIED SUDDENLY.

The life of Helen Farnsworth Mears, also a sculptor, likewise
was allegedly cut short by disappointment over the loss of a coveted
commission. Born in Oshkosh, Wisconsin, in December of 1872,
Mears was recognized as a precocious talent while still in her
twenties. Her colossal sculpture *The Genius of Wisconsin* was
selected to represent the Badger State at the 1893 World's Columbian
Exposition. A marble version, derived from her 9-foot-tall plaster
model and carved by Piccirilli Brothers of the Bronx, makers of the
famous Edward Clark Potter–designed New York Public Library
lions on Fifth Avenue, is today displayed in the Wisconsin State

Friday, March 29, 1913.

HENRY G. DEARTH, ARTIST OF NOTE

Henry Golden Dearth, artist and a member of the National Academy, is dead at his home, No. 116 East Sixty-third street, at the age of fifty-four years. One of his best known paintings is "Boulogne Harbor," in the Metropolitan Museum.

The artist was born in Bristol, R. I. He was a pupil at the Ecole des Beaux-Arts and of Herbert and Aimé Marot in Paris. He was the winner of the Webb prize of the Society of American artists in 1893, received a bronze medal at the Paris Exposition of 1900, and a silver medal at the Buffalo Exposition.

He was a member of the National Academy and of the Fencers, Lotos and Century clubs. He married Cornelia Van Rensselaer Vail, of New York, on February 26, 1896. Mr. Dearth is survived by his wife and a daughter, Nina Van Rensselaer Dearth.

HENRY G. DEARTH, PAINTER, DIES AT 53

New York Artist, a National Academician, Who Won Several Medals, Expires Suddenly.

Henry Golden Dearth, a distinguished American artist and winner of several medals, died suddenly yesterday from heart disease in his home at 116 East Sixty-third Street, in his fifty-fourth year. His painting of "Boulogne Harbor" is in the Metropolitan Museum of Art.

Mr. Dearth was born in Bristol, R. I., and was the son of the late John Willis and Ruth Marshall Dearth. He was a pupil at the Ecole des Beaux-Arts and of Herbert and Aimé Morot in Paris. He was the winner of the Webb prize of the Society of American Artists in 1893, received a bronze medal at the Paris Exposition of 1900, and a silver medal at the Buffalo Exposition of 1901. He was a member of the National Academy and of the Fencers, Lotos, and Century Clubs. He married Cornelia Van Rensselaer Vail of New York on Feb. 26, 1896. Mr. Dearth is survived by his wife and a daughter, Nina Van Rensselaer Dearth.

Sultan of Turkey by the then President; the Prince of Wales, later Edward VIII.; James J. Hill, Cornelius Vanderbilt and "Buffalo Bill." Fifty of his paintings are hung at the Historical Society rooms.

EVANSTON VOTES TO TAKE IDLE LAND FOR GARDENS

. . . arib, Canada, on August 27, 1843, and spent several years of his early life abroad, studying his profession and the processes now extensively used in this country in modern photography and art reproductions. He studied in London, Paris and Munich and brought to the United States many original methods that he used here for the first time. His studio was at 292 Fifth avenue, Manhattan.

Mr. Cooper made a specialty of reproductions of the paintings in the galleries of American millionaires, and some of the notable collections that he photographed were the Weidner, Elkins and Johnson . . .

WISCONSIN ARTIST DIES.

Miss Katherine MacDonald Well Known Over Nation.

La Crosse, Wis., Jan. 17.—Miss Katherine MacDona'd, well known as an artist, discoverer of the present method of painting glassware, died at her home here today. She was born May 14, 1839, in Picton, Nova Scotia, and was a sister of the late Captain D. A. MacDonald, one of the pioneer figures on the Mississippi river and a lumberman of note.

. . . or Queen Henrietta Maria in Warwick Castle, England, and her work now adorns the Maryland State capitol at Annapolis. She also copied the portraits of Lords George and Cecilius Calvert, First and Second Barons of Baltimore. Her life-size painting of Cardinal Gibbons was exhibited at the St. Louis Exposition.

NOTED ARTIST DEAD

Henry Golden Dearth Was Native of Bristol, R. I.

Bristol, R. I., March 28.—Henry Golden Dearth, American artist and winner of several prizes, died yesterday at his home in New York. Mr. Dearth, who was 54 years old, was a native of Rhode Island, being born in Bristol, the son of John W. and Ruth . . .

Orion Frazee, Jersey Sculptor, Buried at Chatham---Molded Features of Dead Jefferson Davis.

ACTED AS H. W. GRADY'S PROTEGE

Special Service of the NEWS.

NEW PROVIDENCE, Feb. 17.—The funeral of Orion Frazee, the sculptor who made the death mask of Jefferson Davis, president of the Southern Confederacy and of other famous Southerners, took place yesterday afternoon at the undertaking parlors of E. P. Burroughs & Son, Springfield avenue, Summit. He died Monday in a sanitorium at Belle Mead. Services were conducted by Rev. J. Adam Oakes, pastor of the East Summit Methodist Episcopal Church. Burial was in Fairmount . . . bronze medal at the Paris Exposition in 1900 and silver medals at the Buffalo Exposition in 1901 and at the Charleston Exhibition in 1902. He became a member of the Associate National Academician in 1902 and of the National Academician in 1906. He was a member of the Fencers', Century and Lotus clubs.

NEW YORK, March 28—Henry Golden Derth, a distinguished American artist and winner of several medals, died suddenly at his home here yesterday.

Mr Derth was born in Bristol, R I, 54 years ago. He was the winner of the Webb prize of the Society of American Artists in 1893, received a bronze medal at the Paris Exposition of 1900 and a silver medal at the Buffalo Exposition of 1901.

. . . ARTIST IS DEAD

Succumbs Suddenly to Heart Disease in His Home in This City.

Mr. Henry Golden Dearth, artist, died suddenly yesterday morning of heart disease in his home, No. 116 East Sixty-third street, in his fifty-fourth year.

Mr. Dearth was born in Bristol, R. I., son of the late John Willis and Ruth Marshall Dearth, and was a descendant on his grandmother's side from Governor Bradford, of Massachusetts. He studied art in . . . and was a pupil of the Ecole des Beaux Arts and Aimé Morot. On February . . .

township is . . . every person over 14 years of age is a member of the Bay Lake Red Cross auxiliary.

WELL KNOWN ARTIST DIES.

La Crosse, Wis., Jan. 18.—Miss Katherine MacDonald, well known as an artist, discoverer of the present method of painting glassware, died at her home here yesterday. She was a sister of the late Captain D. A. MacDonald, one of the pioneer figures on the Mississippi river.

HAWLEY COPPER QUITS.

GUILFORD.

Remains of Ralph S. Mosher Brought Here for Interment—Other Notes.

(From Our Regular Correspondent)

GUILFORD, April 2—The body of Ralph Strout Mosher was brought to Guilford for burial Monday morning, from Bangor where his death occurred on Saturday. Mr. Mosher was born in Nashville, Tenn., and was brought to Guilford by his mother at the age of six months, they residing in this town until he was nearly thirteen years of age. He was 25 years of age at the . . .

NOTED SCULPTOR WHO DIED SUDDENLY.

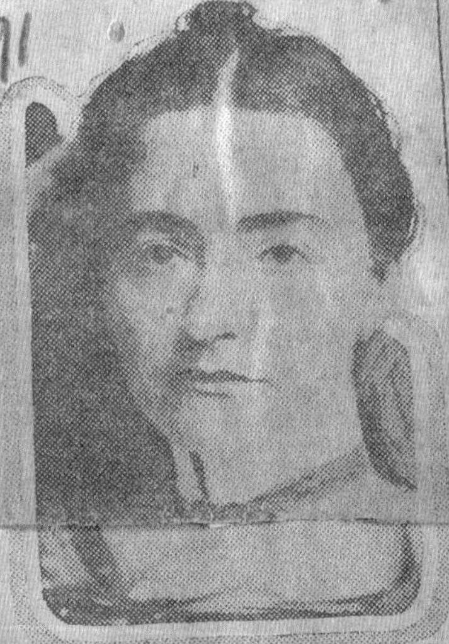

Helen Farnsworth Mears.

HELEN MEARS, SCULPTOR, DEAD IN HER STUDIO

Collapses Beside Unfinished Statue of "Youth."

Helen Farnsworth Mears lies dead in her Washington Square studio near her unfinished statue "The Fountain of Youth." Heart disease attacked her so suddenly last night that she died before a physician summoned by her sister, Miss Mary Mears, an author, could reach her. She was 38 years old and had made an international name for herself.

Capitol. Mears came to New York to study with Augustus Saint-Gaudens and worked for a time as his assistant. After a European sojourn she set up her own studio on Washington Square and produced marble and bronze portraits.

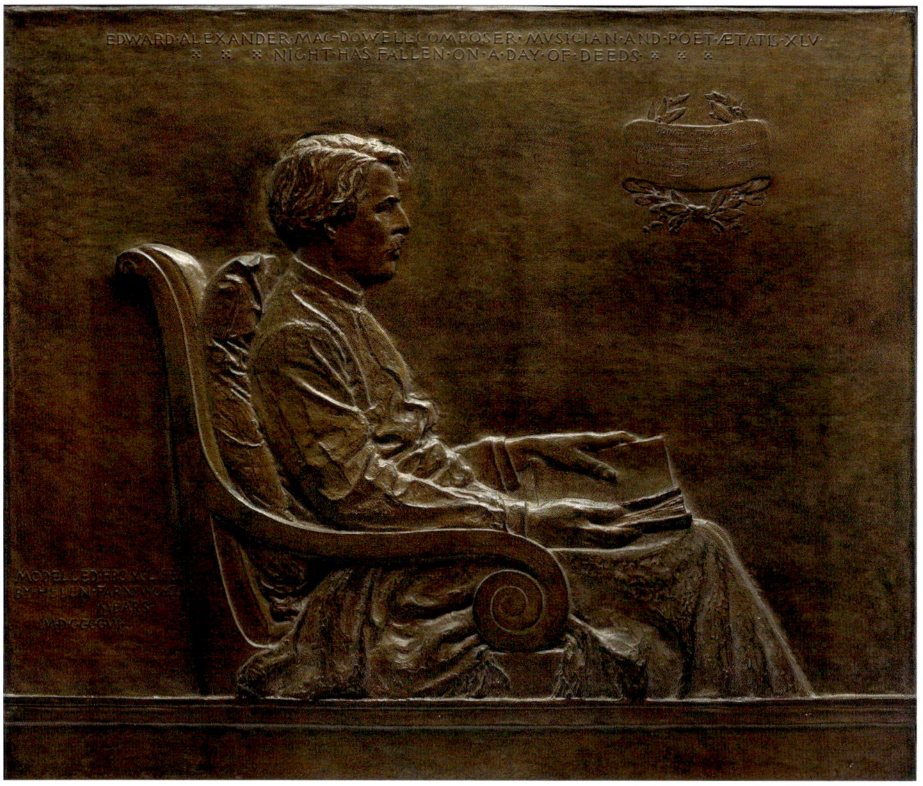

Helen Farnsworth Mears, *Edward Alexander MacDowell*, 1906, cast 1907.
The Metropolitan Museum of Art, Gift of Alice G. Chapman, 1909 (09.147)

The Metropolitan Museum has a fine example of her bronze work, a 1906–7 relief of the musician and composer Edward Alexander MacDowell, cofounder, with his wife, Marian MacDowell, of the MacDowell artist residency. For the state of Illinois, Mears carved a life-size marble statue of woman suffragist Frances Willard, later installed and still on view in the United States Capitol's National Statuary Hall.

Mears died unexpectedly in her studio at age forty-three (erroneously reported as age thirty-eight), possibly of a heart ailment.

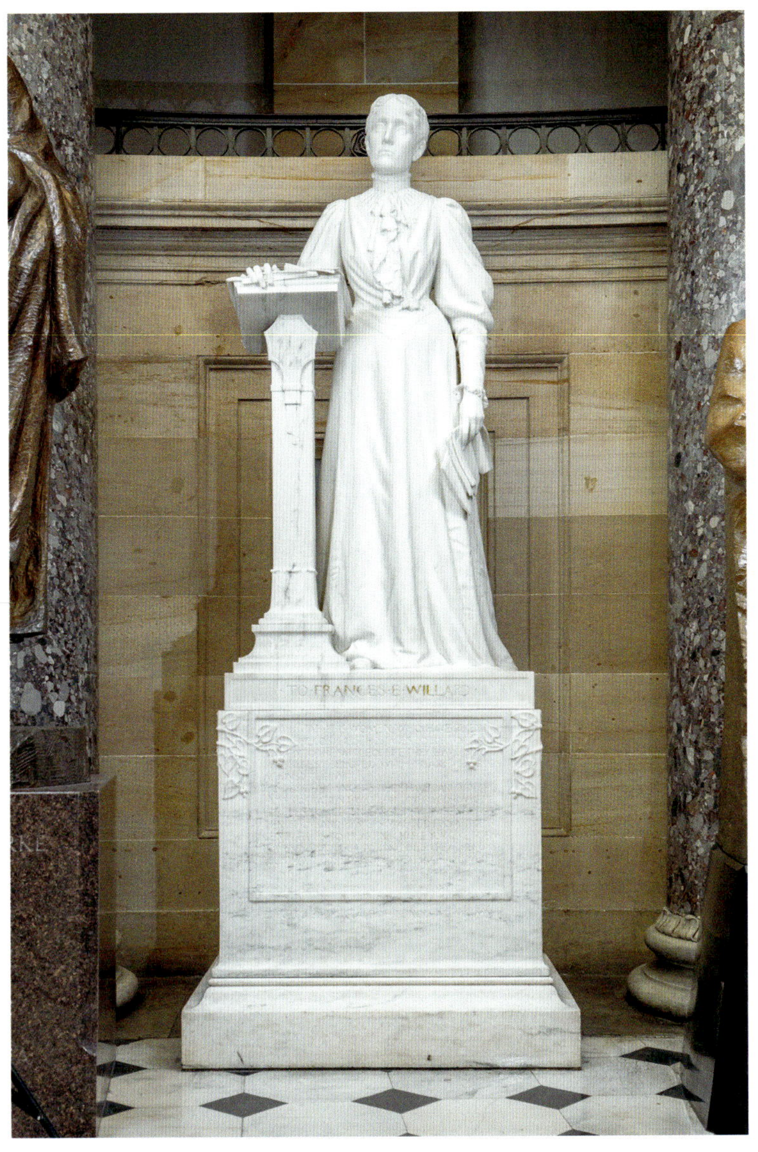

Helen Farnsworth Mears, *Frances E. Willard*, 1905. National Statuary Hall, United States Capitol

Some reporters speculated that overwork, the stress of financial hardship, and the loss of a public commission awarded instead to Daniel Chester French ruined her health and drove her to an early grave. She expired in the shadow of an incomplete sculpture titled *Fountain of Youth*.

. . .

Viewers of the scrapbooks today can study, interpret, and respond to them in many ways. These fragile memento mori, composed of dense, decaying layers of folded browned paper, black ink, and dried glue, have an intrinsic, aesthetic worth as physical objects and are deeply redolent of time's passage. Their accounts, though often embellished, are clear depictions of how the lives of a past generation of American and European artists ended. Their sensationalist techniques, typical of the heyday of yellow journalism, ramped up newspaper sales and influenced how millions of readers thought about what it is to be an artist. Irresistibly entertaining, the stories they hold are written in a literary style that is by turns blunt, satiric, and laudatory—even comic at times—and seldom dull. Their pages harbor abundant source material and inspiration for new as yet unimagined creative endeavors.

By 2022 I myself had absorbed all I could from the scrapbooks, and I turned my attention to writing this book and working on ways to widely disseminate their contents. Scrolling back through hundreds of iPhone snapshots of jarring tabloid headlines that I had made during my research, I recognized there was an imperative need to photograph systematically and professionally every page of the scrapbooks at high resolution to preserve them in digital form. Although the inevitable disintegration of many folded-up clippings prevented capturing the full text of their stories, a visual record now exists of how all of the scrapbook pages look, just as I found them. Working with expert colleagues in The Met Imaging Department, I have overseen the making of a full set of these documentary images, which in time will be made freely available on the Museum's website.

My study of the scrapbooks has also led me to think in a new way about artists who have died during my own lifetime. Many of them, I realize, would have been fine fodder for a 1910s tabloid writer— such as outsider Ray Johnson, who deliberately swam out to sea and drowned, or acclaimed Neo-Expressionist Jean-Michel Basquiat, who overdosed on opiates and cocaine. But the artist's death story of my own time that most moves me is enviably peaceful and well befits its enigmatic subject. On October 3, 1968, *The New York Times* published a front-page obituary of Marcel Duchamp. After hosting a small dinner party, the eighty-one-year-old artist-provocateur was preparing for bed just after midnight on October 2 when he dropped dead in his bathroom. His wife Teeny later recalled that when she looked upon her husband's fallen body, he had a "calm, pleased expression on his face." She said his instantaneous passing was "almost magic" and believed "he did not know when it happened, and that was the way he always wanted it." Duchamp was cremated, and his ashes are buried in the family plot at Rouen in his native Normandy, beneath a tombstone with a cryptic epitaph.

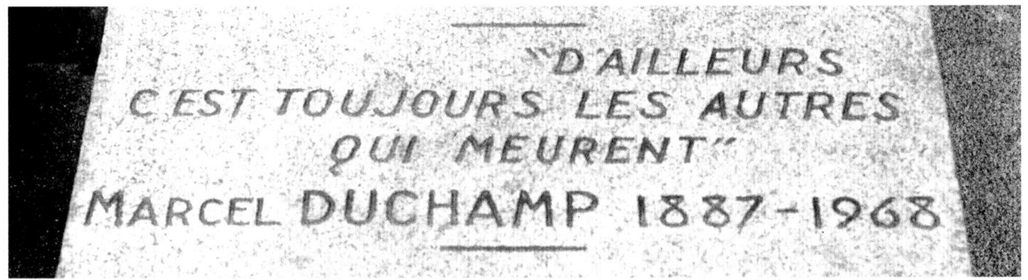

D'ailleurs
c'est toujours les autres
qui meurent

Besides
it is always the others
who die

ACKNOWLEDGMENTS

I am deeply grateful to many people and institutions that helped me make this book. Artist Lenka Clayton and writer Christine Coulson inspired me to recognize the creative potential of what was right in front me. Corinne Segal expertly edited my first essay about the scrapbooks, published by Literary Hub in 2022. Eve Kahn steered me toward informative genealogical sources and, through the Victorian Society of New York, provided an early opportunity to present my research in public.

At The Metropolitan Museum of Art, Scott Geffert and the Imaging team made available a good camera and taught me to use it. Intern Maggie Nevison picked up where I left off and completed shooting a full photographic record of the scrapbooks for the Met website. Staff in the Thomas J. Watson Library and the Onassis Library for Hellenic and Roman Art shared a wealth of research material online and in the stacks. In the Museum Archives, Melissa Bowling, Barbara File, Cormac Fitzgerald, Angela Salisbury, and Sarah Rappo kept our team's daily work on track while this project absorbed my attention. Marica F. Vilcek Curator of American Paintings and Sculpture Thayer Tolles sharpened my recounting of Met history. Senior Vice President, Secretary, and General Counsel Sharon Cott has always encouraged my research interests and warmly supported this effort.

I consulted collections of the Library of Congress, New York Public Library, HaithiTrust Digital Library, Internet Archive, and Philadelphia City Archives, where K. Edward Rice was especially helpful. Andrea Gallagher and Judy Mitchell of Kensico Cemetery led me to the graves of Arthur and Ida D'Hervilly and Luigi Palma di Cesnola.

Laura Lindgren and Ken Swezey, publishers of Blast Books, fostered a collaboration that has been fun and exciting every step of the way. I am honored to join the eclectic roster of authors, photographers, and artists whose work they have shared with the world in beautifully designed editions. I'm grateful to Robert Storr for his keenly insightful foreword. Don Kennison expertly proofread the pages and offered much-appreciated commentary.

My dear friends Eric Marc Cohen, Elizabeth Felicella, Jim Freeman, Marlene Hennessey, and Denise Mecionis viewed pictures, read drafts, brainstormed narrative strategies, and gave keen advice. My children, Nina Moske and Wendell Moske, were intrigued from the first evening I came home from work buzzing with news about two weird scrapbooks I'd found, and they sensitively shared their thoughts about many artists whose stories I related to them. It meant the world to me that they believed their father could turn this all into a good book.

My partner, Sara Heinonen, and I met each other at a turning point in my work on the project, and I benefited greatly from her encouragement to follow my instincts. Her acuity, honesty, and creative example inspired me to find my way to an ending, and our love now ensures I'm ready to start something new.

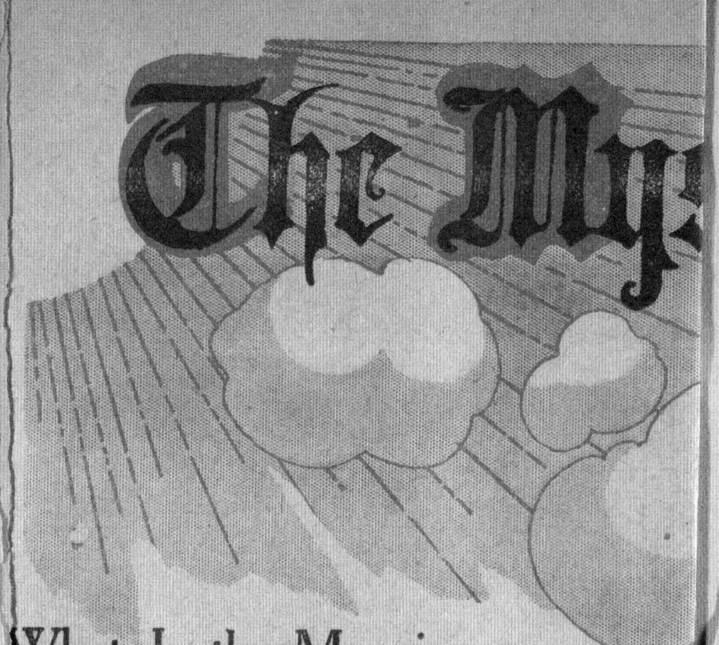

What Is the Meaning in the Famous Sculptor's Studi of Creation Now Shown at the Metropolitan Museum and Eliciting Unusual Public Curiosity?---Some Opinions by New York Clergymen.

By Henry Tyrrell.

AUGUSTE RODIN'S sculptured poem in purest white marble, titled "The Hand of God," is a recent accession which takes extraordinary hold upon the imagination of the crowds who the Metropolitan Museum of Art. This spontaneous apprecia perhaps unexpected, as Rodin is not an "easy" sculptor with ral public, and the two or three other works—"Primitive Man" e Thinker," for which latter G. Bernard Shaw is said to have pose which he is represented at the Museum have never caused a riot h This "Hand of God," presented to the Museum by one of its trust ard D. Adams, is a small replica in marble of the original grou ze purchased for and owned by the French Government. It represe n's conception of the creation of man, as derived from the Bibl of Genesis. While mankind is symbolized in Adam and Eve, ative "hand" of God is rendered literally. The sculptor has mode ge hand, with all the combined science of anatomist, physiologist mancer that Rodin knows so well how to press into the service rt when he happens to feel in the mood of doing so. Held lig e palm of this Divine Hand are seen the pigmy, worm-like figu lam and Eve, still partly mixed with the original clay out of wh lmighty has fashioned them. These two figures, vague and dimi s they are, reveal an exquisitely poetic beauty of form and sugg the man in a characteristic attitude of protection, the woman in

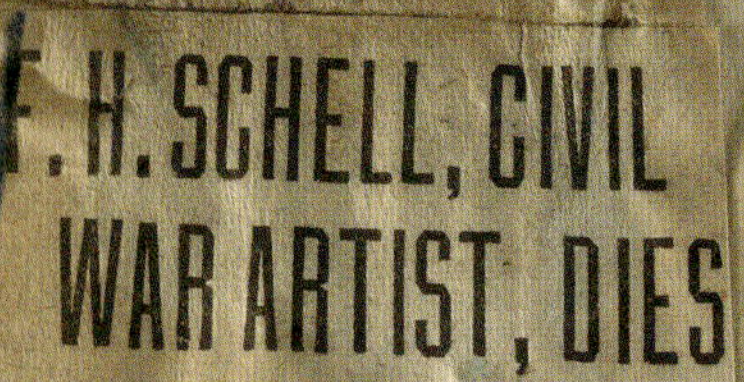

F. H. SCHELL, CIVIL WAR ARTIST, DIES

He Was First Man to Use Balloons to Sketch Encampments of Enemy.

JASPER R. RAND IS DEAD

Vice President of Ingersoll-Rand Company Is Victim of Pneumonia In Salt Lake City.

PHILADELPHIA, Pa., Wednesday.—Francis H. Schell, who gained national fame through his sketches of civil war spectacles, died in his home, at No. 5,227 Archer street, Germantown, to-day, of heart disease. He was seventy-nine years old. He had been known as an illustrator for nearly a half century.

At the beginning of the civil war Mr. Schell was sent to the front by Frank Leslie's magazines and later was made chief of the staff of artists for that periodical in the field. He was the first artist to make use of the balloon to draw pictures of the enemy's encampments.

After the war he was in charge of Leslie's art department but resigned and entered into a partnership with Thomas Hogan. For thirty years the work of these artists was well known throughout the country. Mr. Schell was one of the first illustrators to draw for photographic processes. He left a son, F. Cresson Schell, an artist.

N. Y. World
APR. 7, 1909

Copyright, 1909
Company.

Noted Easter[n] [Artist] Whose Life [...]

Art lovers of Cincinnati join with [...] United States who are mourning t[...] of the Albright Art gallery of Buffa[lo...] 21. Mr. Kurtz had many close frie[nds] and art collectors throughout the c[ountry...] many who knew and loved him to [...] reavement.

Born in New Castle, Pa., March [...] Washington and Jefferson college in [...]

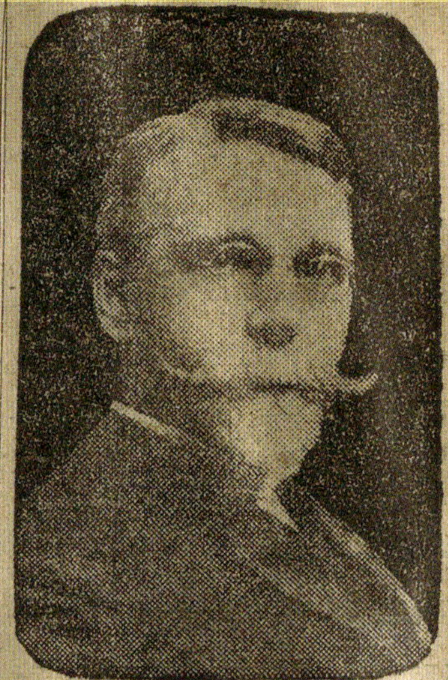

The Late Charles M. Kurtz.

best methods of stirring up public in[terest...] characteristics. When seized with th[e...] gaged with Senor Sorolla, the famous [...] the latter's pictures. He died three d[ays...]

MME. RONNER DEAD.

Madame Henriette Ronner, who in [the] eighties of the last century, had [a] wide reputation as a painter, died [the] other day in Brussels at the age of eighty-seven. She was a Dutch woman—she was born in Amsterdam— who made Belgium her home. Dogs and cats were favorite subjects, and in depicting the latter, she was considered, even in Paris, a strong riv[al] of Louis Lambert.

From PHILADELPHIA, Pa. - [...]
MAR. 30 1909

TUESDAY

Anton Hess, Sculptor, Dead.

Munich, Bavaria.—Anton Hess, the sculptor, died here. He was seventy-one years old and held the Professorship of Plastic Art in the Munich Technical High School.

Mrs. Bessie Eisby Scott, widow of William Wallace Scott, the miniature painter, died yesterday at the home of her daughter, Mrs. Stone, at 7 John street, New Rochelle. Mr. Stone died in 1905 at Nantucket, Mass. Besides her daughter, Mrs. Stone, Mrs. Scott leaves a stepdaughter, Miss G. H. Scott, also an artist, and a step-grandson, who is a Lieutenant in the navy.

From N. Y. Herald
APR. 3 1909

WALTER FLORIAN, PAINTER, IS DEAD

Was a Young Artist Who Attracted Much Attention with His Portraits.

CHARLES C. MELLOR EXPIRES

The Rev. Joseph A. Owen and John Nicholas Riggins, Pioneer Coal Man, Pass Away.

Walter Florian, a well known young artist of this city, who attracted much attention by the promise he gave as a portrait painter, died Thursday, in the Post Graduate Hospital, of kidney disease. He had been ill for two years, his malady reaching an acute stage within two months.

Mr. Florian was born in this city thirty-one years ago. He studied at the Art Students' League here and then went to Paris, where he was a pupil [...]

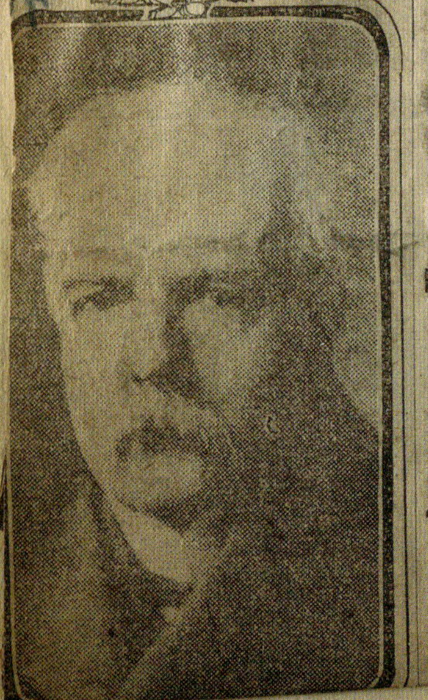

Born
1878

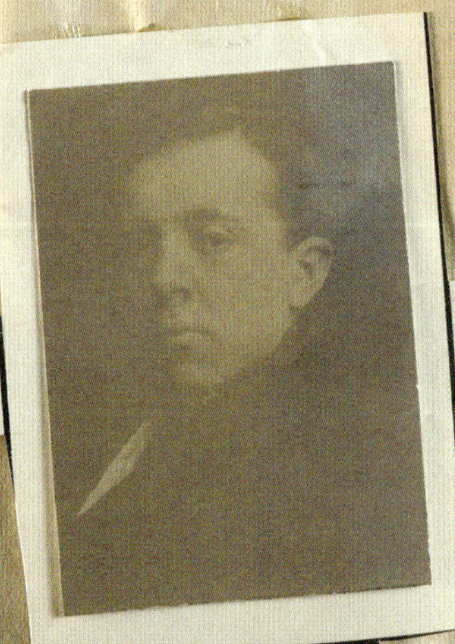

Walter Florian

ABOUT THE AUTHOR

Jim Moske is an archivist and writer based in New York City. He was Managing Archivist of The Metropolitan Museum of Art from 2008–23, and in earlier years was Archivist of the New York Public Library. Jim has published on topics including artwork provenance and transformational moments in the Met's past. In his creative practice, he explores the visual qualities and unintended meanings of historical documents through research, writing, and picture making. *Deaths of Artists* is his first book.

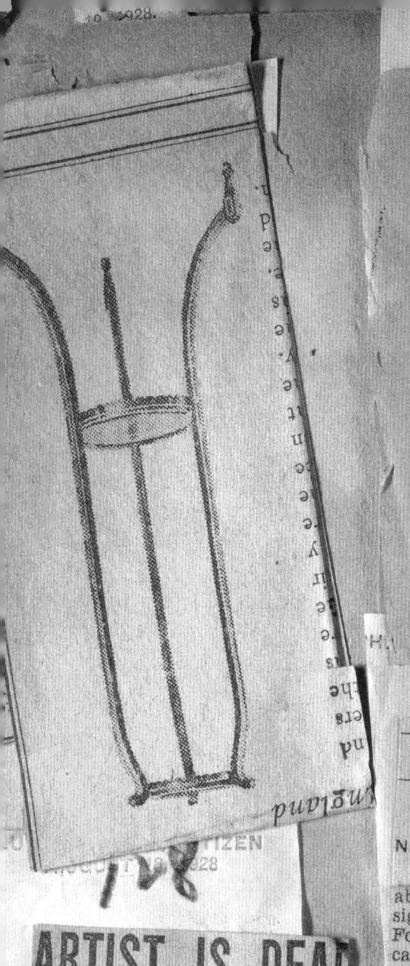

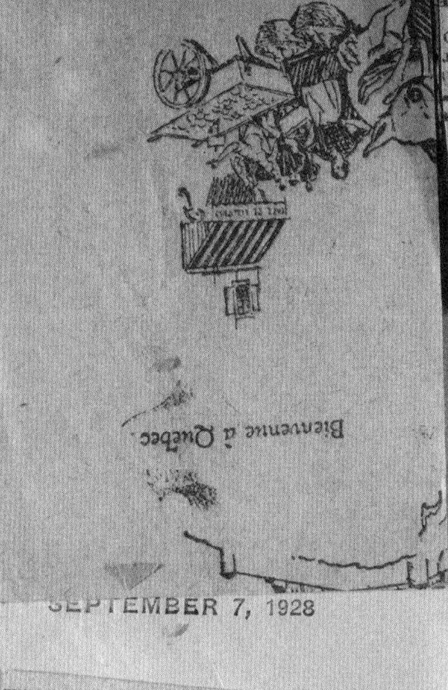

SEPTEMBER 7, 1928

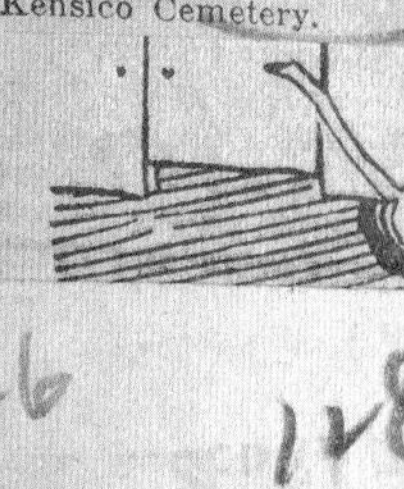

Deaths of a Day

JOHN J. MAENE

Noted Sculptor and Wood Carver
Came of Family of Artists

ably known to architects and designers throughout the United States. For a time Mr. Maene taught wood carving at Drexel Institute and Princeton. He was a member of University Lodge, No. 610, F. and A. M., and of the Unity Art Club.

Tschule, Quebec, Sept. 7.—(AP)—

SPEAKMAN, ARTIST AND AUTHOR, TAKES LIFE AT BELLEVUE

Tells Taxi Driver of Date With "Man on White Horse" at Hospital

HAD BEEN IN ILL-HEALTH, IS WIFE'S EXPLANATION

Wrote Books of Travel on China, Ireland and the Mississippi River

Harold Speakman traveled in many foreign lands the better to write books about those he encountered and to illustrate his books with sketches of things he saw. Yesterday he embarked on another journey and of this one there will be no record. If death is what he expected it to be, he is voyaging into the unknown astride a white horse behind a phantom rider.

"Quick," he told Frank McGlynn, a taxicab driver whom he hailed at the corner of 83d Street and Broadway at 5.05 o[clock] yesterday morning, "take me to [Bellevue]."

"Mr. Speakman," Mrs. Speakman said, "has been ill a long time. He was operated on several times for an internal trouble. At the end of his Trip through China, on which he wrote 'up Beyond Shanghai' in 1921, he was operated on in Shanghai. He has undergone operations several times since. His illness probably upset his mind.

"He arose early this morning and went out. There was nothing unusual in that—he often walked along Riverside Drive in the early morning—and he usually did not waken me."

In addition to the book on China, Speakman, who was thirty-nine, was the author of "Here's Ireland," published in 1925 and of "Mostly Mississippi," published in 1927. He had just returned from a trip through India, on which he was writing a book.

He drew the illustrations for his own books. He and Mrs. Speakman drifted down the Mississippi in a houseboat gathering material for that book, and its illustrations were [by] both of them.

BOSTON EVENING GLOBE

AUG 27 19[ ]

BOSTON ARTIST DIES AT SUMMER HOME

Miss Martha Silsbee Was of Old N. E. Family

Miss Martha Silsbee, 69, of 12 Lime [street], died yesterday at her Summer home at Dublin, N. H. She was a widely known artist and a descendant of an early New England family, which passes with her death.

Miss Silsbee was a descendant of Capt Nathaniel Silsbee of Salem, one of the famous sea captains of that port, who later became United States Senator from Massachusetts.

Miss Silsbee was a member of the Mayflower Club, the Water C[olor Club] and the Chilton Club, and w[ ]

ARTIST IS DEAD

August Lundberg Succumbs To Cancer in New York.

August Lundberg, 52, well known Columbus artist, is dead in New York from cancer, according to word received Saturday by Jorg Fasting. Mr. Lundberg moved to New York a year ago.

He is survived by his wife, a son, Arne, who is connected with the Famous Players-Lasky Corporation, and a daughter, Violet, a former dance pupil of Mr. Fasting, who now is with the Greenwich Village Follies.

Mr. Lundberg's last Columbus painting were the mural decorations in the Keith-Albee Palace. [ ]

ARTIST DIES [AT] HOME IN [ ]

XENIA, Sept. 19.—Fun[eral serv]ices were held in Spring[field this] afternoon for Oscar E. Gr[ouch] artist, who died Monday [at his] summer home in Clifton. [Mr.] Grouch studied in Germany [and] travelled considerably abroad. [Dur]ing the winter, he and his fam[ily] spending their summers at Clifto[n]. He is survived by a daughter, Mrs. Williams, New York city and a son, Oscar, jr., both of whom were at Clifton when he died. Burial was made in Ferncliff cemetery, Springfield.

DAYTON (OH[IO])
SEPTE[MBER]

York Jo[urnal] [in which he drew for The New] York Journal in 1896 and 1897. Then came, in 1901, "Pore Lil' Mose," and in 1902 "Buster Brown," both done for The New York Herald. In "Buster Brown," the artist achieved his greatest triumph. During the adventures of "Buster Brown," there was scarcely a little boy and his faithful dog or, indeed, scarcely a grown-up, who was not familiar with the little boy and his faithful dog. For a time "Buster Brown" was a powerful influence. The clothes for boys called "Buster Brown," the characters, present Mrs. [ ] son, Richard F. [ ] final of "May Jane," [ ] characters, was his [ ] present Mrs. Pershing [ ] After he left The New [ ] cault was for seven [ ] staff of The New [ ] gave up professional [ ] ten years ago, and [ ] only used his [ ] joyment in pai[nting] [ ]
